by colour of law

THE UNIVERSITY OF CHICAGO PRESS • CHICAGO AND LONDON

Howard Nenner

by
colour of
law

Legal Culture and Constitutional Politics
in England, 1660–1689

HOWARD NENNER is associate professor of
history at Smith College.

For Jennie and Lou

The University of Chicago Press, Chicago 60637
The University of Chicago Press, Ltd., London

© 1977 by The University of Chicago
All rights reserved. Published 1977
Printed in the United States of America
81 80 79 78 77   987654321

Library of Congress Cataloging in Publication Data

Nenner, Howard
  By colour of law.

  Bibliography: p.
  Includes index.
  1. Great Britain—Politics and government—1660-1688.
I. Title.
JN201.N46   320.9'41'066   76-25631
ISBN 0-226-57275-7

Contents

Preface

THIS IS A BOOK ABOUT ENGLAND'S LEGAL CULTURE IN THE SEVEN-
teenth century and some of the ways that culture was expressed in the constitutional politics of the period 1660–89.
The study began as an examination of the debates in the
Convention of 1689. A much shorter version of chapter 6,
dealing with the Convention alone, was published in the
American Journal of Legal History in 1966. It seemed to me
then, as it does today, that, irrespective of place on the
political spectrum, members of the Convention tended to
address constitutional issues with a common legal vocabulary and a common disposition of legal mind. And if this was
true for the time of the Revolution, it seemed probable that
the same patterns might be found over a wider chronological
range. The book, then, is not so much about the political
differences which divided men as it is about the cultural
assumptions they shared, their common belief, in the generation following the Stuart restoration, that problems of
constitutional politics ought, at least in the first instance, to
be approached and explored as matters at issue in the
private law.

Along the way I have had the kind of professional help
without which a project of this sort would be impossible to
achieve. I am especially grateful to the staffs at the Institute
of Historical Research, the Public Record Office, the Manuscript Room of the British Museum (now the British
Library), and the libraries of Lincoln's Inn and the Inner
Temple. I am also grateful for the considerable financial
support received from the University of California at
Berkeley, the Social Science Research Council, and the

Smith College Committee on Aid to Faculty Scholarship. Most of all I am indebted to those scholars — Thomas Barnes, David Berkowitz, Louis Cohn-Haft, Felix Gilbert, Jack Hexter, Morton Horwitz, Stanley Katz, Paul Lucas, Sherry Marker, Lois Schwoerer, and Simeon Wade — who have read all or parts of my work at various stages and whose suggestions for change have made this book better than it would otherwise have been.

For three people I have very special thanks: Hilda McArthur, whose paleographic and typing skill produced successive revisions of this work, always under considerable pressure of time; Thomas Green, who read all parts of the work at every stage and whose critical scholarship and encouraging friendship are in evidence throughout; and Sherry Marker, who always knew how, and in what proportion, to combine criticism and forbearance.

HOWARD NENNER

1 July 1976

Introduction

THE ONE ELEMENT OF CONSTITUTIONAL CONTINUITY IN SEVEN-
teenth-century England was the acceptance by king and
Parliament of a political rule of law. Law was the touchstone
of politics. No matter how men might differ as to what the
law said or what it might be made to mean, all were
committed to a legal standard in the conduct of their
political affairs. This is not to suggest that both king and
Parliament adhered without exception to the substance of
the law; yet for each there was an unbroken reliance upon
its structure, its arguments, its procedure, and its forms.
The common law provided a constant conceptual framework for political action. Throughout the century virtually
every important controversy was formulated, and every
position justified, in legal language and common-law
paradigms. The law was the one constant in an era otherwise
marked by constitutional uncertainty and political disarray.
It afforded the one structure, both institutional and intellectual, which rendered the issues intelligible and which provided a forum for political debate. Never in question were
the existence and utility of a rule of law. Law instead was an
instrument and a prize: he who would control the constitution would have first to control the law.

Historically, the instruments of legal control belonged
predominantly, if not exclusively, to the king. Law was the
king's law, judges were the king's surrogates, Parliament
existed only at the king's pleasure. As the century progressed, the place of law in politics became even more
important. Force, as a lever of political control, no longer
seemed to be a creditable option. It had been supremely

difficult to lay two civil wars to rest and to restore a legitimate king to his rightful throne. A repetition of that process and of the mistakes that would make it necessary was almost unthinkable. It was thus that the fear of anarchy and the spectral horror of regicide were more than sufficient after 1660 to deter men from any course that might impel them once more to inconsiderate action. Political energies were now, more than ever before, to be concentrated upon the uses of the law and the opportunities for legal manipulation. This was as true of the Crown as it was of Parliament. The attempt to suspend the law generally or to dispense with its effects in particular cases is evidence of Stuart legal sophistication. It is testimony to their imaginative and often effective use of the law rather than to their disregard of it.

The law was ready at hand. By the seventeenth century, England had developed a political culture completely comfortable with sophisticated legal concepts and no less at ease with the intricacies of legal form. Lawyers may have been mistrusted, but it was always a mistrust born of the practitioner's ability to convert the richness of the law to his own or his client's use. Law, in expert hands, was a powerful device, one that might also provide a paradigm for parliamentary politics. Crown and Parliament, both proficient in the legal craft, sought with consummate skill to control and to use the law. As a result, a legal disposition of mind which had been forged initially in the intricacies of the private law was being increasingly brought to bear upon political and constitutional problems. It conditioned men's thought and language and ultimately their actions. It found expression in every area of political life, and in 1688–89 it so determined the shape of events that revolution was made to seem respectable. What was to emerge was a revolution that was constitutionally palatable because of its overwhelming appearance of exacting legal form.

It was of little consequence that the law itself might sometimes be distorted. What was at the heart of constitu-

tional development was this important matter of legal
configuration. Substance, if necessary, could always be
sacrificed to form, reality to fiction, and law to the "colour
of law." In this effort the entire arsenal of the private law
was brought to bear upon political issues; and as long as
political behavior could find workable analogues in the law
of contract, trust, real property, or inheritance, it would be
able to claim a preeminent respectability.

In this way the law exercised a powerful hold over
seventeenth-century constitutional politics, and it is for this
reason that the culture, possibilities, and uses of the law
need to be examined. Although we speak easily and correctly of the impact of the common lawyer upon the
seventeenth-century constitutional crisis and of his role as an
architect of the evolving seventeenth-century constitution,
we need to know more of the impact upon politics of the
common-law culture itself. To have been bred in that
culture meant much more than having a knowledge of
principles and rules. It meant having, as well, a ready-made
vocabulary of political discourse and a particularized view of
the political world.

IT IS UNFORTUNATE THAT AN UNDERSTANDING OF STUART
England is often confused by the erroneous supposition that
law and prerogative were opposed, that, at the beginning of
the century, law, in the person of Coke, is properly to be
seen as the relentless adversary of the prerogative, in the
person of James I. The seductive danger of this assumption is
that, once the struggle is so defined, it becomes compellingly
easy to skip to the "conclusion" and to reason backward
from the perspective of 1689. This, of course, is the Whig
position: Constitutionalism, locked in mortal combat with
Stuart despotism, gains impressively throughout the century
until the English common law and the liberties that it
guaranteed emerge victorious from the Glorious Revolution.
Personal rule and all other manifestations of Stuart contempt for legally limited monarchy are washed away in an

overwhelming Whig tide. By the end of the century, popery and tyranny have been vanquished, Protestantism and law have triumphed.

It can, however, be argued that the seventeenth century makes greater sense, is rendered more intelligible, when the Stuarts and their parliaments are viewed in the context of a somewhat different constitutional struggle, a struggle which was not for the ascendancy of law but for the ascendancy of king or Parliament, and which was at all times circumscribed by law. In this light the personal rule does not become an eleven-year tyranny. It emerges instead as a period in which the king resorted to the available processes of the law. Ship money, after all, was a battle fought in the courts. Benevolences, forced loans, and all the components of fiscal feudalism, those current and those revived, were based upon legal precedents. Charles pushed back the limits of the law, but he rarely went outside them. And when the only solution to the nation's ills seemed to be war, it was not because the law was opposing tyranny; rather it was because Charles had effectively demonstrated that he could use the law *ex parte* and to his own advantage. The Long Parliament went to war, not to preserve the law, but to win it back from Charles.

The reality of the struggle for command of the law was often obscured by the larger constitutional fiction of *preservation* of the law. The reasons for this are striking. Throughout the Stuart century, law and history assumed an overwhelming pride of place. Truth was derived from the past, particularly the legal past, and there it was, waiting to be discovered, demanding to be respected, and insisting on being preserved. Innovation in all things was thought certain to weaken and eventually to break the bonds of society. The belief in the tension between preservation and innovation, this dialectic of good and evil, was so pronounced that no one politically sane dared challenge it. The irony in this construction is that throughout the Tudor-Stuart epoch the enormity of change is what English politics was all about. The monumental shifts in religion under the

Tudors were all carried forward under the banner of restoring the past. In this respect the seventeenth century was no different. The processes of political alteration were conducted in the same constitutional idiom as that which had characterized the preceding century. Every new and renewed challenge to monarchical prerogative was, and had to be, confidently characterized as a defense of the "ancient" or the "existing" constitution, even if that existence was to be found nowhere but in the constitutional imagination.[1] This "constitution" may have been contrived, but it could not be ignored. Like "preservation," "precedent," and "law" itself, it was an expression and an assumption indispensable to the language of political respectability, there to be used with equal conviction by parliamentarian and royalist alike.

When Parliament convened in 1640, it went directly to the attack. If it was going to wrest control of the law from Charles, it had to begin with his ministers and judges, those magistrates who had kept custody of the law for the king. Strafford and Laud may have been of greater political moment, but a judiciary which had been obediently doing Charles's bidding was to Parliament no less important. Sir John Finch, recently made lord keeper, had been chief justice of the Common Pleas and architect of the ship-money decision. It was therefore not surprising that he joined Strafford and Laud as a candidate for impeachment. In all, the Commons saw fit to impeach each of the six judges who had sided with the king and had voted in favor of ship money.[2]

The proceedings against Strafford were the most significant. They demonstrated clearly that the real concern of Parliament did not lie with the monarchical threat to law. It rested instead with the Crown's employment of law for undesirable ends and with the tortured interpretations of questionable precedents. No matter that in his impeachment Strafford was charged with subverting the fundamental laws of the realm and with attempting "to introduce an arbitrary and tyrannical government against the law." These charges could never be substantiated. The law was still on Strafford's side, still in the province of the king. However much he had violated its spirit, he had never transgressed its forms. However objectionable his policies, his acts were not illegal. Parliament had no choice. If it were to proceed legally and effectively, impeachment had to be abandoned and an attainder substituted in its place. Impeachment would have succeeded only if Strafford had been guilty of violating the law. Breaking the law carried penalties, while manipulating law for political ends did not. It is therefore in the form of the action that the substance of the grievance is revealed. If Parliament in its proceedings was not always to be governed by what was lawful, it was still very much concerned with what appeared to be lawful.

The proceedings against the king's magistrates were only the first steps toward loosening Charles's hold upon the law. The real task of the Long Parliament, the actual shift in the balance of control, was yet to be accomplished. It remained to appropriate or destroy those legal powers which the king had so tellingly employed. An assault upon the so-called prerogative courts swept away Star Chamber and the Court of High Commission, and along with them went the "like jurisdiction" in the Councils of the North and of the Marches of Wales. Ship money was simply declared illegal; but in declaring it so, Parliament was saying something infinitely more important. It was warning the king that the judgments of a sycophantic judiciary could be reversed in a higher court, the High Court of Parliament.

Control was now shifting away from the king. But so long as Parliament was not independent of the king, so long as the words "*Le roy le veult*" were not merely formulaic but meaningful as well, nothing that the two houses did on their own would have any legal effect. It was as if the king and his Parliament held the law as tenants in common, each with an undivided interest in the whole of the estate, each striving for it all, and with civil war only as a forum for creating partition.

When the break came, each side advanced itself as *custos* of the law; but it was the king who had the better *prima facie* case. Unless Parliament could carefully distinguish its actions, it was guilty of rebellion; and rebellion was clearly illegal. To meet this burden, Parliament alleged that it was not offering a challenge to monarchy, to the institution to which it owed allegiance. It was, instead, opposing the person of Charles Stuart, and this was a different situation entirely. It may have been a fine legal distinction to oppose the king in the name of the king, but it was for just that reason—that it was a legal distinction—that it was so important.

Regicide presented a different problem. It would have been too difficult to confront the king directly and assert that he was to be tried and condemned in his own name; yet it was only slightly less difficult to pretend that he could be tried at all. Nevertheless, that pretense was carried out under the color of perfect regularity. When Charles Stuart was beheaded in 1649, it was not as the victim of a conspiracy to assassinate. Nor, like Edward II, Richard II, and Henry VI, was he first deposed and then murdered. He was, as king of England, tried in open court and executed according to law; and however distorted the substance of that law may have been, the forms that were followed employed every pretense of being correct.

Rectitude, however, was no assurance of legality. Despite the suggestion that Charles be indicted and tried in a court of common law, in strict accordance with its procedures, it was eventually decided to place the king before a High Court of Justice, in this case one hundred thirty-five commissioners who would perform the functions of judge and jury. Although at variance with the prescription of the common law, this court, and the others throughout the Interregnum which were modeled upon it, paid scrupulous attention to legal form. Designed to cope with political offenders, these special courts, like the prerogative courts before them, were often more attentive to the needs of the accused than were their common-law rivals.[3]

The king too was aware of the forms. It was these that he contested throughout his trial. Never once did he deign to reply to the charges against him. He denied the jurisdiction of the court and refused categorically to enter a plea. As a result, no witnesses could be produced to testify to his crimes. He was deemed, according to law, to have admitted his guilt, and the court moved directly to judgment. For levying war against Parliament and people and for attempting to subvert the law by ruling according to his will alone, Charles Stuart, king of England, was sentenced to death. Parliament, acting through the court, confirmed that its control was complete. It had seized the law from Charles and used it to destroy him.

The period between the death of Charles I and the restoration of his son was a time of constitutional experiment, but always within the larger framework of an established legal tradition. There was, for example, considerable agitation for comprehensive legal reform, a movement which assumed the appearance of a popular cause; yet most of this reforming activity was with the purpose of strengthening, rather than undermining, the common law.[4] In matters bearing more directly upon the constitution, the House of Lords was abolished, but eventually the "Other House" appeared in its place. Cromwell, in frustration, turned out one Parliament after another, but he was never content to allow his rule to rest upon conquest alone. Throughout the period he was striving constantly for a legitimate base, for the return to a legally acceptable constitution. He was searching for a constitution which would be flexible in substance but recognizable in form. For that reason the institutional forms never lost their importance. Parliament, whether it functioned improperly or functioned not at all, was always in evidence. Cromwell may have driven out the Rump and the Barebones during the Commonwealth and dismissed two more parliaments during the Protectorate, but it was the restored Long Parliament which, according to the law of 1641 (16 Charles I, c. 7) dissolved itself and called the Convention into being. In this light the tragedy of the republican experiment was that it was, from the beginning, disposed to failure. The only institution which could meet the test of legitimacy was monarchy, and it was back toward monarchy that England rapidly began to move. By 1657 Cromwell was monarch in all but name. Probably he would have accepted the crown had it not been for the pressures from the army. And, in 1660, when Monck started his march from Scotland, restoration was more than desirable; it was the logical conclusion to the previous twelve years. It was as if monarchy had never been intermitted. Indeed, it had not. In law the Interregnum had been a nullity. At the very moment that Charles I, by ancient formula, was "alive and dead," Charles II succeeded to the throne of England. Although Charles II did not ascend that throne until the twelfth year of his reign, it was on 30 January 1649 that his title vested. It was, by operation of law, both immediate and automatic.

As a result of the Interregnum experiment, Parliament had won and retained the right to make the law. There would be no more impositions, no more benevolences, no more forced loans. Fiscal feudalism would not be revived. King in Parliament, and king in Parliament only, would make the law; king in Parliament, and king in Parliament only, would control supply. But though the civil wars had effected such significant changes, the changes were not complete. King in Parliament might make the law, but Parliament alone had yet to perfect the power to control the law. So long as the king, on the authority of law and history, could claim the law as his own, so long as equity was still the king's conscience, justice his justice, and the judiciary his surrogates, so long also would he be able to assert his sovereign will—and in so doing remain within his legal right. His prerogative was contemplated in law; and through the use of that prerogative, the law, in turn, was his to control. To wrest that control from him would be the struggle of the Restoration and the one that would take another generation to win. As it stood in 1660, a king who could no longer in theory make law could yet do so in fact. If he could not legislate *ex parte* he could nevertheless suspend the law or dispense with its application—or at least, with considerable legal justification, he might try. And if, within the confines of the law, he could no longer control finances in the jurisdiction of England, he could always appeal to the jurisdiction of France. The Stuart kings did not need to defy the law so long as they might cleverly and successfully get round it. This, quite simply, was what Charles II was able to do when he became the client of Louis XIV. Irrespective of the financial or political wisdom of such a policy, that it was sound in law is incontrovertible. A king in need of money might no longer bypass Parliament and go directly to the country; but if he were to look for support outside the country, Parliament would have no legal basis for complaint. It had not been so long, after all, since the king had been expected to live entirely of his own; and even if this were no longer feasible, the idea still retained a large measure of political appeal.

These were the ways in which Charles II and James II would mold the law to their own ends. They were different devices from those employed by the earlier Stuart monarchs, but not so different as to constitute any new or radical departures. There was no greater disregard of law in the 1680s than there had been in the 1630s. If anything, monarchy was gaining in legal sophistication. Where Parliament could not be defied directly, it could still be successfully circumvented. If law was not in the exclusive province of the king, it was yet within his effective control. Dispensation from the effects of the law and suspension of the law itself were clearly injurious to the spirit of the constitution, but they were not destructive of its forms. The law that Charles II and James II would leave to William and Mary would be left intact. It would be in need of change but not of repair. It would have to be made to conform to the new realities of political existence; but in the true common-law tradition, as enunciated by Matthew Hale, that was clearly to be expected. For centuries before and in centuries to come, the measure of the common law had been and would be its ability to adapt, to meet new situations as they arose. Seen in this perspective, the seventeenth century, and the years 1660 through 1689 in particular, do not mark any breach in constitutional or legal continuity. They are, instead, very much a part of it.

The Revolution of 1688 and its attendant settlement did, however, mark an important constitutional watershed. The fiction of regularity was advanced and this time retained. When it was all over, the pretense was seen to have succeeded. The nation was persuaded that James II had abdicated and that the principle of hereditary succession had been preserved, though that was palpably untrue. Whatever else may have happened, there was no revolution in institutions. There was no rupture in constitutional continuity. The contemporary perception of events had supplanted reality. The truth of the Revolution was what the society believed it to be, which is to say that it was no revolution at all. The myth of 1688 would become part of England's historical legacy in a way infinitely more important and lasting than the earlier fiction of the "ancient constitution." As early as December 1688, before any settlement of the Revolution had been achieved, Gilbert Burnet delivered before Prince William a symbolically important sermon, more prescient in its analysis than Burnet could possibly have realized or William could possibly have understood. "We have before us a work," Burnet said, "that seems to our selves a Dream, and that will appear to Posterity a Fiction."[5] It was an amazingly accurate interpretation of both present and future. Yet despite the distortions worked by historical legend, there was a resolution of the central issue of who was to control the law. In this respect Parliament had won the day, and, in this respect particularly, the Revolution would emerge as an event of singular importance.[6]

That a resolution came when it did seems understandable in view of the narrowing and focusing of argument between 1660 and 1689. Civil war in the middle of the century was paradoxically successful because it had failed. It had had the effect of invalidating open rebellion as a viable corrective to repressive monarchy. By 1660, force as an instrument of permanent and effective change had been discredited. It was no longer accepted as an alternative, or even as a complement, to legal procedures. For the next generation the battle would have to be waged in the available arenas of the law. It would be there that issue would finally be joined and a decision ultimately rendered. How that came about, and a suggestion as to why, is the purpose of this study.

Part One

the
political culture
of the law

1   *Attitudes*

AN AMATEUR KNOWLEDGE OF THE ENGLISH LAW SERVED SEVERAL
purposes for a seventeenth-century gentleman of quality. It
permitted him, in the first instance, to manage his own
affairs with a style and assurance that were socially necessary. Matthew Hale, who, like Coke before him, was dis-
dainful of amateurs meddling in the law, affirmed
nevertheless the value of a general legal education for all
gentlemen. Such study, he believed, would "fitt a man with
so much knowledge as will enable him to understand his own
estate, and live in some repute among his neighbours in the
country."[1] As an extension of this ideal, a knowledge of the
law was deemed essential in the conduct of local government. It was expected of a gentleman that he would
participate in the administrative and judicial responsibilities
of his community, usually in the capacity of justice of the
peace. He was, on the parish level, to be both symbol and
enforcer of an ordered society.

For these reasons alone the Englishman's familiarity with
the law was an essential part of his equipment for society.
Yet there was something more. In addition to its value in
matters of private property, social standing, and local
governance, the law was used continuously and effectively as
a frame of political reference. As Christopher Hill has
noted, "Most gentlemen had a legal education of some sort,
and thought of politics in legal terms."[2] The cumulative
result was for law to become central to the society's cultural
conditioning, for law to move far beyond the narrow
confines of a professional discipline and to assume the
dimension of a contemporary disposition of mind. Law had

3

4   become so much a part of the educated Englishman's culture and of his assumptions about society that in every area of discourse and thought he drew automatically upon its vocabulary and relied instinctively upon its forms.

Although this attitude of legal mind was pervasive and intense, it was not unique to seventeenth-century England in either time or place. Medieval philosophy, in general, was largely predicated upon laws, sacred and profane, which dictated men's obligations and behavior. And in England, specifically, a legal culture based largely upon the common law had been in existence for centuries.[3] What set the seventeenth century apart, and especially the period in England after 1660, was the degree to which a legal disposition of mind was used, naturally and unself-consciously, to explain, to rationalize, and to facilitate political change.

Stretching beyond politics proper, the influence of the law was felt in the area of political thought. Like the legal mind itself, the study of natural and divine law was by no means new; but from James I at the beginning of the century through Locke at the end, interest in those principles which informed men's moral behavior was being intensified — and to some extent changed. Hobbes, in particular, provided a new dimension to moral philosophy. Not content with the theological categories of good and evil, he was to examine with painstaking care the laws of social and political conduct which he believed were observably verifiable and upon these laws would construct a legally exacting version of the social contract. For Locke the terms of the contract were different, and for Filmer there was no contract at all; but for these two, no less than for Hobbes, political society was fundamentally explicable in the obligations and relationships imposed by law. John Selden, early in the century, saw the great and complex constitutional issues of his day in what were surely the simplest and most compelling legal terms. "To know what obedience is due to the prince," he said in his *Table Talk,* "you must look into the contract betwixt him and his people; as if you would know what rent is due from the

tenant to the landlord, you must look into the lease."[4] It was   5
a politically comforting and useful formula because it
brought a fundamental constitutional relationship into the
conceptual purview of the private law. It made an exalted
obligation no more difficult to understand than one that was
totally mundane. The inference to be drawn is important:
the development of a consensual theory of government had
first to be grounded in a knowledge of the private law. As a
result, any *right* to revolution was rendered much less
dependent upon philosophical justification than upon an
understanding of the legal consequences which would follow
upon the breach of a particular contract. This is what
happened in 1688-89, in the Revolution itself and in the
constitutional effects that the Revolution produced. It was
frequently argued in the debate over the new oaths of
supremacy and allegiance to William and Mary that
James II had forfeited the obedience of his subjects because,
by his own acts, his contract with them had been broken. As
asserted by one publicist, "it is evident that in compacts if
one party neglect or act contrary to his part of the obligation, He forfeits all right which he might claim by vertue of
the compact from the other party."[5] It was just that simple.
And it seemed to suggest that political action, if it was
dependent at all upon intellectual justification, derived that
justification not from philosophy but from law.

Another intellectual current of the seventeenth century
was provided by the scientific revolution. Like the law, the
new science gave rise to a conceptual order capable of
widespread application. Transported beyond the boundaries
of its own immediate concerns, scientific methods of inquiry
would be addressed effectively to the problems of other
disciplines. Hobbes's empiricism, as already noted, transformed moral philosophy, while Matthew Hale's scientific
attempt at an English jurisprudence was the first attempt to
order the ambiguities of the common law. It has even been
suggested that law and science were complementary facets of
the same seventeenth-century culture, that each was affected by a new and pervasive impulse toward the systematic

6

organization of knowledge, and that each was growing more concerned with degrees of probability than with absolute truth.[6] Although this thesis may be suggesting more of an equivalence than in fact existed, it is certain that science, as much as law, was becoming the common property of every educated seventeenth-century man.

The probable result was to raise science to the level of intellectual discourse enjoyed by the law, but, unlike the law, the scientific revolution did not carry over into the arenas of practical political debate. Political and constitutional controversy continued to be cast, almost exclusively, in paradigms and metaphors drawn from the law and reinforced by history and Scripture. Whatever the popular currency of a new empiricism and a new rationalism, science would face a more difficult task insinuating itself into a political perspective which abhorred innovation. Law, history, and Scripture had been forged into an intellectual synthesis which derived authority in part from its status as revealed truth, but that synthesis also relied upon its collective genesis in immemorial time. For the new science to succeed, it would first have to overcome the most deeply ingrained assumptions of the age: it would have to oppose precedent with reason successfully. This, eventually, it was able to do, and even to effect some influence upon the patterns of legal thought; but for most of the century, scientific method would have no appreciable impact upon politics. This was particularly true in the generation after 1660. Following the failure of the republican experiment, there would be a renewed suspicion of radical constitutional change. The result was for politics to stand aloof from science while increasing its reliance upon the law.

Yet science, particularly as an intellectual guide to problems of organization, was having an effect upon the development of law itself. As experimentation inclined more toward scientific laws that were usable, so too did it allow lawyers to consider foreign legal systems when their precepts seemed applicable to English conditions. The appeal of the civil law was that of an exact jurisprudence, a formulaic scheme which would articulate the important restraints upon human conduct. Matthew Hale, chief justice of the King's Bench and preeminent among the later Stuart jurists, was a common lawyer who could perceive the value of the civil law and who himself at times inclined toward "Scientifical Principles."[7] He recognized the attraction of a multiplicity of cases and decisions reduced to a finite number of workable rules. This, Hale believed, would be particularly important in equity jurisdiction.

Equity was regarded as "a Trust committed to the Kings Conscience";[8] but to protect against conscience being arbitrary, rules for the effective dispensing of justice would have to be applied. By the period of the Restoration, although Chancery jurisdiction was becoming increasingly systematic, "the principles of equity were still far from fixed."[9] For this reason there was the possibility of capricious administration, a danger that Hale, and later Nottingham, took to be serious. Hale believed it necessary to reduce equity to "certain Rules and Principles, that men might study it as a Science,"[10] while Nottingham declared that "if conscience be not dispensed by the rule of science . . . men's estates should depend upon the pleasure of a court which took upon itself to be purely arbitrary."[11] This implied a belief in a sense of system in the common law. Yet Hale would not carry his belief in "scientifical principles" to its logical extreme. He thought that the study of the law was not susceptible of the same certainty as mathematics. The common lawyer would only be deceiving himself if he presumed that he, like Euclid, could demonstrate "an unerring Systeme of Lawes."[12]

For all of Hale's vision, he was still a cautious man of his time.[13] Attracted to the merits of the civil law and the canon law, he was not unappreciative of the political problems that these legal systems might pose. An acceptance, in any degree, of a foreign jurisprudence suggested the acceptance of foreign authority. Clearly, this would never do. It was a truth abundantly confirmed in the historical memory of 1533 and Henry VIII's break with Rome. Any substantial

8   intrusion of the civil law or the canon law, Hale had said, was to be guarded against; and if any such principles were to be permitted to cross the Channel, it was to be understood that they did not have the "Authority of Laws from themselves, but from the authoritative Admission of this Kingdom."[14] It was a way of recognizing and incorporating the usefulness of a competitive jurisprudence without falling prey to a non-English jurisdiction. Unlike Blackstone in the eighteenth century, who feared that resort to the civil law, in any degree, carried with it the risk of "the despotic monarchy of Rome and Byzantium," and those of a later era, who believed simply that it would never be necessary to look beyond "our own municipal system," Hale was capable of a more objective view.[15] Yet he remained, at the same time, convinced of the superiority of the common law. In this conviction he was precisely representative of his age. Although the common law was not without defects, still it was believed to be the most viable support of English liberties. It was, for Hale, "the great Foundation (under God) of the Peace, Happiness, Honour and Justice, of this Kingdom."[16] Law was the support upon which government rested, and government, in return, was obliged to preserve it.

It is equally significant that these attitudes and assumptions focused inward upon England. "Our Trimmer," wrote Halifax, "as he hath a great veneration for laws in general, so he has more particularly for our own."[17] It was a sentiment symptomatic of an English reflex of mind, one that tended to emphasize those distinctive qualities of English law which set it apart from the code of the civilians — the doctrine of consideration in the common law of contract, the common-law rules of descent and distribution, the refusal of the common law to countenance torture,[18] and, most important, the common-law right of trial by jury. On this last point of difference the English common lawyers were particularly convinced of the superiority of their system. John Maynard regarded this "indifferent way of tryal" to be as much the subject's "right, yea his birthright and inheritance, as his lands are,"[19] and Hale called it simply "the best Manner of Trial in the World."[20] Hale knew that juries were subject to error and corruption, but for him, as well as for his common-law colleagues, the commitment to the English jury was an article of faith that was rarely to be shaken.

As a base upon which society rested, law was regarded as at least the equal of religion. This was especially true after 1660, when the common law, which had become suspect and had been criticized during the Interregnum, stood vindicated. Hobbes, who had otherwise been out of favor with his contemporaries, had written that "religion is not philosophy, but law," an assessment with which the Restoration political community could readily agree.[21] Halifax saw law and religion as partners in the constant struggle "to subdue the perverseness of men's wills," a necessary "double chain" to safeguard the peace.[22] Yet these were common-place assumptions about the law and, except for becoming more firmly implanted after 1660, were otherwise unremarkable.

Much more remarkable, although no less a commonplace, was the recognition that it was from the law that the Church of England derived.[23] Here was one important area in which a nation accustomed to investing its law with mythical properties in order to afford it greater strength could draw that same strength from historical reality. The Anglican rite, that curious mixture of Protestant faith and Catholic ritual, was not rooted solely in the ordinance of God; it was also established in English law. From the acts of the Reformation Parliament through the Restoration settlement, it was by law that the church had been defined, amended, and controlled.

This was not only historically true, it was also politically comfortable. Although in popular estimation the Anglican rite may have expressed "the one *true* faith," political Englishmen who were wary of abstractions and increasingly conscious of change were not content to rest their religion upon absolutes and intangibles. References after 1660 to "the true reformed protestant Christian Religion . . . as it is

10   contained in the Holy Scriptures of the Old & New Testament" did not disappear, but they were less in evidence.[24] The excessive claims of absolute truth during the religiously aberrant era of Cromwell were receding from view, and receding with them was the more reasonable, but no longer workable, religious dichotomy of the earlier Caroline church. In his answer to the Grand Remonstrance of 1641, Charles I had equated Anglican doctrine with "true religion" while recognizing church "government and discipline" as having been "established by law."[25] After the Restoration this distinction could no longer be profitably drawn. With Charles II's leaning, and James II's commitment, to Roman Catholicism, there was growing danger of a reversion to Rome. To suggest that such a reversion would be a violation of *truth,* that it would be adopting Antichrist, was unacceptably reminiscent of civil war. The response to the king's religion would have to be different. As religion again became a divisive political issue, protection against religious change was increasingly sought in the assurances of the law. There would still be those who would equivocate by referring to the "true Protestant Religion, established by Law,"[26] and others who would cling to a logically Fundamentalist assertion that "there is no such thing in Scripture, as religion established by Law,"[27] yet the trend in politics continued to move toward the increased reliance of theology upon the weight of legal, and not divine, injunction. Nor was the formula used only by the critics of royal policies. Just as the later Stuarts were accepting the parliamentary arguments of the "ancient constitution,"[28] so were they now open to accepting a religion subject to the procedures of the law rather than to the prerogatives of a king. In 1681, Humphrey Gower, vice-chancellor of the University of Cambridge, could celebrate Charles II as a king who derived his title from no one but God, yet could, in the next breath, applaud the king's "zeal for our most Holy Religion, as it is professed, & by Law established."[29] To Gower, as to all royalists, there was, in this, no inconsistency. The king

might be responsible to God alone, but his religion was 11
founded in law.

Placing law on a par with religion and acknowledging the
legal foundations of the Anglican church were unobjection-
able exercises, provided, however, that the Englishman's law
and his religion were used as complementary rather than
conflicting supports for his politics — but that was not always
the case. During the Exclusion Crisis, in the constitutional
dispute over the distinction to be drawn between an heir and
an heir apparent (or an heir presumptive), it was submitted
that the common law of England had greater authority than
Scripture. The Bible was taken to be indiscriminate and
inexact in its use of the word "heir." It may have been, as
was suggested by one who looked to Coke, that "the Holy
Writers formed their Language by the vulgar idioms
amongst the People of the Jews, and never intended to write
Law Cases, much less to expound the Common Law of
England."[30] That, however, did not detract from the significance of the argument advanced. In matters of constitutional interpretation the Bible was not to be taken as the
paramount sanction.

This was an unusual juxtaposition of religion and the law,
and it suggested, to the limited extent that it was employed,
the highest possible testimonial to legal authority. Much
more normal were the frequent and highly acceptable
confrontations between law and religion where the religion
in question was Roman Catholicism. In such a contest the
line of battle would be clearly drawn. No one questioned
which was on the side of right and which on the side of
iniquity. Law was good and popery bad. Similarly, it was
law which was compatible with truth. For Catholics to meet
the burden of such an attitude was nearly impossible, and it
is significant that, when they tried, it was never by way of
alleging the older faith to be the greater crucible of Christian
values, or the true religion, or even the equal of the
Anglican rite. Instead there was always the assertion that
the papist had a worthy respect for the law. It was indicative

12   of a society in which a man's attitude toward law determined his place in the community. When all else was stripped away, the papist was persecuted and despised because he was accused of abominating the law or, at the very least, of misinterpreting it. The Catholic religion proceeded in error because it was founded upon a legal misconstruction. The Catholic believed that Christ had devised his earthly kingdom to Peter and the remainder to Peter's successors in perpetuity, whereas the Protestant position, as Sir William Petty had noted, was otherwise: all Christians could claim the inheritance of God because Jesus Christ had expressly disowned this world and, by so doing, had impliedly delegated it to all mankind.[31] And, if this reasoning could be extended further, as indeed it was, then even the Nonconformist held a better and more certain estate than did the Catholic. "Here the protestant Non conformist (whom I will not call the Phanatick) hath a better title, for he holds immediately from Christ, but the Roman Catholick onely from his vicar."[32]

Such an imperfect understanding and such an abject lack of appreciation of the law were firmly believed to be part of the Roman Catholic tradition. To call a man a Jesuit conjured up little about his theological position; it implied, rather, that he lived by a code of treachery and fraud and took no heed of the legal ground upon which England stood. In the 1683 *quo warranto* proceedings against the City of London it was important that the prosecution deny any legal difference between acts done in a corporate, as opposed to an individual, capacity. To suggest otherwise, said the attorney general, would be to propose a distinction "framed in the Jesuits Schooles to incourage Subjects in religious orders to rebell against their Princes."[33] There was really no effective counter to this polemical assumption so long as Catholics owed any allegiance to foreign authority. Within the boundaries of England it would be politically acceptable to vie for control of the law, but the contest was limited to those who would accept the confines of the jurisdiction and who would not invite *praemunire* by stepping outside. The

Catholics were not to be trusted because, in looking to Rome, they were accused of trying to see beyond the law. Pleas for Catholic toleration attempted vigorously, although futilely, to get round this popish impediment. They were based, as they had to be, on respect for all the legal props of the English constitution. The "Romish Religion" was alleged not to be "att all Inconsistent with Propertye, Libertye and our other Good Temporall Lawes; since 'tis to our Roman Catholique Auncestors wee are Indebted for Magna Charta."[34] Even Anne, duchess of York, sought first to vindicate her conversion to Roman Catholicism on legal rather than theological grounds. In her reasoning she was to arrive ultimately at doctrinal justification, but not before she had carefully grounded her thinking in law. Her position was that the English Reformation had been illegal, the illicit act of Henry VIII, who "made the breach upon so Unlawfull a pretence."[35]

THE EMPHASIS ON ENGLISH LAW HAD FOR A LONG TIME BEEN taken as synonymous with homage to the English past. Back in the recesses of time, either unrecorded or recorded and subsequently lost, were the principles of the common law, which for centuries had been steadily unfolding in case decisions and which had the occasional help of an act of Parliament. Coke, at the beginning of the century, had stressed this common-law tone, referring to the law which "sometimes sleeps" until it is awakened by a judgment of the courts.[36] The image conveyed was of an existing law which needed only to be declared. It is uncertain whether Coke actually believed in a dormant, and perhaps fully formed, corpus of common-law principles, requiring for application only the quickening touch of a common-law judge, or whether a rule "awakened" from the past was little more than the exercise of a masterful jurist developing doctrine out of whole cloth. As Samuel Thorne has reminded us, "sentences beginning 'For it is an ancient maxim of the common law,' followed by one of Coke's spurious Latin maxims, which he could manufacture to fit any occasion

14 and provide with an air of authentic antiquity, are apt to introduce a new departure."[37] Yet, either way, the accent is unmistakably upon legal precedent and the animating authority of immemorial time. For Coke, as for most of his contemporaries, there is no surer way to fix a judicial decision with unshakable authority than to anchor it firmly in some prior age.

It was of little consequence that the legal past was so often improperly perceived.[38] The failure to understand that the fact of Norman feudalism was more important than the fiction of an "ancient constitution" did not derogate from the importance of law itself. Quite to the contrary, the result was that the law became shrouded in a mystique which served to afford it a greater prestige. The society looked to what it believed its legal origins to be, and it believed in what it saw. It proceeded upon the premise that legal authority rested in legal antiquity. The law was not only ancient, it was immemorial, dating back beyond the reach of historical memory.[39] That precedent which could demonstrate the greatest age could claim the greatest force. There was, as yet, little suggestion of the modern jurisprudential principle that it is the most recent, and not the oldest, precedent which should govern. It was still the remote, and not the immediate, past which counted. Instances of this kind of thinking are to be met throughout the entire period. Representative legal commonplace books of the 1670s, for example, make consistent use of the earliest precedents that can be found. In dealing with constitutional issues such as the position and power of the king, there is almost never any mention of an authority later than the reign of Henry VIII. Most references are set somewhere in the thirteenth through the early sixteenth centuries, and a citation to an Elizabethan precedent is rare.[40]

The past was commended for more than age alone. It incorporated within it the sum of English experience, and it was upon experience that the common law had been built. Time, as a guide to action, was far better and infinitely more effective than any philosophical abstraction removed from its historical context. Long experience represented the collective and accumulated wisdom of the English past. It was, as Hale had said, "much more Ingenious Subtill, and Judicious, than all the wisest and acutest Witts in the world coexisting can be."[41] It was only in time that laws could be tested, only in experience that both the suitabilities and the inconveniences of the law could be found.[42]

> Ancient Laws, Especially that have a Common Concerne, are not the issues of the Prudence of this or that Councill or Senate; but they are the Production of the various Experiences and applications of the wisest thing in the Inferior world, to wit time, which as it discovers day after day new Inconveniences, so it doth successively apply new Remedyes; and indeed it is a kind of aggregation of the discoveries, Results, and applications of ages, and events. So that it is a greate adventure to goe about to alter it, without very greate necessity, and under the greatest Demonstration of Safety & Convenience imaginable.[43]

Only reason might be an alternative to the accumulated wisdom of time, and reason had proved unworkable.[44] The epoch of the Restoration was not yet the age of English rationalism. It was a time when greater guidance was sought and found in established institutions, especially in the law. It was the law which contemplated untold years of English custom and which had, like no other institution, this virtue: it could explain England to Englishmen.

Implicit in the attitude of experience was a new sophistication. Toward the end of the century there was the discernible shift away from that adamantine view of the common law which, despite internal contradictions, had been enshrined in the writings of Coke. It had been a two-pronged turn. First, there was the movement away from the law as sacred. Law was becoming, to the legal mind, more of a secular tool to be addressed to the needs of the community at large. It was still regarded with inordinate deference, but a deference based more upon its

16   extraordinary applicability than upon any inherent sanctity. Hale, for example, was willing to pay a token respect to the sacredness of the law; but in suggesting that veneration was due to it because of the accretions of time, he was making of it a more human institution. Thus, the values of inviolability and expedience were being merged. "Every Law that is old," he wrote, "hath this advantage over any new; ... it is better knowne already to the People who are concerned in itt then any new Law possibly can be without some length of time."[45] It was the aggregate wisdom of the law, gathered over centuries, that accounted for its mystery on the one hand and explained its utility on the other. Hale, in recognizing that old laws were preferable to new because of social and practical considerations rather than because of the antiquity of their origins alone, was reflecting the progress of a new common-law direction, a gradual shift in attention from the status of the law to its function.[46]

As a concomitant of the new emphasis upon practicability there was a new comprehension of the process of change. This was the second prong of the turn from rigidity. It was clear that if law was a collective corpus of experience to be applied to changing conditions, there would have to be an allowance for change in the law itself. Even more importantly, there would have to be a recognition of such change as essentially for the good. No one doubted that the law could change or, indeed, that it had changed; but the open question continued to be whether such change was wise. Coke, for one, had grave doubts. He acknowledged the right of Parliament to introduce new law but was wary of its use.[47] Committed, as he was, to the existence of an ancient common law, he believed that the principal obligation of Parliament and the courts was to see that that law was declared. It was paradoxically consistent with his own excursions into judicially created law that he would repeatedly invoke, as incontestable authority, the immutable legal patrimony of ancient Britain. He wanted Parliament, in particular, to refrain from making new law. He didn't believe it necessary, and he was further convinced that

Parliament's proper role, as a High Court, was to correct the unfortunate divergences from the common law that had been mistakenly made in the past.[48]

If Coke and his common-law colleagues spoke guardedly about alteration of the law, the reforming activists raised up by the civil wars did not. In the period 1640-60 there were the beginnings of widespread agitation for basic legal change. Rather than individual critics expressing dissatisfaction with some aspect of the law, a phenomenon frequently observed in the past, there was now, for the first time, the appearance of what has been seen as "a series of actions by a body of persons"—in short, a *movement*—for reform.[49] What distinguished these men from their predecessors, and from their contemporaries, was not only their activism but their refusal to believe in the common law as the repository, sanctified or otherwise, of justice and of truth. With the successful assault on royal authority and the dismantling of the machinery of prerogative government there came the realization of the law's inherent limitations: any defects remaining in the legal system might well be regarded as the fault of the law itself.[50] Therefore, from the more radical of the critics came the call to complete the revolution and to wipe the slate clean. In 1650 the Digger, Gerard Winstanley, urged Parliament not to "put new wine in old bottles; but as your government must be new, so let the law be new."[51] Yet even Winstanley, who never wavered in his condemnation of the common law, could not divorce himself from the cultural impact of that law upon the pattern of his own thought. One year earlier, in 1649, he could have been seen to use the law, rather than to condemn it, when he made his plea to Lord Fairfax in behalf of "wee poore oppressed Commoners [who] claime freedome in the common land." His were the claims and the language of the law rather than the demands of some abstract equity. He spoke therefore of Parliament's offer, upon which the people did justifiably act and rely. "Wee conceive it," he said,

a firme bargaine betweene you and us; for you and the

18

Parliament in effect said to us, "Give us your taxes, free quarter, excise, and adventure your lives with us to cast out the oppressour Charles, and wee will make yow a free people"; therefore by the law of contract as wee expected was firmly made and confirmed on our part by performance, wee claim this freedom to enjoy the common land for our livelihood.[52]

The people had been made the offer of a unilateral contract, a promise in consideration of their performance. The offer had been accepted, they had performed, and Winstanley was now demanding that the contract be enforced.

Most of the other reformers were not so extreme; yet they all acknowledged existing areas in which English law might be altered and improved. Criminal and civil procedure, prisons, debtors' law, land law, Chancery administration, and ecclesiastical jurisdiction all came under attack. The results, however, were disappointing. Under Cromwell's republican administration there was considerable visible activity with only minimal effective result. Neither the parliamentary committee for law reform established in 1649 nor the Hale Commission, created for the same purpose in 1652, was capable of generating substantial legal change. Whether this was principally because of the resistance of the legal profession itself or was due to a lack of reforming commitment on the part of the government is not altogether certain, but what does seem sure is that the Interregnum impulse toward law reform among the landed and professional classes — the political nation — was both limited in scope and insufficient to the task.[53] It is therefore hardly surprising that the Restoration served to invalidate the minimal strides that republicanism had made. Ecclesiastical jurisdiction was reintroduced, as were Latin and French as the recognized legal languages, while most of the inequities of civil and criminal procedure, partially cured during the Interregnum, were allowed to return.

Nevertheless, the movement for reform did not pass without effect, even if the effect was largely negative. The result of some twenty years of experimentation was a return to known and settled institutions, most obviously to the monarchy but also to a reinvigorated common law. The earlier progress made by the civilians had been halted and reversed largely because theirs had been a system too closely identified with arbitrary government.[54] Another result, more difficult to measure but no less important, was the enlivened awareness of the possibilities of change. This became apparent in politics and also in the law; and it was Hale who once again reflected the shift. Hale agreed that law might indeed be immemorial, but only in the sense that its origins in custom were too distant in time to be known. Otherwise, the law was quite fluid, perpetually adapting to the continuing, if imperceptible, movement in conditions and circumstances.[55] Acts of Parliament could still be, as Coke had preferred, declarative of the common law, but there was now the much more confident recognition of statutes as introductive of new law as well.[56] All this was consistent with the law's being brought into closer harmony with a more practical and more empirical view of the world. In this new understanding it would be permissible to say that laws might be "laid aside as useless, because the Reason of them is ceased" and to recognize the law as an imperfect instrument of man's creation.[57] The myth of immutability was therefore no longer so important, since there was a greater admission of the reality of change. The result was for a sharper focus on movement and adaptation — an acknowledgment that the spirit of the common law was not to be located in its substance but in its continuity and process.

The idea that law could change was both appealing and ominous. Hale, particularly, was conscious of the need to proceed with care. More as a practical jurist than as a legal philosopher he appreciated the myth of an immutable law. "Not soe much to gaine observance, as firmeness," he said of the "Pretence that their Laws were given from Heaven; and therefore not to be changed by any Inferior Authority."[58] Hale knew that the law was alterable, but he feared the consequences of either sudden or basic change.[59] Any

20   reformation of the law was therefore "to be done with greate Prudence, advice, Care and upon a full and cleare prospect of the whole business ... least the whole Fabrique be Endangered."[60] His fear was of change so radical and ill considered that it would be destructive of the law's essential form. To provide against this, Hale wanted the processes of change to be controlled by the legal profession. Like Coke he believed in the capacity of the courts to expound the law and thereby to develop it; and also like Coke he was conscious and suspicious of Parliament's legislative powers. Hale admitted that the common law could not be "authoritatively altered or changed but by an Act of Parliament,"[61] but he had also proposed that what should be done in the first instance was "what can be done by the Power and Authority of the Courts and Judges without troubling a Parliament."[62] It was therefore when the judiciary could not act and when there was no usable alternative that Parliament should be invited to bring about a necessary legal change. But, even then, king and Parliament would be advised to do nothing without first consulting "the Judges and other Sages of the Law," who would "prepare Bills, that may be fitt for the Reformation of the Law, against the next Session."[63] Hale's attitudes, then, were not much different from those of Coke.[64] In the reformation of the law, each would assign the controlling role to the professional lawyers, in general, and to the judiciary, in particular—those who had achieved a mastery of the law, who appreciated its form, and who could be expected to preserve it.

The recognition of mutable law raised the question of possible exceptions. Was there any law which was fundamental and which could not be changed? Was Magna Carta, for example, so basic to the English legal structure that it could not be denied? Was the common law superior to statute and therefore to be the standard by which legislation should be judged? These were difficult questions to answer conclusively or address dispassionately, since any resolution would be charged with overwhelming and highly controversial political implications. At stake was the ultimate control of the direction of the law and, with it, the direction of the constitution. Repeatedly in time of political crisis Parliament would cite the ancient constitution as a restraint upon the king's actions, thereby suggesting that the one area of the law was of a higher value than the other. And even when king and Parliament were in legislative accord, their agreements were sometimes challenged by, or in behalf of, the courts. The king's courts, by invoking the standard of the common law, might seek to countermand and invalidate an incompatible act of the king's Parliament. And if the judiciary was able to render an act of Parliament void because in derogation of the common law, what was to prevent the king, by using his suspending or dispensing power, from effectively doing the same? Coke, in *Dr Bonham's Case* (1610) had said that "the Common Law will controll Acts of Parliament, and some times adjudge them to be utterly void."[65] Whether he meant to enunciate a doctrine of judicial review or was only stating a position of strict statutory construction is uncertain, but in either event he was clearly reluctant to allow the development of the law to escape into the unregulated province of Parliament.[66] It was a position with which Hale, on jurisprudential grounds, and many of his contemporaries, on political grounds, could well agree. In 1677 the earl of Shaftesbury, attempting to overcome an order of the House of Lords committing him to the Tower, urged King's Bench, without success, to assume jurisdiction of his case. He argued *a fortiori* that, as the court might hold an act of Parliament void if such "be against Magna Charta," it might well invalidate an order of the House of Lords depriving him of his liberty. Although neither assertion was accepted, the issue remained unsettled. While the weight of professional and political opinion favored the right of king in Parliament to make any law of its own choosing, still there was enough of an emphasis upon political fundamentals and the ancient constitution to prevent any doctrine of parliamentary sovereignty from taking an unchallenged hold.

All of these attempts to harness and cope with a law which

was now admittedly mutable served to underscore the law's protean adaptability to political circumstances. The aura of sanctity was no longer its exclusive strength. At least part of its power was now to be found in its application, its use as an instrument to remedy the bad and preserve the good. The problem, of course, was, as always, to reconcile conflicting political and social values. In the disputation aroused by James II's first Declaration of Indulgence (1687) it was argued in favor of James that the king, by right, could suspend the penal laws. They were, like all human laws, to be regarded as "expedients of mans invention for the good ends therein proposed and therefore alterable by the same counsels according as the same ends may in different circumstances vareously require."[67] In this instance it was a matter of Catholic special pleading, but it was no more self-interested than the utilitarian argument implicit in the Exclusionists' position, some years earlier, that James should be legally removed from the hereditary succession in order to accommodate the public good. It was, in fact, characteristic of the late-seventeenth-century disposition of mind that greater voice was being given to what the law could be made to do. More persuasive and conspiciously more malleable than the mystery of a hovering omnipresence was the notion that "all laws are but Contracts where the people agree one with another that such things shal be done."[68] To a society attuned to the protection of its contractual rights, private and political, it was an idea easily understood. Even Coke, at the beginning of the century, was busily adapting the law to the changing needs of society, as he recognized those needs to be.[69] Yet what was markedly different toward the end of the century was the relative ease with which the admissions of instrumentalism could be made.

The shift in understanding from a fixed to a flexible law was to have far-reaching constitutional results. If the law was not static, not always with us and wanting only to be declared, if it would in fact change and if Parliament could control that change, then it was at least possible that the same might be true for the constitution, which was based upon it. In 1689 such an appreciation of constitutional mutability was a persuasive inference to be drawn from the recently concluded Revolution. In March of that year John Somers, the future lord chancellor, said of the constitution that although it "be as good as possible for the present time, none can be good at all times."[70] For that reason the constitution, like the law, should be open to reform. From the ideal of an ancient constitution Somers had signaled the shift to a reality of fundamental change. The shift, however, was in keeping with Hale's view of an adaptive common law.[71] Despite a sharpened taste for sovereignty, the older fiction of a supreme law, independent of human control, had not been abandoned. It was modified and retained for the larger numbers who were as yet unaccepting of constitutional alteration. For this majority of the political nation there was a greater reliance upon the pretense of regularity and procedure by color of law; and when the fact of change was so overwhelming that it could no longer be denied, there could still be the redeeming image of Parliament, not as legislature but as High Court, meeting an unusual case upon its individual merits. The members of the Convention were not seen to be rending the constitution; they were adapting it instead to a distinctive condition. The common law was so rich that it might contemplate almost any eventuality; so, likewise, by the late seventeenth century, was the English constitution.

BETWEEN THE COMMON LAW AND THE COMMON LAWYER A careful distinction had to be drawn. The law, even at the height of the agitation for reform, was widely respected. The lawyer, however, was not. The general attitude toward him was ambivalent. He was, on the one hand, recognized as a man of specialized and valued learning, but a learning conspicuously devoid of classical tradition. For that reason the common law was not considered appropriate to the liberal-arts curriculum at Oxford or Cambridge, and the professional lawyer, by extension, was regarded as vulgar.[72] Matthew Hale reportedly stated "that he came from the

24   University with some aversion for lawyers, and thought them a barbarous sort of people, unfit for anything but their own trade."[73] Yet for a society that focused so intently upon hierarchy and form, the study of law assumed an agreeable place in the educational order. With the emphasis upon grammar at school and logic at university, it was a progressive next step to continue in the law. Moreover, among the professionals themselves it was considered as an ideal that the well-educated lawyer would be a rigorously educated man. He would prepare for his further legal training, as Coke had prescribed, by first learning at one of the universities "to discern between truth and falsehood, and to use a good method in his study."[74]

But legal education, like higher education in general, was in a noticeable process of decline. Roger North, in his *Discourse on the Study of the Laws,* criticized generally what he believed was the appalling lack of preparation received by common lawyers,[75] while William Prynne, in his *Animadversions on . . . Cooke,* specifically deplored the erosion of instructional standards.[76] These were judgments borne out by the post-Restoration conditions of education at the Inns of Court. The Inns, after 1660, had virtually ceased to function as learning institutions and had instead become much more recognizable as professional associations of practitioners and acolytes. Instead of the earlier concentration upon a system of aural exercises—of case-puttings, moots, and readings—there was now the primary reliance upon private self-instruction through the use of printed materials, a process that had been evident for more than a century and which had gained considerable momentum with the onset of civil war. The cause of this change is not entirely clear; but the result was that admission to the Inns after 1660 became increasingly limited to those who were set, not upon the trappings of gentility, but upon the minimal requirements of a legal career. Although the Inns may have had little left to offer to gentlemen of quality, they retained exclusive control over entrance to a profession at the bar.[77]

The result of increased professionalization in the late seventeenth century was not regarded by the lawyers themselves as altogether unwelcome. Jealous of what they understood to be their own specialized preserve, they were more than willing to widen the gulf between the professional and the educated layman. Unlike seventeenth-century science, which was being advanced by a talented corps of "virtuosi," common law was not considered a fit subject for amateurs—those whom Hale had characterized as "moral philosophers." It might be desirable for gentlemen to be educated in philosophy or mathematics, but such studies did not suit them to the task of legal interpretation.[78] This was a severe judgment to accept in a kingdom where most men of quality still thought of themselves as capable, even if amateur, "common lawyers." Despite the falling-away of the standards of legal education, the culture of the law had remained. Although the gentry were receiving less exposure to institutional legal study, there was no evidence of a commensurate decline in their legal self-assurance. Hale, taking note of this, expressed the generalized distaste of his fraternity for men who had "only taken pains to read over the titles of the statutes or indexes or repertories of some law books" and thereby conceived themselves to be learned in the law. Hale's attack, although specifically directed against Hobbes, was extended to all men who regarded themselves as "born common lawyers."[79]

Hale's concern was specifically professional. He was insistent upon separating the legal practitioner from those laymen who dabbled irresponsibly in legal opinion. Yet the society at large did not share Hale's sense of differentiation, nor did it endorse his confidence in the professional lawyer. If anything, there was a palpable uneasiness about the definitive pronouncements that lawyers seemed to make as a matter of course. In this regard no one was immune from suspicion, not even Coke. The *Institutes* and the *Reports,* after all, were so protean that they could be used, like Scripture, to support almost any constitutional position.[80] Coke, therefore, could be cited with equal ease both by those

26   who would advance and by those who would retard the use
      of the prerogative.[81] In the pamphlet war at the time of
      Exclusion it was argued, upon the authority of Coke, that
      even if James, as heir presumptive to the throne, were
      attainted of treason, that treason would automatically be
      cured at the moment of his accession. Such was the teaching
      of Coke upon Littleton, and normally it would have been
      enough to settle any argument — but not here. Exception to
      Coke's authority was taken on two significant counts. It was
      suggested by one pamphleteer that we "inquire, first,
      whether these words be Law, or his [Coke's] Notion as a
      Lawyer," and, second,

> if it should appear they are Law, whether it will agree
> with the Wisdom and Safety of any King (whether
> Protestant or Papist) to let such a Law be unrepealed,
> seeing a Successor may be a Traytor, and yet must have
> the Crown. Pray, Sir, consider, it is no breach of Law to
> Repeal a bad Law, and make a better.[82]

From these remarks it was evident, at least in some quarters,
that any authority, Coke included, was subject to question.
No lawyer could be trusted always to be right, nor any law
always to be wise. Law and lawyer alike were open to error
and therefore to change.[83]

Perjury was one example of a crime which many contemporaries agreed did not carry a fit punishment and
which, therefore, ought to be changed. Titus Oates, for
having perpetrated the Popish Plot, was sentenced to a fine,
prison, and the pillory, but his life and limb remained
intact. As a result, the law was exposed to serious criticism.
There were those who clamored for retribution in kind as
the only punishment appropriate to a villain whose false
accusations had claimed five lives. To some reformers it
seemed to be a clear defect in the administration of justice
that Oates should be allowed to live, that there should be no
"just recompense and satisfaction to the law of God for
shedding innocent blood."[84] Even the judges echoed this

lament. At the time of Oates's sentencing in King's Bench, Jeffreys, presiding, specifically regretted that there was no legal way to return to the older penalties of death or mutilation; and Sir Francis Wythens remarked, "I do not know how I can say but that the law is defective that such a one is not to be hanged."[85]

Yet it was not the law itself or even the lapses in the law that were most often being faulted. More times than not it was the "abuses, and Corruptions, . . . that doe adhere to the law and will in time strangle and stifle it."[86] There was therefore a sharpened awareness of the law as an instrument of manipulation available to those who could use it for both social and political ends. And perhaps even more important, there was a similar awareness of the lawyer as a trained, well-paid, and often devious specialist in the manipulative arts. This was how the lawyer made his living. He was educated to see the subtle distinctions that often obtained between things which, upon the surface, appeared to be the same. It was a valuable skill to possess, useful not only to the lawyer but to all who would claim a discriminating intelligence. In a letter from an anonymous correspondent commenting on England's relative military strength in 1675 there is the exhortation always to distinguish, "for he that does not distinguish well can never Judge well."[87] But it was also felt that distinguishing could lead to sophistry, to pettifogging, and, what was worse, to jesuitical distortions. In a popular polemic of the period, "Heraclitus Ridens Redivivus: Or a Dialogue between Harry and Roger Concerning the Times," Harry is depicted as the hypocrite noted most for his inconstancy. He once was vehement in his reproach of the papists, but, in 1688, he is supporting the king's policy of Toleration and repeal of the Test Act. Criticized for shifting position in a shamelessly expedient way, Harry is content to reply that, like the lawyers, he is merely "distinguishing."[88]

At no time more than the period of the Exclusion Crisis was the art and practice of distinguishing in greater evidence. The Exclusionists were treading a very thin line. They were mounting a direct attack on the next in line to the

28   throne, and they had to be mindful not to go too far. Every step of the way they were required to demonstrate that they were committing no treason, that attempting to disinherit one who would be king was not to be construed as rebellion. In this they were successful, even though Exclusion was to fail. The points had been made carefully and well, so much so that it was remarked, of one Exclusionist, that "if he cannot demonstrate so well, yet he can put Cases, like Littleton."[89] This was not intended as a compliment. It was at the cost of having his arguments labeled as lawyers' tricks and deceptions that the otherwise respectable comparison had been made.

It was apparent that the legal profession depended very heavily upon form and appearance. "The End or Aim of a Lawyer," wrote Roger North, "is duple: 1. to know and 2. to appear to know; the latter brings in clients & the former holds them."[90] In one sense, this might appear to be a cynical appraisal, but it is unlikely that North intended it that way. Every lawyer knew that not only his profession but the administration of the law itself was reliant upon what could readily be seen by all of society. Justice, to be done, had to be seen to be done. Otherwise, a barely visible fabric of paper laws and judicial decisions could not command the respect necessary to its function. It would, therefore, be a mistake to assume that appearances were divorced from reality. It was, on the contrary, from appearances that the law, the lawyer, and the constitution drew their greatest strength.

Yet not everyone could be expected to appreciate the value of legal appearance, least of all those who had fallen victim to some of the more unfortunate contrivances of which lawyers were capable. As a direct result of the Rye House Plot, William, Lord Russell and Algernon Sydney, among others, were tried and executed for conspiring the death of the king. Lord Russell had been silent throughout his trial. Not until he was upon the scaffold did he attempt any sort of defense, and then, of course, it was too late. After maintaining that he might, at most, be guilty of misprision

of treason, he proceeded to condemn those who had distorted the law in such a manner as to be guilty themselves of
legal murder:

> Nor did I ever pretend to a great readiness in speaking:
> I with those Gentlemen of the Law who have it, would
> make more Conscience in the use of it, and not run Men
> down by Strains and Fetches, impose on easie and willing
> Juries to the Ruine of innocent Men: For to kill by Forms
> and Subtilities of Law, is the worst sort of Murder.[91]

So the emphasis upon form could be as generative of evil as
it might be productive of good. Adherence to form could be
perceived as both the lawyer's weakness and his strength.

The ambivalence was resolved by associating all the good
things in the law with the greatness of the common-law
tradition, while all that was bad was due to the law's
avaricious practitioners. The lawyers were often seen to
reflect all that was wrong in the society. They were understood to be forever available to pander to the gross passions
and ill designs of anyone who might have the requisite fee.
Burnet wrote of Hale that he "used to say it was as great a
dishonour as a Man was capable of, that for a little Money
he was to be hired to say or do otherwise than as he
thought."[92] And if Burnet is to be believed, Matthew's
father, Robert Hale, himself a barrister of Lincoln's Inn,
gave up the practice of law because it did not comport with
his conscience as a Christian. He "could not understand the
reason of giving Colour in Pleadings, which as he thought
was to tell a Lye."[93] Matthew Hale also reported that at the
central courts at Westminster there were always those who
were "ready . . . to gratifie the Spleen, Spight or Pride, of
every Plaintiff,"[94] a problem exacerbated by what was
believed to be the existence of too many laws. "When there
are but few Laws there are fewer Law Suits," wrote one
commentator during the reign of Charles II;[95] and, in 1675,
Shaftesbury warned that "a land may groane under a
multitude of Laws (& I believe ours does) & when laws grow

30

so multiplied, they oftener prove scares, than directions & securities of the people."[96]

But to accuse the "long robe" of being parasites was not the ultimate condemnation. There were those who were less afraid of the multitude of lawyers prepared to do another's evil than of those lawyers who went further and generated business on their own. It was a common image for critics to conjure when they spoke of "the great number of Attorneys who do so swarm that they can hardly subsist but by setting their Neighbours at variance."[97] This, after all, was the way an attorney made his living. He was in greatest demand in areas of discord, and he was suspected of creating that discord where it did not otherwise exist.

Once in the courtroom the lawyer was to be scrutinized with a wary eye. It was known that his arts were many and that he had a characteristic manner of avoiding truth and finding refuge in duplicity. It was in this regard that he was suspected of being truly "jesuitical." The trial of Baron Delamere for high treason, in 1686, is a good case in point. Delamere had first been implicated in the Rye House Plot and, two years later, in connection with Monmouth's Rebellion, was brought to trial in Westminster Hall before Jeffreys, by then lord chancellor. He had made a plea to the jurisdiction to the effect that he ought not to be tried by a number of peers and a lord steward, under commission. Rather, he contended, he should be tried by the whole body of the House of Lords in Parliament.[98] The attorney general demanded that the plea be rejected as not being in proper form and that the defendant be made to interpose a plea in chief. Delamere then asked for counsel. The request was granted, provided that the defendant produce counsel then and there, which he was unprepared to do. He asked for time, which was denied. Jeffreys ruled that in a trial for a capital crime it was inappropriate for the defendant to have counsel until such time as the court determined that it was proper. That time would come only when there might be a question of law on which it would be deemed beneficial by the court to have the opinion of counsel. Jeffreys continued:

For if in case any Prisoner at the Barr shall beforehand
be allowed to have Councel to start frivolous Objections,
such as this (and we all know that there are some who
will be easily prevailed with, to endeavour to pick Holes
where there are none) and to offer Matters foreign from
the things whereof the Party stands accused; and upon
the Prisoner's bare Request, Councel must be heard at
every trivial Point, the Courts of Law would never be at
an end in any Tryal; but some dilatory Matter or other,
would be found to retard the Proceedings: But it does not
consist with the Grandeur of the Court, nor your Lordship's Interest, to let such a frivolous plea interrupt your
Lordship's Tryal.[99]

The dictum is instructive, for it expressed a good measure of
the general attitude toward the legal profession: the lawyer,
as often as not, was an impediment rather than an aid to
justice.

It is not altogether surprising that the lawyer was held in
such suspicious regard. Although many of the criticisms
leveled against him were either exaggerated or false,[100] it is
at least certain that the lawyer was particularly expert in
those skills and contrivances which made his art more of a
weapon than a shield. He moved professionally in a world of
arcane mysteries which he alone claimed to understand, but
a world in which the educated layman felt nonetheless
competent and privileged to participate. The problem was
that the law was not, and could not be, solely an occupa-
tional preserve. It was part, instead, of a wider culture
which encompassed all of the political nation, professional
and amateur alike.

2   *Analogues and Metaphors*

IT IS SOMETHING OF A FICTION THAT TIME ALLOWS FOR A faithful perspective upon the events of history. What seems to contemporaries to be confused, chaotic, and disordered at the moment of a particular event is not usually capable of being viewed in truer light from a distance. All that time really permits is the opportunity to impose a meaningful order upon the past so that, to an often confounded present, what has gone before it may appear more intelligible. Moreover, men do not do this to their past alone. As great as their need may be to perceive an order in what has already been, there is a greater need to regulate and explain the world and time that are part of the here and now. In this regard they have a small measure of choice. They can seek to impose an order of their own creation upon the bewildering world, or they can borrow an order that is already apparent and well understood. The first approach is clearly more imaginative, but the second is infinitely more comfortable.

It was the second address that political Englishmen chose in the late seventeenth century, a method which happened to explain the past and present in precisely the same way, by reference to a preexisting frame. This frame, in larger compass, was the law; in most instances, particularly, it was the common law. Stated simply, the familiar concepts of English law were used to shape men's ideas of their constitution. It was not at all times a very conscious process, nor was it ever a calculated design. Instead, it was a cultural instinct which reflected the strong and basic assumptions of the society. England was a realm that was founded in law; and, regardless of who controlled that law, the law itself was the acknowledged standard by which constitutional politics would be guided. In the same way that law explained men's relations with one another, so too would it explain their relations with their state and sovereign. It was an attitude which, unlike moral philosophy, was tied less to abstractions and more to institutions. The law was already there, and in its fundamentals it was easily comprehended by all within political society. This intellectual posture was expressed not only in a knowledge of rules but in a way of thinking and of viewing the world. It existed as a legal disposition of mind which invited constitutional problems to be understood in fixed, often formulaic, private-law terms.

Among the private-law principles to be applied to politics and the constitution, inheritance was the most common. Englishmen spoke easily and with conviction of legacy and birthright. Everyone knew that the common law protected a man in the inheritance of lands from his father. By the same reasoning there were political rights, common to all Englishmen, which sought the same protection. There was, in fact, nothing in normal parlance which carried a greater guarantee of acceptance than a reference to the heritable quality of the English laws, liberties, and religion. William Petyt, the late-seventeenth-century archivist and antiquary, extolled English law as "the birth right and the most antient and best inheritance that the Subjects of this Realme have."[1] Here, as in other constitutional matters, he characteristically supported his own views with a range of authority. With enthusiastic approval he cited Bacon for the proposition that Englishmen "take themselves to have as good a title to their Lawes, as to the Common aire they Breath in,"[2] and Coke for the observation that the nobility and kings of England held the law in precisely the same regard.[3] Heritable rights were secure and unquestioned because they were part of the patrimony of time assured by the common law. It was a mark of that respect for the past which characterized the law itself.

An inheritance could even have the effect of transforming an uncertain into an indisputable holding. For men to know the truth of their inheritance would serve to "establish and settle them in quiet and lawful possession."[4] By this process Magna Carta meant more in the seventeenth century than it had in the thirteenth. King John's barons held the Great Charter as a tenuous conveyance, but the whole English people, some four hundred fifty years later, held it by inheritance as a secure and indefeasible estate. However limited it might have been when originally granted, it was now, by all accounts, something more. In the earl of Shaftesbury's case,[5] in 1677, Shaftesbury propounded an eloquent, even if disingenuous, argument for his constitutional inheritance. "I hope," he said, that "my beinge a peere or a Member of either House shall not loose my beinge an English man nor take away my birthright nor make me have less title to Magna Charta and the other Lawes of English Liberty."[6] Magna Carta had come that far, and it had come by way of inheritance. From a feudal document which had been wrested forcibly from a reluctant king, it had become a fundamental charter of English liberties.

Despite the haven afforded by inheritance, the fact of any given legacy could be, and often was, disputed. Daniel Finch, a member of Parliament from 1673 through 1682,[7] questioned the House of Commons for asserting their "Priviledges to be as much their right and Inheritance as their Land,"[8] and Sir Joseph Williamson, keeper of the state papers under Charles II, made the same critical observation. "The Priviledges of the H. Commons," he recorded in his notebook, are "not properly said to be their inheritances.... They are rather the grace of the Prince."[9] And, in a jury charge at Middlesex Quarter Sessions in 1682, Sir William Smith reviled those Dissenters from the Church of England who "contended for the Conventicles, as if they had been their Inheritance."[10] In each instance the protective quality of the principle was never at issue. Indeed, in withholding its coverage from the Commons and the Dissenters, respectively, first Finch and Williamson, then Smith, were reinforcing its value. Inheritance was not being applied as a metaphor to the matters of constitutional issue.

The legacy was deemed instead to be both literal and real. It was necessary to each argument that such a firm stand be taken because, once it could be established that something was indeed part of a man's inheritance, there was little more to be said. It was his as of right and could not very easily be taken away.

Not, that is, so long as the heir was legally competent, so long as he was of full age and sound mind. He would not be competent if he were adjudged in law to be an infant, an idiot, or a lunatic. In such cases the heir would not be capable of governing his affairs or of managing his estates. The first category presented little difficulty. A man's age was a matter of fact to be determined by reference to an agreed and certain standard. Either he had or had not attained his majority. Idiocy and lunacy were not so simple, but in those cases, as well, there were accepted definitions to be applied. An idiot was a "fool naturally from his birth," and a lunatic "mad or frantick at a certaine time of the moone."[11] One was permanently affected, the other temporarily; but each, for the duration of his affliction, was "of soe weake an understanding that he cannot governe or manage his inheritance."[12] That, of course, was the significant common denominator. Although a man's inheritance was usually secure, an heir could forfeit the administration of his patrimony if he were ruled incompetent for that purpose. It was the one important proviso that was to have far-reaching constitutional ramifications in two critical periods of the era, first during the Exclusion Crisis and, a decade later, at the time of the Revolution. In each instance the same argument was advanced: James Stuart could be made to give up the management of his inheritance because he was, in law, incapable of the necessary control. To those who tendered the argument, it made no difference that the inheritance in question was the English Crown. The same rules could be made to apply. No one would suggest that James had been incapacitated from birth; but "if a King's Heir be so mad as to be of any Perswasion different from the People,"[13] a case might be made for his lunacy. It was, after all, a credible way in which to account for James's abhorrent religion. It had, on the one hand, the attractive advantage of equating Roman Catholicism with a defect in reason; and it allowed, on the other hand, for a valid legal procedure by which James might be divested of his inheritance. It was an extreme construction but one that nevertheless derived from the principles of the common law.

The most confusing of the common-law concepts were those that applied to property. To begin with, property was associated with an immensely difficult area of the law. There was the seemingly endless complex of rules and principles which had no intrinsic logic and made sense only when applied as specific solutions to specific problems. Yet the confusion stemmed from something more. The word "property" itself could be subject to a great deal of ambiguity and misinterpretation. Everyone knew that it was important; everyone used it with ease; but it did not always mean the same thing. The word could be then, as it is today, equated with a man's possessions, both personal and real. When Charles II, in February 1672, assured Parliament, as he often did, that he would preserve the established church and further guaranteed that "no Man's Property or Liberty shall ever be invaded,"[14] he was seemingly speaking in just that way. Property could simply be viewed as the corporeal object of ownership. A man's land, his home, his chattels— this was his property. But property might also be something more. As a legal word of art it was infinitely broader in scope. In law what was contemplated was something which might be peculiar or proper to any person, something which, in the strict legal sense, was viewed as an aggregate of rights. By this definition it would be meaningful to speak of a man's property in his life, his liberty, and his religion. This, certainly, was what Petyt intended when he wrote that men "had a right and Property in their lives and Estates"[15] and what Hale intended when he wrote that "Every man hath an unquestionable property in his own life and in his own self";[16] and it may very well have been what Charles meant as well. In the debates on the Declaration of Indul-

gence following the king's February 1672 address, Sir Robert
Howard argued in support of the Crown's assurances.
Answering those who challenged the king's guarantee,
Howard observed that "life, liberty, and estate is property"
and denied that any of these would be invaded by the
Indulgence.[17]

The distinctions to be drawn between one use of the word
and the other were often unclear. The duke of Buckingham,
in an address to the House of Lords in 1675, began
by saying:

> There is a thing called Property, (whatever some men may
> think) that the People of England are fondest of. It is that
> they will never part with, and it is that His Majesty in his
> Speech has promised to take particular care of. This, my
> Lords, in my opinion, can never be done, without an
> Indulgence to all Protestant dissenters.[18]

It was the reference to the Dissenters that conveyed
Buckingham's construction of the word. He was suggesting
that each man had an estate in his religion and that, by
denying that estate, Parliament would be guilty of an
infringement of property. It was a sensible argument, one
which an assembly that valued property so highly could not
fail to appreciate. An Englishman's religion, like his life and
his liberty, was as much his property as was his land, and to
deny one would be no different from denying the other. The
problem, of course, was that the same reasoning might also
be applied to the Catholics, and only a very few were
prepared to extend liberty of conscience quite that far.

It was more a matter of politics than of legal interpretation, but, in denying the same rights to papists, the property
concept was not to be abandoned. To those who opposed
Toleration, the Roman Catholic was to be deprived of the
advantages of the law because property was something that
he abused. Papists, after all, particularly those involved in
the "Plot," were justly guilty of conveyancing evil. Left
unchecked, they were certain to entail their "devilish

38   principles" upon the posterity of the realm. "And so, if God, by his Providence do not cut off the Entail, and cut off those Evil Doers also, our Nation can never be Safe."[19]

References to property were invoked even when they could not be justified. Gilbert Burnet, in 1687, ranging himself against James II's first Declaration of Indulgence, tried to reverse Buckingham's argument by simply labeling the Declaration itself an invasion of property. Yet what was most important was that he too thought of property in terms other than, or at least more than, land and chattels. In the same letter in which he condemned the Declaration, Burnet wrote that "the first branch of property is the right that a man has to his life."[20] This by no means excluded other things from the property concept, but it did establish a hierarchy in values. It was consistent with the anonymous treatise which began: "The use of the Lawe consisteth principally in theis 2 thinges, the one to secure mens persons from death and violence, and th' other to dispose the propertie of Lands and goods."[21] All of a man's possessions were deemed by the law important, but it was to the property in his person that primary consideration was to be given.

John Locke's thought was subject to the same ambiguity. A careful reading of his *Second Treatise of Government* reveals that he too used "property" both ways. In chapter 5, "Of Property," Locke speaks at some length of man's creating private possessions by mixing his labor with nature.[22] "Thus labour, in the beginning, gave a right of property, wherever anyone was pleased to employ it upon what was common."[23] But property did not end, nor did it begin, with this explanation alone. Like Burnet, Locke recognized the proprietary interest of each man in his own life. Locke, indeed, noted at the outset of the chapter that, "though the earth and all inferior creatures be common to all men, yet every man has a property in his own person; this nobody has any right to but himself."[24] Property, then, only sometimes referred to realty or personalty; at other times its object might be religion, liberty, physical well-being, or life itself.[25] All that was certain when Burnet, Buckingham, or any other late-seventeenth-century commentator mentioned property was that, like Locke, he was speaking always of a "private right."[26] In this regard, John Locke was a perfect example of the thinking of his time. However property might shade in meaning, it would always be that which was recognized in law as "dominion," the highest right that a man could have to anything. So to say, with Buckingham, that "there is a thing called Property . . . that the People of England are fondest of" is both true and misleading. It does not support the contention that England in the seventeenth century was concerned less with its religion and its liberties than it was with its land. That misguided argument, which proceeds upon too narrow a construction of "property," is too often advanced as the primary basis of the parliamentary position. This, however, is not to suggest that the "justification of property" interpretation of the period, and particularly of the Revolution, is without contemporary support.[27] In 1675 an anonymous writer alleged that the political upheaval that the kingdom had thus far experienced (an obvious reference to the civil wars of the 1640s) had been due to the growing concentration of land in the hands of the "people." He noted that this had been accomplished by Henry VII's having liberalized the law as to the alienability of estates and Henry VIII's having dissolved the monasteries.[28] And several years after the Revolution a pamphleteer bitterly remarked "That a man hath not the like advantages to defend his Life, as to defend his Right to an Acre of Land."[29]

Yet, what is more to the point, and goes further to explain the period, is that the larger view of "property" was the accepted frame of conceptual reference. What Buckingham's dictum does imply is that the language of property, as understood by the lawyers, was also the accepted idiom in political society at large. It was that which made the greatest sense as a metaphor to be applied to constitutional debate.[30] It was that which helped to dress the radicalism of opposition to the king in the conservatism of adherence to the law.

If "inheritance" was the most common of the applied

40 concepts of the law and "property" the most confusing, "contract" was certainly the most important. More than a polemical device, it encompassed a set of well-known rules which could describe and delimit the relationship between king and people. It was a reflection of a world of reciprocal rights and obligations, a world which was in perfect harmony with an earlier medieval order. Contract was England's guarantee against absolutism. As long as a compact, any compact, existed between king and people, there would be some restraint upon the freedom of the sovereign. He would, at the very least, be obliged to do, or refrain from doing, certain things which the contract alone made incumbent upon him. This, by definition, was in the nature of any binding agreement recognized in English law. A simple contract meant mutuality of obligation, the agreement between two or more parties upon a sufficient consideration from each. Consideration was the crucial element in all agreements except those under seal, the requirement that each party be required to give up something as an inducement to contract. It was this which served in part to distinguish the common law from any other jurisprudence. For the canonists and the civilians, consideration was not nearly so important; for the common lawyers it was indispensable. Without it, a simple contract could not, in law, exist. If a binding obligation was attempted on one side but was absent on the other, the agreement would be merely illusory. It would not, in fact, be a contract. This is why it was argued that the people, as a party to the original contract, could not promise to be bound to the terms of the agreement if the king chose not to be. Obligations had to be mutually binding. If it were otherwise, "the nature of the Act is changed, & it becomes a gift or donation rather than a contract."[31] The people would have no rights at all, but would be reduced to slavery. The political implications were therefore apparent. If the king could not be bound, neither could the people.

Nevertheless, it was possible to reject contract as the basis of constitutional relationships and still rely upon the constructs of the private law. Sir Peter Leicester, for example, was particularly attracted to the conclusions to be derived from a Crown which had originally been conferred as a gift. Although he rejected the suggestion of an elective monarchy, he argued that, if there had ever been an original "election" of a king, it was a power that could be used but once. The Crown had been donated to the king, and the gift could not be revoked. "A donation absolutely made without any condition interposed, cannot be revoked de iure ... , for the right, which before the election was in the Electours, after the election passeth into the Persons elected." It was, by analogy, like the elections to Parliament. "The freeholders of a county may choose a Knight of the Parliament, but not recall him after he is duly elected."[32]

There was never any question but that the people owed obedience to their king. It was how far that obedience was to go, how much it could be taken for granted, and what, if anything, the king owed in return that occasioned dispute. This was the great issue of the seventeenth century, and this is what made the compact theory of government so attractive to those who would place constitutional limits upon the Crown. For the act of obedience and the forbearance from freedom there needed to be a sufficient consideration. As a result, it was often alleged, quite simply and directly, that "the title of our Kings is founded on a proper mutual contract between them & their people obliging them to govern us according to the laws & the people to a correspondent obedience."[33] The king had received a benefit, something of value, and for this he was obliged to render something in return. Yet, too much emphasis could not be placed upon the monarch's obligations without risking the suggestion that the king had not entered the agreement of his own accord. If the contract had been made under duress, even if upon a sufficient consideration, it would be voidable at best and possibly null and void from its very inception. This had long been recognized, and in other contexts as well. When, for instance, during the Puritan Interregnum, an attempt was made to impose the Covenant upon the

42   University of Oxford, it was noted that it would be of no
avail to force a man to swear to any compact contrary to his
conscience. In the Oxford Remonstrance against the Covenant it was argued, as an analogue from the private law,
that such an imposition was "repugnant to the nature of a
Covenant; which being a Contract, implieth a voluntary
mutual consent of the contractors."[34] It was evidence of a
legal sophistication that in the seventeenth century had
come to characterize an approach to religion as well as to the
constitution. Even theology itself could be based upon a
covenant between God and the believer. It was therefore the
case that in matters of church doctrine, as in matters of
church government, as in matters of the organization of
society, the concepts applied were often rooted in the
familiar constructions of the private law.

The problem of contractual interpretation did not end
with the question Has a contract, in law, been created? In
most cases the affirmative of the question could be established. What was more important was the determination of
the point at which the obligations incurred might cease to be
binding. In this regard, what was most often argued was
that a material breach by one party—usually the king—
constituted a forfeiture of the rights that he claimed
pursuant to the agreement.[35] In such instances the people
would be released from their contractual duty to obey. In
legal terms, their obligation of performance would be
excused. The difficulty, of course, was in the definition of a
"material breach." Not every violation would amount to a
breaking of the contract. The king, like any other contracting party, would be allowed some latitude in his actions
before the compact could be considered destroyed. It was an
important distinction to be made, and in 1688 it was to be
an issue of the greatest consequence.

In a constitution erected upon legal principles such
careful distinctions were always to be drawn. Under the law
of contract not all agreements were viewed in the same way,
nor were they to be accorded the same treatment.[36]
Analogues from the private law were therefore selective. It

was in the compact of marriage that the most attractive analogies were often found, for the relationship between king and Parliament could be seen in marital terms. To some who consistently supported a royalist position, it was the king who was the metaphorical husband and who was therefore rendered a superior status. The marriage contract, as everyone knew, was not an accord between equals. There was, as a result, the expected warning of punishment by the king of his occasionally disobedient "wife." Even dissolution of a perfidious Parliament, as a last resort, could be explained in this way. This was what was carefully outlined by the lord chancellor in 1672 so that there would be no mistake. He told Parliament that its marriage to the king was one "according to Moses's Law, where the husband can give a Bill of Divorce, put her away, and take another."[37] Yet, it was not quite that simple. Everyone recognized that, with reference to marriage, it was the law of God rather than the common law of England that was primarily involved. It was therefore argued by some that, since matrimony was ordained by God, there could be no unmaking of it by man. The bond, once made, was indissoluble.[38] Now, if this could be applied to Parliament, it would mean that, once having been summoned by the king, Parliament was his for life. This clearly would never do; and although Charles II's Cavalier Parliament went on for more than eighteen years, no one seriously questioned the king's right, under the prerogative, to prorogue and ultimately to dissolve.

Where the argument based upon matrimony had the greatest currency was in the discussion of the "original contract." On this issue it was politically expedient for the king to allege that, if there was a compact, it could not be dissolved, and for the Parliament to allege the contrary. And so long as the marriage metaphor was to be applied, it would be vital to determine whose interpretation was right. Unfortunately for the Stuarts, history, in addition to law, was working against them. Henry VIII had focused too much attention upon the possibility of divorce. The only suitable compromise seemed to be to envisage the marriage

44   contract as one that could, in law, be broken, but not easily or lightly. So too would it be for the contractual obligations between the king and his people.

> Whereas in matrimony there is a contract of mutual Love & cohabitation till death do them part, it is not every act of unkindness between man & wife, that nulls the obligation: But in case of Adultery in the wife or extreme cruelty in the husband the Innocent party may sue out a Divorce & be separated from the other. So not every Transgression of the Law putts the Subject out of protection, but Treason does &c & so not every maleadministration or illegal Act in the prince disengages his subjects from their obligation to Him, but such only as subverts the essentialls of the government.[39]

As in marriage, dissolution was possible, but only when there was no longer an open alternative. "So long as any part of the constitution is preserved in such manor as to be able to rectify the male administration of the rest ... Arms ought not to be taken up."[40] It was possible, therefore, for the king to be guilty of a breach of the contract so serious that the people might legally be relieved of their obligation to obey. The point at which a royal act, or failure to act, would constitute such a subversion of an essential part of the constitution, and thus amount to a material breach, was a matter of serious dispute, but there was little doubt among those who would apply the principle that the king was liable to a forfeiture of his throne.

To most who believed in an original contract, and to those who hoped to use it for political advantage, the king was to be regarded as a contracting party; he had bound himself to the terms of the compact and could be held to account for his performance. This, however, was not the view of the contractarian philosophers, Thomas Hobbes and John Locke. For Hobbes and Locke the original contract was among the people alone, and did not include the king. In the Hobbesian reconstruction of the agreement the contract called for each man to surrender his individual sovereignty to the ruler in consideration of every other man's doing the same thing, while in the Lockean re-creation there were two contracts, of which only in the second was the king to be included. For Locke the original contract was the instrument by which men entered political society. Then, by a second agreement (which, in law, was closer in form to an instrument of trust), the corporate people transferred limited powers to their monarch.

Neither the Hobbesian nor the Lockean original contract is anywhere in evidence in the parliamentary disputations of the later seventeenth century. When, in 1688, James II was forced to flee the realm and the political nation was called upon to settle the government, the issue of whether James had broken the original contract was immediately and repeatedly raised. To those Whigs who invoked and interpreted that contract it was certain that the Crown was a party. For this reason the rationalism of Locke, like the more obviously unacceptable absolutism of Hobbes, was, in 1688–89, of little political moment. The contract that was then so extensively discussed derived from the private law and not from political theory. The Whig compact was between king and people. It was the only compact of which the Convention of the Revolution ever spoke.[41]

What was comforting in the use of this private-law analogue was something more than the liability it placed upon the king that, as a contracting party, he could be faulted for a material breach of his obligation. By such a construction it could also be demonstrated that the contractual standing of the people as parties was legally superior to their roles as subjects. Indeed, it was as a result of the contract that their status as subjects had been established. They were parties first, and in asserting their contractual rights they could never be guilty of treason. As long, at least in theory, as they restricted themselves to an interpretation of their agreement, and could prove that the king had dishonored that agreement, they could feel secure that they were on safe legal ground: A basic principle of the private law could be used, almost as a matter of course, to excuse the act of

46   treason, the most heinous crime known to the realm. It was an interesting paradox, and one which in the decade of the 1680s was to find repeated and urgent expression.

The use of the law as analogue and as metaphor was current throughout political society. Particularly as applied to the constitution, the forms of the law were everywhere in evidence. It could in fact be said that constitutionalism was more a matter of form than of substance. The way in which things were done rather than the things themselves counted for far more in the sum of English experience. Just as the Elizabethans, as part of their medieval heritage, had sought out "correspondences" between the different planes of existence, so too did they pass on to their descendants the same need for structural unity and order.[42] It is this that suggests why law, legal forms, and legal procedures, all designed for the regulation of man and his society, would be so important to the age. Nothing else proceeded so naturally from the traditional patterns of thought. Nothing else reflected so accurately an ordered view of the world.

In much of medieval political thought Parliament was understood to be nothing but a court, not unlike the courts at Westminster. It was deemed responsible for hearing pleas and for discovering and declaring the law. It had, therefore, definitive judicial responsibilities but, in a technical sense, no legislative function. That Parliament could, in fact, make law was only slowly to be admitted. Certainly, in its origins, Parliament had enjoyed a conspicuous judicial role, even if it is still unclear whether the first parliaments were essentially political or essentially judicial bodies.[43] The earliest forms of the law were, as Matthew Hale had recognized, in the nature of petition and answer;[44] and by the seventeenth century the style "High Court of Parliament" was still an appropriate characterization of its function even though the assembly had long since ceased to entertain private suits.

Whenever a judicial metaphor was employed to describe constitutional relationships, the king was cast in the role of judge,[45] and Parliament, particularly the Commons, in the form of petitioner or lawyer. It was therefore understood that Parliament's purpose was to press its own demands or those of its clients, the nation. It was not uncommon to hear references to Parliament as "the Atturneys of the people," called upon to do their bidding and to protect their rights.[46] Bracton, it has been noted, "thought of the nation in terms of a common element in civil litigation — the joint and inseparable interests of a number of parties to the same suit,"[47] and the same perception continued throughout the seventeenth century. Beyond this, the components at times became a bit confused. Part of the Parliament, the Commons, might be viewed as a grand jury, and the Lords, as in the matter of impeachment, in the posture of judge. Or, in cases where complaints against ministers were made directly to the king, it was the king who once more assumed the paramount judicial role.[48] Yet, throughout the process, what was most apparent was that parallels and corre- spondences were continually being drawn between elements of the private law, on the one hand, and the mechanism of government, on the other. In matters of legislation the analogues were especially useful. Subsidies granted to the king were viewed sometimes as "gifts" and at other times in the manner of a "bill of bargaine."[49] As Hale saw it, every act of Parliament was really in the nature of "a *Tripartite Indenture,* between the King, the Lords and the Com- mons."[50] It was as if every aspect of parliamentary business could be, and had been, outlined in the terms of the private law.

The common law, particularly as it applied to contract, leaned heavily upon the doctrine of mutuality. One could not normally expect to gain from an agreement unless something was given up in return. In the law there was always the striving for equilibrium. Obligation was balanced by right; responsibility was traded for privilege. Politics and the constitution were seen in the same way. As a matter of form, mutuality in the law could easily be converted to balance in government. The nature and the position of the fulcrum might be in issue, but the constitutional ideal of

48   king and people as two forces in working harmony was
continually visible. Sometimes it was Parliament that was
seen as the point of balance. From this perspective, a
common expression of mutuality might be that "Parliament
is assembled for the profit of the King, and of his people."[51]
This was particularly apparent during the time of the
Exclusion debates. Parliament was conceived as the only
hope for insuring the nation against the rule of a Catholic
sovereign. In preparation for the elections to the Oxford
Parliament it was the perpetuation of this safeguard that
was urged by the proponents of Exclusion. Only frequent
parliaments, each meeting long enough to dispatch the
required business of the realm, could guarantee the necessary "adjustment ... betwixt the Kings Prerogative" and
"the Rights of the People."[52] The reference was only thinly
veiled: the delicate symmetry of the English constitution was
in danger of being disrupted by the accession of the duke of
York. More often, however, it was the law that was seen as
effecting the proper balance. In the concluding encomium
to his Trimmer, Halifax describes the law as the great
equipoise "between the excesses of unbounded power and
the extravagance of liberty not enough restrained."[53] This
was the essence of mutuality and the basis of constitutionalism. It was the law that made "a true distinction
between vassalage and obedience, between devouring prerogatives and a licentious ungovernable freedom."[54]

The great effectiveness of the law as constitutional
fulcrum was that all would admit to its value. It was old, it
was respected, and it was adaptable. If properly understood
and carefully treated, there would be very little that it could
not be made to do. Everyone curried its favor and vied to
control it. More important was the fact that by the reign of
Charles II it had lost much of its appearance as the rival of
prerogative. It was not that law had retreated in the face of a
stronger enemy. It was rather that law had shifted to a
position above the battle. This, in itself, was the mark of a
great constitutional watershed. It meant that the struggle
for sovereignty could be understood more clearly as existing

between king and Parliament and that each could appeal to the law for the fullest measure of support.

There were some who would resist this shift, but after 1660 there were few places to which the proponents of an unregulated prerogative might look for encouragement. Sir Joseph Williamson was one who provided an anachronistic voice when he maintained that only the "private Rights" of the king were subject to the law; his "Supreame Rights" were not. These "Supreame Rights," by which he meant the prerogative, were, he contended, inseparable from the Crown and incapable of being either alienated or judged.[55] Williamson's argument, although it had never enjoyed wide acceptance, had at one time been more persuasive. In the first part of the century, *Bate's Case,* Cowell's *Interpreter,* and the *Five Knights' Case* had given currency to the position that some part of the prerogative, at least, stood beyond, if not above, the law. In *Bate's Case* (1606) Chief Baron Fleming pronounced that the "King's power is double, ordinary and absolute." Only the ordinary part was contemplated in law, while the absolute prerogative, which Fleming called "policy and government," was not.[56] John Cowell reinforced this idea when he stated in his *Interpreter* that the prerogative existed above the law; and although James was obliged to renounce Cowell's claims for monarchical absolutism, he went only so far as to say that "there was such a marriage and union between the prerogative and the law as they cannot possibly be severed."[57] In the *Five Knights' Case* (1627) Chief Justice Hyde, refusing to bail Darnel and the four others, found "that if no cause of the commitment be expressed it is to be presumed to be for matters of state, which we cannot take notice of."[58]

This was the legacy upon which Williamson was drawing, but throughout the century it had been steadily losing ground.[59] Its antithesis—that the prerogative, like all other components of the constitution, was to be fully contemplated in the law—was the view that ultimately would prevail. Many of the institutional supports of prerogative rule had been stripped away from the restored monarchy,

50   while the fear of renewed revolution served to focus greater
attention upon the rule of law. The way to support the
prerogative was to uphold the law from which it emerged.
This was one of the more important lessons of the Puritan
Interregnum. It was the only defense against absolutism or
anarchy, and, because each of these alternatives was unthinkable, law was vaulted into an even greater role than it
had ever before enjoyed. Petyt and Shaftesbury underscored
these fears pointedly. Petyt contended that without "the
guard of the Law ... farewell all peace, & happinesse
either, to Prince, or People"; [60] and Shaftesbury explicitly
warned that "the King holds his Prerogative by the Law & if
that be abolisht, the Title is left to be disrupted by the
sword, & he who has the sharpest, will prove to have the best
Title."[61] It was a position that even the judicious Matthew
Hale could easily support without giving offense to the
king,[62] and it found favor with others in positions of
influence and importance. The earl of Danby, in a notebook
of his memoranda, could quote Coke with approval in his
observation that the "prerogative has its orig from the
Comon Law."[63] And Lord Chancellor Shaftesbury, upon
the installation of Serjeant Thurland as baron of the
exchequer (1673), could admonish Thurland thus: "Let not
the Kings Prerogative, and the Law, be two things with you.
For the Kings Prerogative is Law, and the Principal Part of
the Law; and therefore, in maintaining that, you maintain
the Law."[64] In 1682, by which time Shaftesbury's fortunes
had changed, a polemical comment on the recent proceedings against him made the same point. "No kind of procedure," it was observed, "is further for the King's Honour
and Interest, than as it is according to Law, which is the
standard of the King's Prerogative, Glory & Safety."[65] It was
clear that the time was rapidly passing in which anyone
could take for granted that the prerogative might be placed
outside the law, let alone above it. There was still a long way
to go, and prerogative as a potent force was not to retreat
willingly; but the signs of its vulnerability were already there
for those who cared to observe. By the end of the century, a

statement by William Petyt that, at the beginning, had appeared highly contentious could be accepted as close to definitive. Petyt, echoing Coke, wrote that "the King of England hath no Prerogative, but what the Law of the Land allows him."[66] As a statement of sound constitutional principle it was unequivocal and in need of no further explanation.

Once the doctrine of mutuality gained the ascendant, prerogative was lowered onto a par with privilege. Both were seen as valid and competing forces, each having its place in the political order, each contributing to the furtherance of justice. The privilege referred to might be that of the people at large or, more specifically, the privilege of Parliament. In either case it called the prerogative into a more visible balance. As a result, the doctrine of mutuality could be seen to adumbrate and even express a growing political reality, the mounting challenge to the power of the king. Bulstrode Whitelocke, in his *A Treatise on Parliament,* had written that the king was obliged to be mindful of the privileges of Parliament because in that way only could his prerogative be assured. Each was necessary to the support and defense of the other, and both, together, were the foundation of a prosperous society.[67] This was a theme which was to continue throughout the period. The prerogative which under Elizabeth and the earlier Stuarts had been inflexible and unyielding was now more than ever to seek justification and ultimately to be justified by its responsiveness to the needs of the political community. It was not that the prerogative had been substantially diminished. Rather, it was that justification, once attempted, would in the future always be required. The "Kings prerogative," it was alleged, "extends only for the good of the people, never to their prejudice or great inconvenience."[68] It was an assertion of political mutualism in which many were ready to concur. Petyt perhaps expressed it best when he wrote, in "Jus Parliamentarium," "That the Kings prerogative is to defend the peoples liberties, and that the peoples libertie strengthens the Kings prerogative."[69] It was a gospel of mutual dependence in which prerogative had to accept not only a parity with privilege but also a place under the regulation of law.

The balance that existed between prerogative and privilege received expression in the rule of law. This was a concept that could be accepted easily. There would be no quarrel with the idea that the law is "the Rule by which we are to be protected in our Reputations and Lives if innocent, as well as cast and convicted, if upon Trial we be found to · have Capitally offended."[70] It was the notion that law alone could provide the necessary standards and guides for the direction and security of the entire people, what Shaftesbury called "a blanket of justice and certainty which belongs to every man."[71] This need for legal certainty, "the just, known, and common Rule of Justice and Right,"[72] accounts in large measure for the accelerating appeal of the doctrine of *stare decisis*. Matthew Hale was one who had recognized that judicial decisions, though they might be binding only between the parties to an action, would still "have great weight & Authority Directive in cases occurring after the like Nature." Departure from the judgments of a prior age should not be ventured lightly lest the result be a "perpetual uncertainty and unsettledness."[73] Men needed to have and to know, unequivocally, the limits and bounds of acceptable behavior. They needed to feel secure in their actions even though those actions might be severely restricted. "Better to live under severe Lawes," Joseph Williamson noted, "than under uncertaine Lawes."[74] It was the expression of a popular sentiment, one to which king and Parliament, at least in theory, could both subscribe.

Where there was agreement in theory there was also dispute in fact. Over the dispensing and suspending powers, issue was finally to be joined between king and Parliament. Charles II and James II could maintain that in exercising these powers they were operating within the confines of the law, and technically they were correct. Yet, as a result, the nation was being made to face a harmful and potentially destructive paradox. The law could be preserved while the rule of law was being eroded. There could be no certainty afforded by any law so long as the king could dispense with its application or suspend its operation entirely. The struggle was therefore to be cast in the terms of legal interpretation. Were the laws to be as certain as Parliament would have preferred, which was to say that the king could not tamper with law once made, or was the king to have the ultimate control? Not until the Revolution of 1688 would the answer be provided, although the direction already seemed clear to many. If England were to move toward political stability, it would in part be in consequence of the growth of precedent and the maturation of the rule of law.

With the developing strength of the rule of law came a corresponding decline of the doctrine of the divine right of kings and its companion maxim, "The king can do no wrong." Divine right was never firmly entrenched in the English constitution, although one of its component parts — that resistance to the king is a sin — proved particularly attractive to the post-Reformation Tudor monarchy. For as long as Henry VIII's break from Rome introduced into England the danger of a religiously inspired rebellion, it was useful to counter that peril with an emphasis upon the need for absolute obedience to the king.[75]

By the end of the Tudor century, James Stuart, acting on his expectation of Elizabeth's throne, embraced divine right in its expanded form. Giving the doctrine vivid expression in *The Trew Law of Free Monarchies,* he explicitly endorsed the idea that hereditary succession is indefeasible and, further, that the king is accountable to God alone.[76] Yet, by the end of the sixteenth century, an inflated theory of divine-right monarchy was already a glaring anachronism. It could be freely acknowledged by both champions and critics of royal authority that the king was responsible to God, but it was another matter to hold that he was responsible to God *alone*. As suggested by Margaret Judson, "It is essential in understanding the constitutional and political thinking of Englishmen in the early seventeenth century to realize that most of them believed in the divine right of kingly authority; but it is equally necessary to understand that the great majority of them also believed that the king's authority was limited in many ways by the law, the constitution, and the consent of man."[77]

At best, monarchy was part of God's order, as was the whole of the medieval world;[78] and, for English kings particularly, the indefeasible right of hereditary succession smacked more of an estate in fee simple than it did of a grant founded in the grace of the Lord. There had been many attempts to portray England as a realm established primarily upon religion and God's grace, but despite these efforts and the abundant recourse to religious metaphor, the country was to emerge from the seventeenth century much more committed to its basis in law. This, in part, had to be due to the excesses of the Puritan experiment. Just as the specter of regicide was to influence the politics of the Restoration, so too was the fear of unbridled religious zeal to have its effect upon future events. A characteristic sentiment of the time was that of a writer for Toleration who, as late as 1675, was still denouncing the "wild Principle of the Fifth Monarchie men that Dominion is founded in Grace." He then proceeded to note, as an extension of such irresponsible thinking, the even more dangerous possibility of "makeing Propertye, nay Libertye, nay life itt selfe, to be built on Grace."[79] Divine right was unacceptable because it invalidated the rule of law. It was certainly not, as Shaftesbury had charged in a speech to the House of Lords, the creation of Archbishop Laud; but the allegation itself was enough to cast the doctrine into sufficient disrepute. It was, he said, "the most dangerous destructive Doctrine to our Government and Law, that ever was." If ever it were to prevail, "our Lawes [would be] but Rules amongst our selves during the Kings pleasure."[80] Yet there were those who would have had it just that way. James I had contended for the proposition that it was the king who made the law and not the other way round, and there were many who would concur. Sir Orlando Bridgman, in his charge to the jury at the arraignment of the regicides in 1660, adopted the position that the king is supreme and answerable to no one but God; [81] and Humphrey Gower, vice-chancellor of the University of Cambridge, in an address to Charles II in 1681, assured the king of the university's belief "that our Kings derive not their Titles from the People, but from God; that to Him only they are accountable." [82]

"The king can do no wrong" was a different matter, one that could be properly set into a temporal context. It was close to saying that the king need answer to God alone, but it never went that far. It was much more palatable to a society committed to law because it was a maxim which itself claimed to be a part of that law. "The laws provide for that," said Bridgman; " 'the king can do no wrong; it is a rule of law; it is in our law books very frequent,' 22 Ed. IV. Lord Coke and many others." [83] Indeed, for centuries, it had been held, as joint maxims of the common law, "first, that the King of England is always a Minor; and secondly, that he can do no wrong." [84] For this reason the constitution allowed for, and even demanded, that the king be equipped with sworn and qualified ministers. In that way might there be someone held to account for the malfeasance of executive power. Certainly the king could not be held, even if he were to be bound to a standard of legal responsibility. There was no way, legally, for him to be tried, because as a man without peers he could not be judged. [85] So it was that the maxim had endured, not in defiance of the law, but as an anomaly in the structure which the law had incorporated and was required to countenance. But at all times it was a part of the law, whereas divine right was not.

Seen from this aspect, "The king can do no wrong" becomes compatible with Bracton's dictum, "The king is under the law." The law might not always insure perfect justice, but it was all-encompassing. It comprehended the king as well as the meanest of his subjects, because the alternatives, as it was sometimes argued, would have the king above the law and therefore outside it; and to be outside the law was to be an outlaw, by definition. [86] As an argument it was an awkward piece of sophistry, but it did express what most of political society preferred to believe. It was precisely in the same vein as Shaftesbury's pronouncement, "My principle is, That the King is King by Law, and by the same Law that the poor Man enjoys his Cottage."[87] It represented a seventeenth-century turn of mind, one that understood the law as the great common denominator and was prepared to apply it to every class and situation. Even Sir William Petty, in writing in *The Powers of the King of England* (1685) that "the King by ceasing or forbearing to administer the Severall Powers above nam'd can doe what harm he pleases to his Subjects," was making an important concession to the force of the law.[88] He was, in effect, arguing that the king, by virtue of his position, could use, manipulate, and control the law to such a degree that he might do injury without doing wrong. It was, on its face, a seeming contradiction, but it was not inconsistent with the conceptual direction of the age.

Eventually the king would have to be called to a personal accounting, but not before an interpretation of the applicable law could be made to undergo some necessary change. Along these lines, the first suggestion was that the king might in fact be capable of error, if the error were committed unintentionally. Queen Elizabeth, at the end of her reign, thanked Parliament for bringing to her attention the facts in regard to monopolies, "whereby you have called us home from an Error proceeding from ignorance not willingness."[89] Implicit was the idea that the monarch could do wrong if, as later commentators were to point out, the error was inadvertent and not deliberate. It was a point made in defense of a sovereign, but one that admitted to the possibility of a negligent mistake. This, however, was not enough. Elizabeth's success in managing her Parliament was not to be enjoyed by her Stuart successors. There would be too many times during the seventeenth century when the king would force an issue rather than admit to an unwitting error. If the maxim that "The king can do no wrong" was to survive at all, it would have to be buttressed by a stronger defense, a defense which not only would meet the needs of the king but would refrain from any challenge to the structure of the law. If the king were not privileged by law to commit an illegal act, the act itself would have to be nullified.[90] This is what Hale meant by the *Potestas Irritans,* that which "bindes the Kings Acts and makes them void if they are against Law."[91] The maxim was thus employed as a defense of the king, a defense of the people, and a defense of the king from himself. It was to the everlasting credit of the law that "by a kind restraint [it] rescueth him from a disease that would undo him."[92] Petyt was another who followed this line of reasoning; but he was prepared to go even further. He argued that it was the prerogative that defended the king from error. Petyt allowed for the possibility that the king might be seduced into commanding something con-trary to law, but, like Hale, he contended that the command would be void. This was so because the maxim that "The king can do no wrong" was part, indeed "the Highest Point, of Prerogative."[93] It was precisely because Petyt was, for the sake of his argument, accepting the proposition that the prerogative was unassailable that he was able to interpret the maxim in the same way as Hale. What Petyt added was the notion that, if the prerogative was still too formidable for a direct attack, it could nevertheless be turned to a different political advantage. It was a consequence of the attempt, first begun by Coke, to limit and control the prerogative and, in so doing, to attenuate even further the ability of the king to control the law. It was thus in a very few years that the king, James II, was finally to be undone; and the law which had preserved him, and those before him, was now to work his undoing.

Part Two

the
political possibilities
of the law

3   *Control of the Law*

AN INTERPRETATION OF THE SEVENTEENTH CENTURY WHICH focuses upon political conflict in the context of law may well be described as a qualified return to Whiggism. Certainly it is a rejection of that view which fixes property at the base of the struggle and which all too easily dismisses law and religion as superimposed idioms of polemical convenience. It is an interpretation that is Whiggish at heart because it neither avoids nor deemphasizes the basic accomplishment of the century, the triumph of Parliament and Protestantism. But it is qualified, and importantly qualified, because it does not pit absolutism against constitutionalism or law against prerogative. It is an interpretation which understands the political rule of law and a commitment to known and settled forms as constitutional constants throughout the century. Law, in this view, is not seen as a contestant for survival; rather, it is the politically acknowledged prize in the battle for sovereignty between king and Parliament. It is not a party to the struggle but the object for which the struggle takes place.

Past generations of Whig historians have seen the common law on the side of Parliament alone. Even when some degree of sympathy could be generated for a king who had been striving in vain to ward off Parliament and the common lawyers as they encroached upon the Crown, there was still the well-defined and exclusive association of Parliament and the law. It was as if law were alien to monarchy, a thing apart, something employed to check the king but never to aid him. When, therefore, in 1688 William of Orange descends upon England, it is as much for the deliverance of

62   the law as it is for the salvation of religion. Macaulay, rehearsing Burnet's account of the dramatic first meeting between William and John Maynard, England's elder legal statesman, underscores this dominant Whig theme. " 'Mr. Serjeant,' said the Prince, 'you must have survived all the lawyers of your standing.' 'Yes Sir,' said the old man, 'and, but for Your Highness, I should have survived the laws too.' "[1] The clear implication is that law, itself, was very nearly a casualty of Stuart rule. G. M. Trevelyan, carrying the argument further, was even persuaded that the "Revolution Settlement was first and foremost the establishment of the rule of law. It was the triumph of the Common Law and lawyers over the King, who had tried to put Prerogative above the law."[2]

It is this view which is both Whiggish and wrong because it suggests an alliance between Parliament and the law that does not square with historical reality.[3] In a society where kings paid such scrupulously close attention to the law, where they were as attentive as any Parliament to the intricacies of legal procedure, a simplistic polarization of law versus monarchy would not be valid. What is closer to the truth is that king and Parliament both had a salutary respect for the law and what it could be made to do. It was, for each, much too valuable an ally to be courted by one side and rejected by the other. The Stuart monarchs may well have perverted and abused the law, but it is certain that they never ignored it.

Nevertheless, when any English king in his assertion of authority was both successful and politically efficient, he was immediately subject to the label of tyrant. The term has been applied to the Tudor dynasty in general and to Henry VIII in particular, to the Stuarts at various times during the seventeenth century and, most particularly, to the eleven years of personal rule of Charles I. It has also been used to characterize reigns which were somewhat less than politically successful, such as the nearly four years of misadventure of the second James. Yet in none of these cases is the label especially applicable, because in none of these cases was the monarch ever to rule unchecked or was the standard of the law ever to be submerged. To suggest that any or all of these monarchs had a predilection for tyranny is as meaningless as it is vague. The fact of absolutism is at all times subject to the opportunity for absolutism, and for the Tudors and Stuarts that opportunity was never really there. As long as each monarch in question recognized in the law a threshold of inviolability beyond which he was unprepared to go, "tyranny" could be nothing more than a hollow, although dramatic, allegation. It is, for example, probable that Henry VIII, Charles I, and James II would have delighted in rule by proclamation alone. What is also likely is that every other monarch of the Tudor-Stuart period would have been similarly pleased by such an arrangement; and we need not stop there. We can range both backward and forward in time to include the Angevins and Hanoverians as well. It would, in fact, be difficult to maintain that the members of these dynasties were so willingly committed to a political rule of law that they would have been offended by the opportunity to rule solely by royal fiat. The critical distinction would seem to be that, whereas the opportunity for undivided sovereignty in the king alone may be a reasonable constitutional measure of any reign, the mere attractiveness of such sovereignty is not. For the Tudors and the Stuarts, absolutism might always have been a hope; but so long as law went unchallenged, it could never have been much of a prospect.[4]

The contemporary critics of Stuart monarchy may not have thoroughly understood this, but they were aware of the unending profusion of regal encomiums to the value and sanctity of the law.[5] They invariably sought to hold their kings to account because of it. If it could be demonstrated that the king, by his own pronouncements, carried the law in such high regard, he would always be open to attack when he and the law appeared to be at variance with each other. Yet the matter was always more a question of interpretation than of patent divergence. Throughout the Stuart century the charge of monarchical infidelity to the law was easy to

64   make but difficult to prove. What seems closer to the truth is
that in the seventeenth century the law of the constitution
was not yet settled, that this is what the struggle was largely
about, and that, as monarchy resorted to ever greater
extremes in legal manipulation, the cries of "tyranny" would
invariably become louder.

But if law might not be violated, it might certainly be
controlled. The real constitutional question of the period,
and particularly of the time before the Revolution, was to
whom that control would finally fall. In retrospect the
answer inevitably seems clearer than it did during the years
between Restoration and Revolution. It is, in fact, because
the victory seemed to be going to the Stuarts that the
Revolution became a necessity. Charles II and James II were
dangerous because they were legally effective, because they
never lost sight of the worth of the law. Their adherence to
form was usually impeccable, even when their treatment of
substance was brought into question. It was a contest for
control of the law being won by a monarchy always mindful
of recognized procedures. It was a monarchy which promulgated no law except in full Parliament of king, Lords and
Commons and which went upon no man except by the law of
the land. To be sure, the dispensing and suspending powers
might be employed to their fullest potential, and judicial
interpretation might be twisted and strained, but it could
never in truth be said that the Stuarts operated in disregard
of the rules. Instead, they used the law and, with the help of
a dependent judiciary, maneuvered their way toward an
interpretation of the constitution that was becoming ever
more politically menacing. That interpretation was to prove
ultimately untenable; yet it never transgressed legitimate
bounds. In England the law of the land was nowhere writ so
large or so clear that none could disagree as to its meaning.
Coke had tried to stamp the law with a definitive interpretation — his own — but he was only partially successful. In those
areas where law touched upon politics, he was eventually
made to yield to a more powerful king. Law was still a
matter of interpretation, and a king who controlled the

instruments of that interpretation also controlled the law. It is thus that what has too often been viewed as the Stuart refinement of tyranny may be understood better as the growth of legal sophistication.

Monarchy was being accused of killing by forms because its legal controls were producing unpleasant results. Unpleasantness, however, is not illegality. In a commonplace book from the reign of Charles II an unknown compiler recorded a line attributed to Tacitus: "There is no Tiranne so bad as he that pretends much to observe the Law."[6] As an allegation applicable to Restoration England it was somewhat extreme. If the label of tyranny were to fit, it would first have to be shown that in law the Stuart exercise of power was arbitrary. Even if all would agree that such exercise was severe, this alone would not be enough.

Moreover, the condemnation of legal form as a weapon of political persecution was used not only against the king but by him, as well, as an offensive device. In the *quo warranto* proceedings against the City of London, the corporation was charged with the "oppression of the Kings Subjects by Colour of Law." It was alleged that the City was pretending, and indeed seeming, to act in compliance with law but in fact was not.[7] It is probable that the City was less guilty than the king of the pretense of legal regularity and was therefore less open to the charge. But what is more important is that these allegations were being directed from all sides against those who, far from being indifferent to the law, were, to the contrary, using it with particular skill.

It has already been observed that the prerogative throughout the seventeenth century was under considerable assault and that much in evidence by the 1670s and 1680s were statements attributing the strength of the prerogative to the sustaining force of the law.[8] It was the law, said Bishop Burnet, that set the executive power of monarchy into motion and, for which purpose, had "clothed him [the King] with a vast prerogative."[9] As a philosophic position, Burnet's statement was arguable. Certainly, it was the very antithesis of the Hobbesian postulate that law is the will of the

66   sovereign. But this was not a place or time receptive to the thinking of Thomas Hobbes. Burnet, a far less creative intellect, was much more representative of his age. There seemed to men like Burnet, men who were increasingly in the majority, little alternative to the proposition that prerogative was part of the law. If it were not the case, the king might be regarded as absolute, a possibility which all shades of responsible opinion treated as unthinkable. Even the mere suggestion of absolutism was regarded as a repugnant innovation. A writer who addressed himself to the use of the words "absolute power" in the Royal Proclamation of 1687 for Liberty of Conscience in Scotland recoiled at the prospect of anything so alien and so unlimited. "Prerogative royal & souverain authority," he wrote, "are terms already received & knowne, but for this absolute power as it is a new terme, so those that have coyned it may make it signify what they will."[10] The fear was of a temporal power removed from the law and therefore no longer subject to control. This is why the placing of prerogative under the law was so important. It is also why a polemicist like William Petyt would devote a substantial part of a treatise to disproving the "erroneous" assertion, attributed to Filmer, that the "Kings prerogative is a preheminence in cases of necessity above and before the law of property or Inheritance."[11]

Nevertheless, the problem of regulating the king's discretionary powers continued. One difficulty was that the prerogative was also considered to be inalienably attached to the Crown. It belonged to the monarch only by virtue of his office and would therefore descend, along with the throne, to the next in line of succession. As Hale had observed, "things, which are of their own nature testamentary, yet if possessed by the king in right of his crown, they are not devisable; neither do they go to the executors."[12] Yet this did not speak to the question of what the king might do while still alive, by way of an *inter vivos* conveyance, nor did it address the more important issue of whether the prerogative could be limited by another power. If the prerogative might not be given away, might it, nonetheless, be taken away? If not, if the prerogative was something more than a discretionary instrument of government, it would hold dire implications for Parliament. If kings were allowed the possession of absolute rights beyond the regulation of law, they would own an advantage impossible to overcome. It would suggest that the prerogative was above the law and therefore sovereign. This was part of the argument of *The Trew Law of Free Monarchies*. James held that "a good king will frame all his actions to be according to the Law; yet is hee not bound thereto but of his good will."[13] Historically, the supports for this position were tenable. Yet during the course of the Stuart era they were abandoned. It is an irony of the age that the Stuart kings lost control of the law at the same time that they were increasing their commitment to the law. They had suffered the law to contemplate and define the prerogative, in some measure because they seemed at times to have little choice, but also because they believed, in turn, that they could themselves define the law. They knew in theory that the law was theirs. What they did not reckon with was that Parliament, in the end, would take it away.

By 1689 the assertion that prerogative was part of the law had become so well accepted that it was readily employed by the supporters of "legitimate" monarchy. Advocates of the Stuart cause, in an attempt to stop William from assuming the Crown, argued for the conditional recall of James. They reasoned that, since Parliament might set limits to the prerogative, the king could be kept within tolerable bounds.[14] What this signified was the complete acceptance of the prerogative under the law and, even more important, the idea that law might now be deemed to be under the control of Parliament. The constitutional struggle has therefore to be perceived as proceeding in two stages. Only in the first stage was the limiting of the prerogative the primary consideration. Placing prerogative under law would not in itself be sufficient. It was the second stage, the contest for control of the law, which would be determinative; and it was not until the Revolution had been concluded that it was in any way clear who would ultimately win that control.

Control of the law was not an end in itself. It was the key

68   to sovereignty, the means by which any dominance in political society would have to be achieved. Halifax was one who, seeing this, had noted that, "if it be true that the wisest men generally make the laws, it is as true that the strongest do too often interpret them."[15] He who would be sovereign would first have to command the law, the most important tool of sovereignty.

In the seventeenth century, and particularly in the years following the Restoration of Charles II, when the lines of legal battle were being drawn more sharply than ever, the two aspirants to sovereignty were Parliament and the king. Yet neither of the two, except on rare occasions, laid open claim to that which both really coveted. It was politically safer to speak of the sovereignty of the law or of the sovereignty of the king in Parliament. As to the former, the sovereignty of the law, that was a shadowy image, the amorphous nature of which enabled it to be used in support of any side. It was important and will later be discussed at some length. The latter, the sovereignty of the king in Parliament, enjoyed the same measure of safe respectability and had the additional virtue of somewhat more substance, although it too served more as a facade behind which the real fight took place. So long as neither king nor Parliament after 1660 was strong enough to outmaneuver the other completely, it was convenient to subscribe to an interpretation of the constitution that allowed for sovereignty to be shared. Nottingham, in his *Treatise on Parliament,* acknowledged kings, Lords, and Commons as "the Supreme power by the fundamentall Constitution,"[16] and others, on both ends of the political spectrum, said the same.[17] However desirable and institutionalized the fiction might later become, the fact of shared sovereignty was for a long time a simple political necessity, one that might readily and happily be abandoned if the balance of control were ever to be tipped and a resolution achieved in favor of either contestant.

Political society was accordingly characterized as something other than purely "monarchicall," "aristocraticall," or "democraticall." It was, wrote Hale, a combination of the three, "not a simple form of government, but mixt."[18] But the elements in that mixture, and the proportions in which they were measured, were another matter. There was, for example, the suggestion that the king be considered as one of the three estates of the realm. This was a new line of attack, a shift away from the orthodox notion of the three estates as the Lords Spiritual, the Lords Temporal, and the Commons. Instead, what was emerging with noticeable frequency was the reference to the estates as "King, lords and commons."[19] This had the political effect of raising Parliament to a position of parity with the king and made it increasingly difficult for the king to operate outside Parliament without challenge.[20] Coke had written in his *Fourth Institute* that "the king and these three estates are the great corporation or body politick of the kingdom."[21] He had not included the king as one of the three, but he had subsumed the king under a corporate heading. That, to some minds, was considered enough of a threat. The doctrine was accordingly attacked as a piece of legal deception. As an idea, it was not new; but by the time of the Restoration it was considered to be highly dangerous, and it aroused substantial opposition. The earl of Danby vehemently denied that there was such a thing as "the body politick." It was, he wrote, "a mere trick of the lawyers."[22] Any theory of the constitution which sought to define the king as only one of several interdependent parts was clearly restrictive of the function of monarchy. It meant, in effect, that the king had entered the arena of constitutional debate as an equal. It was a doctrine to be sharply disavowed, but it was a fact that could not be avoided.

The further implication of shared sovereignty was that each of the constituent parts of Parliament would have a hand in the legislative process. Everyone agreed that no law might be made unless and until it was assented to by the king, the Lords, and the Commons.[23] Yet most people also appreciated that there were ways for the king to get around this, ways in which the king might affect legislation through his unilateral, although legal, acts. There was, therefore, an

70   understandably defensive and contentious edge to the observations that "the Law cannot be changed but by Act of
Parliament."[24] In Hale's *Discourse or History Concerning
the Power of Judicature in the King's Council and in
Parliament,* there is the appearance of the chief justice
attempting to hold the line against the king. "By the
concurrent advice of both those houses the King makes and
alters laws and not otherwise."[25] The "otherwise" presented
several possibilities. There were the dispensing and suspending powers, politically powerful and difficult to control.
There were also proclamations, which Hale noted as part of
the prerogative; but these were not to be used to "make or
introduce a new law, or add a new penalty to an old law, or
abrogate any law."[26]

Properly seen, it was all part of the fight to keep the king
from the complete control of the law. Using the same
principle of legislative cooperation but according it only
token acceptance, the advocates of strong monarchy attempted to strip away any real control that the Parliament,
particularly the House of Commons, might have. William
Petyt apprehended this danger. In a "draft work correcting
what he considered to be errors of recent English historians
and writers on Parliament,"[27] he addressed himself to the
problem. He attacked Filmer's assertion that the Commons
has little to do in the legislative process, that by legal and
historical precedent the laws are made by the king himself.
Accordingly, Petyt challenged the theory that laws being
made "by Authority of Parliament" really means that "the
king ordains, the Lords advise, the Commons assent."[28] He
knew that such a construction would have meant an end to
the power of Parliament. In another place Petyt carefully
differentiated between the king who governs "politically"
and the king who governs "regally." The latter, he submitted, was a civil-law construct based upon the principle that
"what the Prince pleaseth to appoint, obtains the Force of a
law."[29] As such, it had no place in England, where the king
had no authority to make or alter the law without the
consent of his subjects.

Where Petyt was direct, Hale, as usual, was circumspect and judicious. The chief justice was not prepared to admit the king's *ex parte* control of the law, but he was willing to abide a formula whereby "the power legislative resides in the King alone, though so qualified, that he cannot enact a law without the advice and assent of the three estates assembled in parliament."[30] It was a concession much more apparent than real. The king was still barred from acting unilaterally. It had the effect of making the king, in the legislative process as he was among the nobility, *primus inter pares.* While nominally impressive, it gave away nothing. All were aware that if the king had truly been allowed the power to make law, the two houses of Parliament would have been reduced to the exercise of a ceremonial function, deprived of any initiative or discretion. As a constitutional force they would thus have been effectively neutralized. It was a politically untenable thesis; but from the perspective of the Stuarts, the thought was conspicuously appealing.

The Stuarts were not to have their way. They were to suffer defeat because, over the span of the century, they were to relinquish their domination of the law. It is curious that, as the Stuarts were expanding their power to the limits of legal acceptability, they were compromising their claim to legal expertise. It was an expensive concession and more than just a symbolic adumbration of the eventual collapse of James II; it was clearly one of the causes of that collapse.

Issue had been joined early in the reign of James I on the subject of monarchical control of the law. In 1605 Archbishop Bancroft protested the use of the common-law writ of prohibition to enjoin ecclesiastical courts, specifically the Court of High Commission, from proceeding with causes adjudged to be properly common-law matters. He asserted that all jurisdiction, spiritual and temporal, belonged to the king and that it was therefore for the monarch, and not the common-law judges, to determine the forum in which any case might be heard.

Even more important than prohibitions themselves were the larger constitutional implications of the dispute. Whether

72   or not he needed Bancroft to persuade him, James was convinced that the king was privileged to decide cases personally in his courts. In 1608 James maintained that he was the "supreme judge," that "inferior judges [were] his shadows and ministers ... and the King may, if he please, sit and judge in Westminster Hall in any Court there, and call theire Judgments in question.... The King beinge the author of the Lawe is the interpreter of the Lawe."[31] Not since the time of Henry IV had a king personally adjudicated a cause at Westminster. Coke, therefore, was eager to challenge this assertion of a direct royal exercise of the judicial function. It is not certain that Coke actually said, as it is made to appear in his *Reports,* that "causes which concern the life or inheritance, or goods, or fortunes, of his [the King's] subjects ... are not to be decided by natural reason, but by the artificial reason and judgment of law, which law is an act which requires long study and experience before that a man can attain to the cognisance of it"; [32] what does seem sure is that James responded to what he properly perceived to be a critical constitutional challenge. It is the king, said James, who "maketh Judges and Bishops. If the Judges interpret the lawes themselves and suffer none else to interprete, then they may easily make of the laws shipmens hose."[33] James understood that to concede Coke's argument would be to deprive the monarchy of its hold upon the law.

After the prolonged controversy between James I and Coke, the issue was quickened, and it emerged several times more during the first half of the century. Then, in 1649, Charles I, on trial for his life, refused to recognize the jurisdiction of the court which had been constituted to try him. In this he was steadfast. Throughout the proceedings he never once abandoned his posture of imperious disdain toward those who would presume to judge him. He denied that any tribunal, no matter how constituted, might ever try "him from whom the law emanates." Like his father before him on the matter of jurisdiction, Charles was right; [34] but this time monarchy was to lose. It is of more than passing interest that at his trial Charles addressed himself to the same question of the king's control of the law. He said: "I do not know the forms of law; I do know law and reason, though I am no lawyer professed; but I know as much law as any gentleman in England."[35] What is particularly interesting about Charles's statement, and what distinguishes it from that of James, made more than forty years earlier, is that monarchy was sounding a partial retreat. Kingship was no longer equating law with reason, nor was it any longer claiming legal competence equal to that of the legal profession. Charles stated only that he knew as much law as any gentleman, and no doubt he did. But he recognized also, if only implicitly and somewhat contemptuously, that the law, built upon forms, was indeed specialized and that lawyers themselves were a breed apart.

What was implicit in 1649 became quite explicit by 1688. At the center of the continued conflict between king and Parliament was the use of the prerogative powers of suspending the law or dispensing with its penal effects. In the period of the Restoration this is precisely where the focus of the legal struggle was to appear. If the king could use the suspending and dispensing powers to defeat the Protestant interest, then any control that his subjects might have of their law and religion would be virtually nullified. That the king could even attempt this is testimony to the potential inherent in the prerogative. But, at the same time that James was employing his powers to their fullest, the apologists for Stuart monarchy were disclaiming the king's personal control of the law. In 1685 Sir William Petty wrote, in his catalogue of *The Powers of the K[ing] of England,* that the "King has a Prerogative which Lawyers must expound."[36] There, at least symbolically, was a critical loosening of legal control. The only real hope for sovereignty to which monarchy might cling was its continued possession of the law. Once it was willing to admit, in a mistaken play for constitutional popularity, that control had passed, any pretense of political dominion could hardly be credible.

At one time the law had belonged to the king. For

74   centuries, opposing political forces had tried to wrest it from him. Now they were on the verge of success. In the summer and early fall of 1688 the invasion of William of Orange was believed to be imminent. In the assault of pamphlet literature that preceded the actual invasion, the prince was either praised as an anticipated savior or damned as a would-be usurper. In one such attack upon William, an increasingly familiar defense of the king was offered. It bears repeating in full:

> Kings are not bred at the Inns of Court, but must trust lawyers for Law, as well as Physicians for Physick. The oppression of Conscience-Laws, deafens his Majesties Ears with perpetual Complaints, and His tenderness of his Subjects prompts Him to relieve them. He adviseth with those of the Profession, and they inform Him, He may, by his Dispencing Power, relieve them Legally, and he does it. Every body is not content, and he refers the whole to a publick Legal Tryal. Pray what better, or other Advice could his Highness have given?[37]

So, on the eve of the Revolution, the monarchy's loss of the law is symbolically complete. Exclusive control as an element of the prerogative has been abandoned. And with this loss, any claim to sovereignty, which of necessity must rest upon it, has been forsaken as well. The law is up for grabs, and he who seizes it will be sovereign.

This is not, however, to suggest that the Stuarts submitted without a fight. It is rather that they were concentrating their energies on the wrong battle. In point of fact, they did fight to keep control of the law, a truth to which their increasingly ingenious use of the dispensing and suspending powers and any number of other legal contrivances bears witness. The problem, and the paradox, is that they were still trying to make maximum use of the law while at the same time yielding up its possession. Thus they created for themselves an insoluble problem and enabled their contemporaries to see more clearly the relationship between legal

control and political sovereignty. If judged by their use of
the law alone, the Stuarts emerge as capable and punctilious
craftsmen. Their mismanagement was of men rather than of
law. Their mistakes and their failures were not legal but
political.

THE SUCCESSFUL WRESTING OF THE LAW FROM THE KING BY NO
means settled the matter of control. Parliament was the
obvious beneficiary of James's abdication; but within that
body the battle between the Lords and Commons, a conflict
which had been growing in intensity throughout the period,
had yet to be determined. It is true that the Commons, in
the 1620s, had laid down a political challenge to the king;
but resolution of their struggle for the law was to remain
uncertain for a long time to come. The House of Lords had
established a jurisdictional preserve which it fully intended
to protect. Then, too, the claims of the judicial establishment had to be considered. Theirs was a demand for possession that had been pushed hard since Coke's early posturings
at the opening of the century; yet it was not to be sufficiently
credible until such time as an independent judiciary could
be established. As a result, while the primary struggle for
control was proceeding between Parliament and the king,
two subsidiary battles of increasing consequence were also
being waged. One, between the Commons and the Lords,
was the more dramatic and important; but the other,
between Parliament and the courts, was as much a cause for
political concern.

It would therefore be mistaken to imagine Parliament and
the common lawyer as consistent allies throughout the
century. At times they did come together, because each
hoped to benefit from the application of their collective
strength against the king. Yet, as long as each was seeking
control of the law as the prize of battle, the alliance could be
only uncertain and temporary. As the power of the king
began to recede, a new friction between his successful rivals
emerged. Much of the antagonism was, for a long time,
blurred by the towering figure of Coke. First as jurist and

then as Member of Parliament, he symbolized the concentration of pressures against the Stuarts. It may even be that it was just this powerful association in the years leading up to 1642 that was responsible for welding together a force sufficient to defeat the king. But circumstances after 1660 were different. Coke was gone; and although there was no want of juridical talent on the same professional level, viz., Nottingham and Hale, neither was there anyone to provide the vital nexus between Parliament and the courts. There was, on the contrary, a new and much different alliance between Parliament and the judiciary — this time in telling support of the king.

The courts once more seemed willing to do the king's bidding; and, as the Restoration years wore on, an image of judicial servility developed and intensified. The evocation of such names as Scroggs, Jeffreys, and Herbert seemed quite sufficient to suggest a lamentably corrupt bench. To some extent this characterization is accurate. There was certainly justification for the political opponents of the Crown to believe that the Stuart kings called upon their judges to reinforce a royalist view of the constitution. The widely suspected purpose of the judiciary was to clothe questionable extensions of the prerogative in precise legal dress; and it was just this aggrandizement of monarchical power that inspired the allegations of judicial immorality. Yet the charge may be somewhat extreme. The depiction of the Restoration judiciary as legally undistinguished political sycophants should probably be tempered by a more realistic assessment of both the quality of the judges' acts and the nature of the judicial function. In the first instance, the judicial appointments made in 1660, although clearly tied to politics, were nevertheless of men largely competent. Moreover, these new judges functioned, at least until 1676, with a noticeable degree of independence. In the treason trials of the early sixties they demonstrated sympathy for the Crown, but they were by no means guilty of wide-scale improprieties. As to the penal laws, the judges can only be said to have accepted responsibility for enforcing acts of Parliament; and in the matter of the Declaration of Indulgence (1672), the negative attitude of the judiciary toward the suspending power probably contributed to the Declaration's having failed. This is not to suggest that Charles II did not at any time exercise a large measure of control over his bench or that that control did not become tighter after 1676; but it is to allow for the balanced accuracy of A. F. Havighurst's judgment that the Restoration bench's understandable support of the king implied neither total subservience nor a "cynical disregard for law."[38] Neither should it be forgotten that the judicial function was properly considered to be one of the powers of the king. Sir William Petty was taking a constitutionally defensible position when he wrote, in 1685, that

> the King makes Judges durante bene placito. They sett fines and punish at their own Discretion in Severall Cases. They govern proceedings at Law, Declare and Interpret the Law. Reprieve &c. & the King can suspend the Law, pardon or prosecute.[39]

It is also clear that contemporaries did not always agree with the subsequent judgments of legal historians. To maintain, as Holdsworth did, that there was, in England, a long-standing homogeneity of law and institutions, of "judicature and legislature," of lawyer and Parliament, is not completely true. In most instances the common lawyers might recognize Parliament "as the highest court which the king has, as the court in which the errors of their own courts could be redressed";[40] but not in all cases was this so readily accepted, because not in all cases was such a proposition clearly in the best interests of the courts of common law. The arguments advanced in the case of the earl of Shaftesbury (1677) operate as an illustration in point. In that matter the vital issue of jurisdiction was examined. Shaftesbury's counsel contended that the court of King's Bench might judge of the validity of the earl's commitment to the Tower by the House of Lords.[41] He implied that the common law would be making a destructive sacrifice if it recognized Parliament as

78   a superior court in all cases. The jurisdictional hierarchy, he said, need not proceed only from the courts of common law to the High Court of Parliament but in certain circumstances might move in the reverse direction. The argument failed because of the overriding motion of political events, but it was not without legal merit. The justifiable fear of the common lawyer was of just that degree of constitutional control for which Parliament was contending. If Parliament were conceded to have jurisdictional supremacy, its lead in the struggle for sovereignty might well be irreversible. For anyone who favored Parliament's cause, this was obviously desirable. It was not so appealing to those common lawyers who saw in Parliament a threat to the common-law courts. The problem, however, was that the courts could not yet stand on their own. They were wedded to the king, and so his cause, in most cases, was of necessity theirs. Such a case was that of Shaftesbury, in which the king's interest was the silencing of the earl. Shaftesbury had maintained, upon the authority of an obscure and long-forgotten statute of Edward III, that the Cavalier Parliament, in 1677, was illegally constituted and should be immediately dissolved. As the power of dissolution belonged only to the king, the summoning of such ancient authority might well be construed as an attack upon Charles.

When the issue of jurisdiction was heard in King's Bench, not all of the king's interest was immediately apparent. Control of the law received much less consideration than the political problem at hand. Accordingly, the judges elected to collaborate with the Lords rather than attend to the reason in Shaftesbury's argument. This, in a sense, was ironic, because it was Shaftesbury who was advocating a position which favored the king. He maintained that it were no "kindnesse to the Lords to make them absolute & above the Law"; [42] nor was such to the advantage of Charles. Shaftesbury was, of course, exercised by his own loss of freedom, but it was not exaggeration when he urged upon the court that his "cause was of great consequence." It was true that "the Kinge was touched in his Prerogative, the

Subject in his Liberty, and this Court in its Jurisdiction."[43] He argued that King's Bench was the proper forum for determining the king's pleasure; and the king, in this case at least, should have realized that Shaftesbury was right. Instead, the judges in behalf of Charles opted for the alliance of king and Lords, a tactical expedient which was not to be enough to sustain the Stuarts in the crisis soon to come. Charles's ability to use the law was still impressively intact, but in this important matter it may have been applied to an ill-considered end. The monarchy would have done better to attempt greater judicial restraint upon Parliament in general and, in this instance, upon the Lords in particular. This is precisely the point that Shaftesbury's counsel was moving: ". . . though the House of Lords be the Superior Court yet their jurisdiction is Limitted by the Common and Statute Law and their excesses are examinable in this Court."[44] It was an argument strongly in favor of the courts of common law and of their ability to place important restrictions upon Parliament. Counsel even went so far as to suggest that King's Bench had within it the power of judicial review of statutes of the realm. It could, he said, hold an act of Parliament void if such "be against Magna Charta, & more may it judge of an order of the house of Lords that is putt in execucion to deprive any Subject of his Libertye."[45] The specific premise, although highly questionable, should not have detracted from the significance of the problem. At stake was a vital question of jurisdiction that meant nothing less than control of the law.

There were other attempts to limit the jurisdiction of the House of Lords, cases in which all the issues were usually much closer to the surface. In these cases the lines of conflict were clearly drawn between the Commons and the Lords. One such case was that of *Shirley* v. *Fagg* (1675), in which a Chancery decree had been rendered in favor of Sir John Fagg, a member of the House of Commons, and was appealed by Thomas Shirley to the House of Lords. The Lords gladly accepted jurisdiction. The House of Commons objected, protesting that the Lords' house was without

80 authority to hear appeals from Chancery. Fagg, however, accepted the Lords' jurisdiction and interposed an answer to Shirley's plea. He was then arrested by the Commons and sent to the Tower. The primary point at issue was the right of the Lords to entertain an appeal in equity in which one of the parties was a member of the House of Commons. To do so, according to a resolution of the Commons, was a clear violation of its privilege. No member of the lower house should be made to submit to a judgment of the Lords. The Lords disagreed. They resolved that it was their "undoubted Right . . . in Judicature, to receive and determine, in Time of Parliament, Appeals from Inferior Courts, though a Member of either House be concerned."[46]

The matter of Shirley and Fagg had already occasioned one prorogation of Parliament when, in November 1675, it precipitated another. By this time the Commons had broadened its attack so far as to deny the appellate jurisdiction of the Lords in any equity matter. Whether or not one of the litigants in a Chancery dispute was a member of the Commons, that house resolved that the Lords would have no authority to hear the appeal. But the Lords were not to be put off quite so easily. Shaftesbury, who would soon find himself railing against the jurisdiction of the Lords in his own cause, was, in 1675, arguing strenuously *for* such jurisdiction. "My Lords," he said,

> this matter is no less than your whole Judicature & . . . Judicature is the life & soul the Dignity & Peerage of England. You will quickly grow burthensome if you grow useless; you have now the greatest & most usefull end of Parliaments principally in you, which is not to make new laws, but to redress Greivances, & to maintain the old Land-Marks; The house of Commons business is to Complaine yours to redress not only the Complaints from them that are the Eyes of the Nation, but all other particular persons that address to you.[47]

Shaftesbury realized full well the implications of control and was, in this instance, intent upon preserving it for the Lords. Yet even after the matter had been quietly resolved in favor of the upper house, the controversy, at least in polemical circles, was to remain alive. The tireless Petyt, in *A Discourse Concerning the Judicature in Parliament,*[48] continued to assault the jurisdiction of the Lords. He delved deeply into the past and resurrected precedents from the reign of Henry IV that allegedly demonstrated the impotence of the Peers in the face of petitions of appeal. It was characteristic of Petyt and of the importance of the issue, but as a plea for the rights of the Commons it was of no avail.

The victory in *Shirley* v. *Fagg* was vital to the Lords, particularly as they had lost a large part of their claim to original jurisdiction a few years earlier. This was as a result of the proceedings in *Skinner* v. *The East India Company.* In this case the matter to be adjudicated arose outside the realm and not upon the high seas. For that reason Charles referred the petition for relief to the House of Lords. Here, too, the issue of jurisdiction was quickly joined. The common-law courts protested the king's action, as did the House of Commons. The Commons resolved that the cause, "being a common plea," was improperly set in the Lords as a court of first instance. Moreover, since several members of the defendant company, including the governor, were members of the lower house, the arrogation of jurisdiction by the Lords was allegedly a breach of the Commons' privilege.[49] The matter was settled in favor of the Commons. The House of Lords eventually conceded and dropped the cause. It was a triumph for the principle, as enunciated by Hale, that the Lords were "not to proceed in civil causes in the first instance that are cognizable in the Courts of Westminster."[50] But it was also something more. It was symptomatic, as were *Shirley* v. *Fagg* and the contemporaneous contest for control of money bills,[51] of the intensified struggle for legal hegemony.

82

It spoke to the significance of the law that he who was in control of its processes commanded, as well, a superior political stature.

Impeachment was one area theoretically susceptible of cooperation between Lords and Commons. Both houses were necessary to complete the procedure. The Commons would initiate the impeachment and the Lords, in turn, would try it. It was, as one Member of Parliament noted, that the "Commons are in the nature of a Grand-Jury to present, but the Lords are the Judges."[52] Yet, what was possible in theory too often evaporated in practice. Impeachment was reserved for political offenders, and more often than not it was employed by the Commons to bring down those who were its own special enemies. The Lords could not always be expected to agree, particularly when the person charged was one of their number. Such was the case of the earl of Clarendon, impeached of treason in 1667.[53] It would, of course, be wrong to suppose that Clarendon's assailants were confined to the Commons, but the House of Lords was indeed reluctant to act. It refused to commit the earl upon a general impeachment alone and demanded the allegation of special treason before it would consent to proceed. Yet more important than the mechanics of the matter were the arguments that they generated. These were arguments which served to demonstrate the wide areas of mistrust between the two houses, specifically in the understanding and use of the law. John Vaughan,[54] one of the more active members in the proceedings against Clarendon, reflected a general attitude of disdain of the Lords in this regard. He charged the Peers with a want of comprehension of the authority of the past. When precedents were urged upon them, they replied "that they cared not for presidents, because it was against the express Law of the Land."[55] For this response Vaughan had only contempt. He said: "I thought Law in a Lords Mouth was like a Sword in a Ladies Hand, the Sword might be there, but when it comes to cut, it would be awkward and useless."[56]

Vaughan might have been overstating his case, but not

without considerable effect. The province of the past was one to which the Commons could often retreat with good result. Moreover, the maneuver was based firmly upon political necessity. Any argument for the jurisdictional supremacy of the Commons had to be grounded in the antiquity of the Commons itself. It could not hope to be convincing unless it could merge with the "ancient constitution" and reach back beyond the limits of memory. This is why men like Vaughan and Petyt rarely let go of the assistance afforded by mystical "time." Petyt, for example, knew that as a "rule in law . . . every Corporation, or Body Politick, must commence either . . . By Prescription, . . . By Charter, or . . . By Act of Parliament"[57] and that a prescriptive right was, perhaps, even more valuable than the other two. Indeed, he submitted an "Argument from Prescription" as "the most unanswerable and binding that possibly can be produced."[58] If this were true — and Petyt maintained that it was in almost everything that he wrote — he could then proceed to announce that "the Commons were an essential and constituent part of the Parliament in the Saxon times."[59] The argument could be completely wrong and at the same time totally convincing. All that was really required was the application of legal principle to the political problems at hand. Of little consequence was the relevance of the legal procedures employed. The "colour of law" was usually quite enough.

It was an interesting road to sovereignty: political supremacy founded upon control of the law, which in turn was based, as it had to be, upon an understanding of what the law could be made to do. Parliament and its champions, no less than the Stuarts, put the law effectively to work. Distortion and abuse were not the province of the king alone. It may in fact have been that Parliament's victory, when it came in 1688-89, was something different from what the Whigs would have us believe. It was indeed the defeat of an "evil" king, but it was less attributable to Parliament's legal right than to the richness of its legal imagination.

4   The Instruments of Control

AT NO TIME IN THE YEARS 1660–89 WAS THE LEGITIMACY OF
the prerogative seriously impugned. Like the law, it assumed
its high and proper place in the constitution. Even its most
passionate critics admitted its right to exist. Instead the
attack was always directed to limiting the prerogative, to
defining and constricting the power of the king. The result
was not wholly successful. By the accession of William and
Mary the prerogative was somewhat more circumscribed,
but it was not yet precisely defined. There was a sense of the
several things that the king ought not be permitted to do
unilaterally, but that was all. The prerogative would remain,
and in the hands of a capable king, viz., William III, it
would continue to be a powerful implement of rule.

Yet by the end of 1689 the monarch was no longer in
effective control of the law, and in this respect the prerogative had been critically diminished. While neither the
dispensing power nor the suspending power disappeared as
an immediate result of the Revolution, the monarch was in
practice deprived of both. The dispensing power was condemned "as it hath been assumed and exercised of late," and
in the Bill of Rights there was the further assertion that no
dispensations would be legal save those provided for in bills
to be passed by Parliament in the present session.[1] Similarly,
the monarchical suspending power was completely neutralized by making Parliament a necessary party to any future
use.

What had been clearly in issue, then, was not whether an
act of Parliament might be suspended or its penal effects
dispensed; the question, instead, was by what authority

these legislative controls might be exercised. The Toleration Act serves as an example in point. Rather than repeal the penal laws, Parliament chose instead to suspend the application of selected statutes[2] to Protestant Dissenters.[3] The penal laws themselves remained in force. The constitutional value and validity of suspending a statute of the realm were recognized, but there could now be no doubt that the power to suspend was to be exercised jointly by king and Parliament rather than by the king alone. This was all part of the scheme of monarchical limitation. So long as the king did not act unilaterally in politically sensitive areas, the prerogative might continue technically intact. What had happened over-all was that a dangerous imbalance had been redressed. A substantial part, and perhaps the most important part, of the prerogative had been transformed into a discretionary power susceptible of abuse and therefore of regulation. And just as it had been Parliament, and not "the law," which had adjusted the specific powers of suspending and dispensing, so too would it be Parliament which would eventually arrogate to itself the remaining instruments of legal control. There could be no doubt after 1689 that what mattered most was not the restraining force of the law but the identity of that component of political society which would activate the law.

For centuries there had been a universal equation of the law of the realm with the law of the king. This had been due initially to the extension of monarchical justice throughout England, effectively submerging all those jurisdictional rivals who could no longer compete with the sovereign. Feudal justice had been steadily giving way to royal justice, and it was this process, when complete, that eventually marked the triumph of a national common law. Yet in thinking of the law as the property of the king there was an apparent danger. From such a base it could easily be argued that "ownership" justified unregulated use. This is an argument that was made after 1660. No longer could "the King's law" be taken as a neutral value. It now seemed to be employed with a new and heightened awareness of the political

86   implications involved in its application. This was evident during most of the Restoration, although it did not reach its logical extreme until 1686, in the landmark case of *Godden* v. *Hales*. It was there that the dispensing power was upheld as an expression of the prerogative and there that the sweeping statements were made that "the Kings of England are Sovereign Princes" and "the Laws of England are the Kings Laws."[4] These were the premises which, once accepted, led the court easily to its decision in favor of James II. It was indicative of what might be done politically with the constitutional proposition that the law of England was nothing less than the law of the king.

"The King's law" could also be used in support of the pardoning power. When Lord Chancellor Finch noted that "the King is the fountain of Mercy, as well as of Justice,"[5] this is precisely what he had in mind. Yet Finch was too good a lawyer to maintain as of course that the law was still in the exclusive possession of the monarchy. He recognized that the king's "Justice is tyed to rules, and runs in known and Certain Channels,"[6] and for that reason the king's control of the law could not be complete. But the king's "mercy" was another matter entirely. There the monarchy's control was most defensible. Finch alleged that the king's pardon was a power that knew no "bounds or limitts but those of his Good pleasure."[7] This appeared logically and least objectionably to follow from the idea that the law belonged to the king. Nonetheless, there were objections. The problem was that, once it was accepted that the king might pardon any offense after it had been committed, it seemed reasonable to suppose that a potential offender might be relieved of the effects of the law before the offense took place. This, of course, was the power to dispense, and it is here that issue was most frequently joined. It was argued for the king that the right of Parliament to legislate was not being infringed. Neither the dispensing power nor the pardoning power had any effect upon the existence of a statute of the realm. The suspending power presented a closer question. Once the king took the next logical step and suspended a statute, the appearance of unilateral repeal of an act of Parliament was difficult to avoid. As long as the king interceded in behalf of one man at a time, whether by pardon or *non obstante,* there was still some semblance of practicable restraint upon the monarchy's ability to manipulate and control the law. Once a law was suspended, however, the effect of its existence was nullified.

No argument by a proponent of the suspending power was ever sufficient to overcome the resistance of Parliament. Three times the Stuarts attempted a Declaration of Indulgence,[8] and three times they met with political failure, a fact which itself speaks persuasively to the myth of Stuart absolutism. Encouragement was understandably negligible as long as "a liberty to tender consciences" was interpreted to mean *Catholic* consciences. Within the ranks of Protestant Dissenters a "papist-influenced" toleration could not really generate any widespread support. Only the Quakers appeared committed to the royal policy, an endorsement of dubious value among the many who regarded the Friends as little more than papists in disguise. In 1687 William Penn tried to demonstrate on jurisdictional grounds that James, in his Declaration of Indulgence, was quite right to suspend "the execution of all and all manner of penal laws in matters ecclesiastical."[9] Penn was arguing not so much in favor of the suspending power as in opposition to the whole range of penal laws, which, he contended, were void. Parliament did not have the power to make any law which infringed God's jurisdiction. It was as if Penn were attempting to cast the Declaration in the guise of a writ of prohibition; but the attempt did not succeed. "Render unto Caesar the things that are Caesars," he said, "& to God the things that are Gods."[10] It was a familiar admonition, but rarely before had it been used as a lawyer's argument to differentiate between jurisdictions and to attack the validity of acts of Parliament.

There was considerable danger in allowing the king to tamper with the law in any way. Anything that increased his control added to his claim to sovereignty. For this reason the pardoning power was placed under close scrutiny, and any assertion of its absolute quality was immediately challenged. Hale considered the king's pardon to be one of the rights of the Crown, but a qualified right only. It was a trust that the king was forbidden to use if such use tended "to the prejudice of the kingdom."[11] The standard, according to Hale, seemed to be the public interest. In those cases where an aggrieved member of the public prosecuted an action to a successful conclusion or where such prosecution was instituted by the king in behalf of the public, Hale doubted that the king might afterward pardon the offense. "The King . . . is by the laws intrusted with the prosecution & punishment of publick offenses, so far forth as they are publick."[12] Therefore, he may not pardon if it is inimical to the public interest. What he may do is "pardon those offences of the highest nature, as against his own suit, though not against the suit of the party."[13] This appeared to mean that the power to pardon was dependent upon the manner in which the action was prosecuted. The action could be begun in one of three possible ways: by the suit of the king (an indictment), by the suit of a private party (an appeal), or by the suit of the House of Commons (an impeachment). Only when the suit was the king's own was he on relatively safe ground to pardon. Appeal clearly did not belong to him, nor, it was alleged, did impeachment.

Impeachments, because of their political nature, presented the greatest problem. Finch, who was contending for an expanded pardoning power, accepted that the king might not intervene in the suit of a party or the suit of the entire people. Yet impeachment, he argued, could be construed as the king's action at common law. "For tho it begin by the Complaint and prosecution of the Commons, who are the Grand Inquest of the Nation, yet the whole process and proceeding of it, is in Law the Kings Suit."[14] In 1678 this was brought to the test when the House of Commons impeached the earl of Danby, and Charles II, before the opportunity for trial, granted Danby a pardon. When, therefore, in April 1679, Danby was brought to the bar of the House of Lords, he pleaded the pardon from the

king. The question was referred back to a committee of the
House of Commons, which reported after several days that it
could find no precedent for the granting of a pardon to
anyone impeached by the Commons of treason.[15] It was not
the gravity of the crime but the nature of the proceeding
that would determine whether the power to pardon might be
exercised.

High treason did not make a critical difference. It could
therefore be argued that the killing of the king, although a
crime of *laesae majestatis,* might justifiably be pardoned
provided that the security of the people was not thereby
compromised. "For though this wounds, yet it destroyes not
the government; for though the King is killed in his naturall
capacity; yet he dies not in his politique as King; for by the
demise of the King, another immediately succedes."[16] This
was an important argument to be considered, because in the
long run it tended more to the constriction of the powers of
the king than to his personal glorification. Although it
allowed for the exercise of the king's pardon in specific cases
of treason, it made of kingship a definable office rather than
a God-given fief; and that which could be defined and
institutionalized could also be more easily controlled. It was
this line of reasoning that was being employed throughout
the century and which reinforced the belief that "king" and
"government" were no longer to be considered interchange-
able terms.

All of this supposed that the crime of killing the king
would be tried as a common-law action in the court of King's
Bench. It was the only circumstance in which the pardoning
power might operate.[17] Just as the king might not pardon an
appeal because it was the suit of a private person, so was he
precluded from pardoning an impeachment, "which is the
suite of all and for the safety of the King, and all his
people."[18] Here was the familiar standard of the public
interest, invoked in an argument that sought to restrict the
immense political power inherent in the prerogative right to
pardon. The danger was that if the king might legally
salvage those allies who had been condemned by Parliament,

90   then the control of the law was still very much in the
possession of the monarchy. Danby's case, which in this
regard was so important, was never resolved. Charles would
not run the risk of seeing the Lords agree with the Commons.
Accordingly, before any agreement could be reached, he
prorogued, and subsequently dissolved, the Parliament.

Any stand taken against the king's right to pardon would
be intensified tenfold against the dispensing power. It was
that much more of a political danger. The king would not
have to wait for the judgment of a court or even for the
commencement of legal process. By the grant of a patent
non obstante he could effectively immunize any man against
the operation of an act of Parliament. This is what James,
and Charles to a lesser degree, resorted to in the struggle for
sovereignty. Constitutionally, it was a subtle but powerful
device. The dispensation, in any given case, did not purport
to remove the obligation of the act in question. Rather, it
effectively declared that obligation to have been fulfilled
and thereby disarmed "the sanction penalty & consequence
of a law as to the person & act dispensed with."[19] The result
was that the king would not have to go so far as a general
suspension of the law in order to achieve the desired end.

An argument for the dispensing power in the reign of
James II poses this question: "Whether the King granting an
Office by his Letters Patent to any person with a Non
Obstante to this act [the Test, 25 Car. II, c. 2] may Execute
performance of the severall things required to be don and
Consequently prevent all the penaltys and Disabilitys for not
doing them." The rhetorical answer was simple:

> I conceive that it is very Clear that he may. For this is a
> penall Law and it was never doubted but that the King
> had always a power of dispensing with penall Laws in
> particular Cases. The House of Commons when they
> Quarelled with the Declaration of Indulgence which they
> called a generall Suspension of the penall Laws against
> Dissenters, yet the King's power of granting Indulgences

to particular persons was always owned and admitted by them.[20]

That the House of Commons always "owned and admitted" the legality of the dispensing power in such matters was not entirely true. Although it may have been good law to say that the king had "a power of dispensing with penall Laws in particular Cases," Parliament was inclined at times to disagree—at least as to the case in issue. When, in 1662-63, Charles II was exploring ways to relieve Protestant Dissenters and some Catholics from the effects of the Act of Uniformity, he encountered overwhelming resistance. Not only was the suspending power denied, but in the Commons' address presented to the king on 27 February 1662/63, it was stated categorically that the Act of Uniformity "could not be dispensed with, but by Act of Parliament."[21] Nor would Parliament, in this instance, agree to ground the dispensing power in its own legislative authority. A bill, therefore, to empower the king to dispense with the Act of Uniformity in limited circumstances, for Protestant Dissenters only, lost support and eventually was dropped.[22] Similarly, in 1685, the House of Commons once again protested the use of the dispensing power, which it claimed the king, unilaterally, did not enjoy. In a petition to James II complaining of Catholic officers in the army, it was suggested that the continuation of such a condition "may be taken to be a Dispensing with that Law [the Test Act] without Act of Parliament."[23]

Broadly speaking, there were three possible ways of viewing the dispensing power. It could be regarded favorably as an unchallengeable part of the prerogative; it could be accepted in principle while any number of attempts were simultaneously made to limit and qualify its use; or it could be rejected outright as beyond the pale of the king's constitutional control. This third view, that the dispensing power was no power at all and therefore illegal, received the least support. Most opponents of an extended prerogative recognized that it was not possible to deny the king all use of the *non obstante,* since the weight of legal opinion was heavily on the side of a limited power to dispense.

Those who did not or would not accept that there was, in some form, a valid dispensing power were not much bothered by the absence of a convincing constitutional argument in their favor. Their thinking appeared to be informed by an apprehension more of political than of legal reality. They were motivated by a strong fear of the power of control in the hands of James II and sought to discredit their Catholic king by condemning his papist devices. The familiar allegation of an alien innovation was thus pressed once again into service. Petyt was one of those who had no difficulty in dismissing *non obstante*s out of hand. It was evident to him that they "came from the Court of Rome, And from Thence only, Having no Foundation at all in the Antient Laws of England."[24] But this was a desperation measure. Even after the Revolution had been accomplished, the power of the king to dispense with the execution of a law in some as yet unspecified circumstances was affirmed by clear implication in the Declaration of Rights. The Convention had been unhappy about the use to which James II had put the dispensing power, but the best legal opinion available still affirmed the *non obstante* as a legitimate expression of the prerogative. In preparing their bill for settling the succession and declaring the rights of the subject, the Lords had consulted the judges specifically in this matter; they were advised by a majority, plus the highly influential Serjeant Holt,[25] that the power, in law, did certainly exist.[26] All that could continue to be said against the power by way of absolute condemnation was that it infringed the Parliament's right to legislative parity. That may have been an unpleasant truth, but such was the force of the prerogative that, unless limited, it still gave to the king a decided legislative advantage.

Nor did the issue cease to be significant after the settling of the Crown. The argument against the dispensing power was to continue into the reign of William and Mary, where it yet proved useful in the attempt to win reconciliation of the nonjurors to William. James, it was insisted, had promised to "govern according to the laws made by lawful authority" and had violated that pledge by resorting to dispensations. It was deemed to be a basic premise of government that the law was made by king in Parliament; and James, who had used the dispensing power to relieve the burdens placed by law upon Catholics, was deemed to have subverted the constitution. The dispensing power was held to be nothing more than a legislative power in disguise, a clear violation of the right of Parliament and therefore contrary to law.[27]

Those who reluctantly acknowledged the dispensing power were intent upon keeping it within manageable bounds. For a long time this had seemed possible, although the exact formula to be employed had never been satisfactorily settled. There would be circumstances in which the dispensing power might be employed to correct the undesirable effects of legislation, effects which had never been intended; and in these instances the operation of the power would be welcome. But if it was agreed that statute law might sometimes be modified by the prerogative, it was not nearly so certain that common law would be subject to the same kinds of alteration. In this respect the common law would be regarded as fundamental, and the argument would be made "that the king cannot dispense with, nor alter the Common Law by a Non Obstante."[28] Yet this was a formula open to wide interpretation. Just as it was possible to argue that anything politically objectionable was a "popish innovation," so it could be said that anything worthy of preservation was part of the "antient Common Lawes and Birthright of the nation." And from there it could go further. The common-law prescription could be applied to fundamental matters of government and the argument be made that those "Lawes that appoint & sett out the manner of Government to the prince cann never be pretended to bee under his dispensitory power."[29] By that reasoning no statute could be the object of a *non obstante* if it could be shown to touch in some way upon the constitution. In this fashion the king's power to dispense might be held in check. The distinction was also

94 referred to as one between *malum prohibitum* and *malum in se*. Anything that was illegal only because it had been so declared by the positive law might be open to dispensation; but any law directed against an intrinsic evil should in nowise be impaired.[30] This had been a shibboleth for many years, but when put to the test it was of little objective help. It was just as easy to place an action under the anathema of *malum in se* as it was to declare it established in the dim beginnings of the common law. But if these familiar criteria were legally imperfect for want of precision, they were politically useful for just the same reason. After the passage of the Test Acts, those who would defend the Protestant interest — and they were clearly in the majority — could ask: "Is not Popery Malum in se?"[31] The answer was obvious, as were its implications. The Test Acts, 25 & 30 Car. II, could not by law be affected by the king's power to dispense.

The case of *Thomas* v. *Sorrel* in 1674 underscored a long-established argument in the controversy. In that case Chief Justice Vaughan, presiding in Exchequer Chamber, noted the inadequacies of the *malum prohibitum–malum in se* distinction and attempted to revive and reshape a more meaningful and exact rule. He spoke of a valid dispensation as that which would affect the king's interest alone. As such, it was to be distinguished from a *non obstante* that might unjustly deprive a third party of a right of action. This was an affirmation of the familiar *pro bono publico* test. If the law involved was one "in which the Subjects of England have an interest,"[32] there would be no power to dispense. Yet the standard was less precise than most others. It opened the reasonable possibility of arguing that, since Englishmen had an interest in all their laws, no law might therefore be dispensed. The construction, clearly plausible, had earlier in the century been emphasized in Coke's report of *Darcy* v. *Allin*. Although it had been adjudicated on other grounds, Chief Justice Popham noted in that case that the king might not dispense with a statute that prohibited the importing of playing cards. The teaching there, as expounded by Coke, was that the dispensing power would not be allowed to operate against the public interest even if the statute in question were proscribing an activity normally regarded as *malum prohibitum*.[33]

If, at any time, this had become a majority view of the law, the dispensing power would have been effectively destroyed. Wrote one defender of the prerogative: "All Generall Laws are made for the benefit of the public and so if this Objeccion should take place the King would have no power of dispencing at all."[34] But this did not happen. Instead, the courts were disposed to rule that the interests affected were the king's only and did not touch his subjects in their rights or liberties. In *Thomas* v. *Sorrel* the narrow judgment of the court was that the dispensation to the Company of Vintners by letters patent from James I was sufficient authority for the defendant, a member of the company, to sell wine at retail without a license within two miles of the City of London. The dispensation was held to have caused injury to no one but the king.[35]

The issues in *Thomas* v. *Sorrel* had first been contested some six years earlier by Francis North, acting as plaintiff's counsel in King's Bench. North's argument was that the statute in question had been promulgated for the public good, as a result of which the king's power to dispense was not available merely as a matter of course. In this instance the prerogative was not absolute. It was to be regarded instead as the "discharge of a trust upon consideracion of circumstances."[36] What was contemplated was a limited power in the king to redress wrongs incapable of being foreseen at the time of a statute's enactment — but a limited power only. It was the attempt to make part of the prerogative a discretionary instrument. If the trust concept were admitted, the dispensing power might then be controlled. "Trust" had long been known to the law and was a fit subject for common-law adjudication. North found support in Coke's *Seventh Reports*, where it was written that "the power to dispence is a trust annexed to the kings person."[37] This, in turn, had a further implication: that if the trust were personal, it might not be delegated. Sorrel,

96   after all, was not the direct recipient of the *non obstante*
from James I. He benefited only by virtue of his membership
in the Company of Vintners, and this is what North alleged
was illegal. To uphold the dispensing power in this set of
circumstances would countenance an improper delegation
of a personal trust.[38]

North's argument did not stop there. He was ready to
allow that under certain conditions the king might be
treated as the "owner of the Law,"[39] but here, too, there
should be strict limitations. However valid the dispensation
at the time granted, it was, said North, terminated by the
death of the grantor, James I. This was again because the
object of the dispensation was more than the king's revenue
alone. It was a matter of the public interest, in which the
king was claimed to have no disposable estate. "The king
may give away his inheritance in land or his treasure, but he
cannot give away his lawes from his successor."[40] Thus there
emerged an interesting construction from the private law. In
the area of the king's revenue, it was as if he were possessed
of an estate in fee. This was his undisputed inheritance, and
this he might freely alienate. But in those areas where
legislation touched in any way upon the government of the
realm, the king was to be limited either to a life estate or, in
the alternative, to a trust in which he had no power of
appointment upon his death. In either event the effect
would be the same. Such was the monarchical control of the
law that North was advocating, a control that was hedged in
by restrictions and which obliged the king to preserve the
estate or trust intact.

Despite the force of North's arguments, the dispensation
was ultimately held to have had no effect upon the public
interest. Vaughan's opinion was in support of the king, and
his statement of the law seemed reasonable upon its face.
But it signaled a shift away from the protection afforded by
an inviolable common law. It echoed Hale's earlier opinion
that, although the king "cannot alter a law, yet he may
dispense with such a part of the common law, as was
introduced merely for his own benefit."[41] Hale did not

intend this as a wedge for the prerogative, but that is how it could be used. In the first instance it would always be the king who would decide what laws had been promulgated for the greater public good, as opposed to those that had been enacted solely for the benefit of the Crown. And then, when the dispensation was challenged at law, it would be advanced in behalf of the king that the statute in question did not touch upon the public interest. This assertion might, of course, be rebutted; but if the test were to be one of legislative intent, monarchy need defer to no one. The area of public good was one in which the king might claim an expertise as great as that of any man learned in the law.

North was abundantly aware of the need to restrict the prerogative. In the very sensitive area of the dispensing power, a king who was allowed to "diminish a law . . . [might] by the same reason repeal it."[42] Charles and James tried, of course, to go just that far in their attempts to suspend the operation of the penal laws; and even though they failed there, the Stuart design was far from frustrated. James was successful in surrounding himself with Catholic followers on every level of government through the extensive use of the *non obstante*. In support of James there was no lack of persuasive legal argument. The legacy of Coke, for example, was as valuable in support of the king as it was against him. The maxim of an inalienable prerogative could be construed as a restricting trust or as a nonforfeitable and unregulated power; and Coke could be profitably searched in support of either proposition. In a citation to the *Twelfth Reports,* "by one whose profession is the Law and whose Communion is according to the Church of England,"[43] the argument was made that the king might use the dispensing power to avoid the Tests. He submitted that, according to Coke, "Noe Act can bind the king from any prerogative which is sole and inseparable to his person, but that hee may dispense with it by a Non Obstante."[44] It had, after all, been shown by Coke and others that the dispensing power was a necessary part of the prerogative. It enabled the king to correct inequalities that arose under the law. Even North

98   had conceded "that there is an impossibility of foreseeing all particulars, and some may be of necessity or profit to be dispensed with."[45] This was in the very nature of the common law; and what made dispensations so useful and desirable was that the law itself contemplated the employment of correctives at such times as they might be needed. Equity procedure was one such corrective; the dispensing power was yet another. It could thus be alleged that to deny the king the use of the *non obstante* was to restrain him "in the Service of his subjects." This, no act of Parliament might do.[46] The denial, itself, would operate as a "violent injustice and a serious breach of the law."[47]

That a statute promulgated for the general good might in some instances work an individual injustice was a persuasive argument for the existence of a limited dispensing power. In *Thomas* v. *Sorrel,* part of the case against the *non obstante* was that it was being extended too far — that, as a result of its being granted, not to an individual but to a corporation, there would be an unknown and unjustifiably large number of people to whom the benefits of the dispensing power would apply. The contention was that the prerogative power to mitigate the burdens of the law had to rest on the king's ability "to weigh the profit or necessity of the particular Case, and by consequence such dispensacions must be in cases certain and ... to a particular person or ... limited to Number and quantity." Otherwise, it was feared that "where A dispensacion is large and generall noe measure can be taken of the Effects of it."[48]

This, by extension, was one of the dangers of the suspending power. Yet, even where the effects could be measured, as in the granting of toleration to Dissenters and Catholics, which would create "schism by law," there was no less an attempt to frustrate the king's purpose. Understandably, because the known effects were deemed to be so completely unacceptable by the parliamentary opposition, the resistance was appreciably greater. The suspending power posed a much more formidable challenge to Parliament than the dispensing power. Not only would far larger numbers of people be relieved of the proscriptions of the law, but the legislative intent of Parliament could be totally defeated. It would be, as the House of Commons had contended in 1673, when it was resisting the king's attempt to suspend the penal laws, that the power of suspending, "if it should be admitted, might tend to the Interrupting of the free course of the Laws, and Altering the Legislative power, which hath always been acknowledged to reside in your Majesty and your Two Houses of Parliament."[49]

Politically, Parliament was far more successful in warding off the suspending power than it was in resisting the dispensing power, but that did not suggest any consensus on the constitutional possibility of the king's suspending some less sensitive law. While Charles II was politically incapable of nullifying the penal laws by simple recourse to the Crown's ecclesiastical supremacy, he might still maintain that he enjoyed a limited power to suspend. This is what he did in 1673. In response to the petition and address of the Commons in which it was stated "that penal Statutes in Matters Ecclesiastical, cannot be suspended, but by Act of Parliament,"[50] Charles explained that he did not "pretend to the Right of Suspending any Laws, wherein the Properties, Rights, or Liberties of any of His Subjects are concerned; nor to alter any thing in the established Doctrine or Discipline of the Church of England."[51] The result was that the legal dispute over the suspending power would be fought over the same ground as the dispensing-power battle was being waged. The question was not whether these prerogative powers existed but in what limited circumstances they might be exercised and, most important, in what ways Parliament would be able to keep them under control.[52]

Although the Crown, by the reign of James II, was still in control of the law, the various attempts to restrain the prerogative had not been without important effect. To nullify that effect, the collusive action of *Godden* v. *Hales* was initiated in 1686. Sir Edward Hales, a Catholic, had already been convicted of holding military office in violation of the Test. He had been informed upon by his coachman,

100   Godden, who was now suing for the informer's reward in
King's Bench. On the basis of the law enunciated in *Thomas
v. Sorrel* it was argued that the defendant was in possession
of a valid dispensation from the king. By granting a
commission notwithstanding the proscription of the Test
Act, James could be said to have injured no one but himself.
Chief Justice Herbert agreed that the Test was not a statute
pro bono publico and that the dispensation was therefore
valid. This, in itself, would have been sufficient affirmation
of the manipulative way in which the teaching of *Thomas* v.
Sorrell might be used; but Herbert chose to go further. He
set down five notorious premises which, although technically
dicta, were so openly factious as to overshadow everything
else. They amounted to the careful, indeed the systematic,
rejection of every point raised in limitation of the prerogative during the preceding twenty-five years. The premises
were these:

(1) That the Kings of England are Sovereign Princes
(2) That the Lawes of England are the Kings Laws
(3) That it is an inseparable Prerogative of the Kings of
England to dispence with Penall Laws upon necessity &
urgent occasions (4) That the King is the Sole Judge of
that necessity (5) That this is not in trust given to the
King, but tis the Antient Remains of the Crown, which
never was nor can be taken from him.[53]

If these premises were accepted, then every attempt to
qualify the dispensing power had failed, and every suggestion of a limit to the king's control of the law had been spent
to no avail.

Yet even if Herbert's philosophical assertions in support of
an unregulated dispensing power were not binding in law,
what had been adjudicated, and correctly so, was that the
power to dispense was, on the authority of law and history, a
usable part of the prerogative. How much further the
Stuarts might have carried this was unclear, but it was
nonetheless settled by *Godden* v. *Hales* that the king had a

legal right, in individual cases, to subvert the purpose of the
Test Acts. By the use of the *non obstante* he might raise to
positions of power as many Catholics as he chose. Equally
important was that every argument employed to harness the
dispensing power of the prerogative to a specific legal
control had now failed of practical effect. Not that the basis
in law of these controls had been found wanting. It was still
presumptively possible to deny to the king the use of this
dispensing power in those generalized instances when the
law to be circumvented was part of the ancient constitution,
a statute in the public interest, or a protection against an act
malum in se. Yet the blanket protection attempted by such
general principles had now been made to yield before the
specific need of the king to employ servants of his own
choosing.

THE PROPOSITION THAT THE LAW BELONGED TO THE KING WAS
an argument from history and, as has been noted, an
argument that was used successfully to establish the king's
quasi-legislative rights to pardon and to dispense. Another
such argument upon which control could be based was
drawn from the right of conquest. Everyone knew of the
Norman invasion of the eleventh century and of the monarchical succession that it had established, but not everyone
agreed as to the nature of that conquest. There were
important distinctions to be drawn. If it could be shown that
William's triumph had been total — a victory over people
and institutions as well as over Harold — then the Stuarts in
the line of succession would have yet another claim to
control of the law. This is what made the constitutional
debate on the Conquest so important, so much more than an
irrelevant antiquarian exercise. This is why to some minds it
seemed vital to maintain that the stamp of the Conqueror
was not, indeed could not be, complete.

Hale was in the van of this effort. To him the question
involved much more than the preservation of the ancient
constitution. That was only part of what was important. The
real issue was the question of control. Hale, unlike Petyt, did

not deny the fact of the Conquest. He did not maintain, as Petyt did, that there was nothing more than "a plaine compact and stipulation" between the English and William.[54] Nor did Hale fall back on the myth of an original contract which could not be obliterated by any manner of foreign subjugation. Instead he proceeded from the known truth that William took title to the English throne by defeating Harold in 1066. But to Hale this was not nearly so frightening as it was to Petyt and others. Hale did not shrink from succession by conquest because he was able to put conquest into a framework of law.

Hale realized the need for limiting the use of the Conquest as an instrument of legal control. If the scope of the Conquest could be narrowed, then the control of the law might be placed, at least in part, outside the king's grasp. The way this was to be done was to argue that a conquest might be either *victoria in populum* or *victoria in regem* and that the triumph of William I had been the latter.[55] Since this was the case, William had succeeded to the Crown and to the right of his Anglo-Saxon predecessor — and to nothing more. If the Confessor had no right to alter the laws of the realm, then the Conqueror would be subject to the same limitation.[56] In this way the Conquest could be rendered less than complete and so brought within manageable bounds. It was a valuable construction because it substantially minimized the Conquest's effect. It transformed a violent and extraordinary event into a slightly unusual, although completely regular, step in the succession. It could be pretended that the rights of the people were wholly untouched. This is exactly the position for which Hale was contending. In such circumstances a conqueror would have

no more Right of altering their Laws, or taking away their Liberties or Possessions, than the conquered Prince, or the Prince to whom he pretends a Right of Succession, had; for the Intention, Scope and Effect of his Victory extends no further than the Succession, and does not at all affect the Rights of the People. The Conqueror is, as it

were, the Plaintiff, and the conquered Prince is the
Defendant, and the Claim is a Claim of Title to the
Crown; and because each of them pretends a Right to the
Sovereignty, and there is no other competent Trial of the
Title between them, they put themselves upon the great
Trial by Battle.[57]

Hale's approach was to place the aberration of 1066 in an
institutional context; and by so doing he provided a valuable precedent for the treatment of the Revolution of 1688–
89. The accession of William III could be viewed in the same
aspect of regularity as that of William I. The circumstances,
of course, were somewhat different, but the rationalizations
were much the same. The Prince of Orange did not speak of
differences between the conquest of a king and the conquest
of a people. Indeed, he did not speak of conquest at all,
except to deny that it was in any way his intention. Yet he
did point out that those who were supporting his cause
would never have committed themselves if it had meant the
subversion of "their own lawful Titles to their Honours,
Estates and Interests."[58] He was therefore demonstrating
what was most important, that the outcome of his endeavor
would neither compromise nor prejudice the rights of the
English. It was an assurance consistent with the teaching of
Hale. Although there might be a new king, England's
institutions, and particularly the law, would remain the
same. By his own declaration William had come to preserve
and not to innovate. Conquest would be tolerable as long as
it went no further than the Crown.

Hale's position constituted a reversal of the radical thinking that had become popular during the Interregnum. It
had long been a commonplace to speak of the Norman yoke
of oppression, but only since mid-century had it been
suggested with any force that the English common law was
in some way part of that burden.[59] This may have been
politically extreme, but it was not without a strong basis
in fact. Much of the Restoration dialogue between Petyt
and Robert Brady centered upon this vital issue, Brady

maintaining and Petyt denying "that our antient Laws and Custums came from Normandy."[60] Here again Hale was prepared to deal with a subject that could not be ignored. There was an uncomfortable correspondence between Norman and English law, one with which generations of lawyers and antiquaries were either unable or unwilling to cope. Just as he had acknowledged that there had been a Conquest, so did Hale allow that Norman law was to be found in England. There was, however, one important qualification. The authority of that law did not derive from the Conquest. On this point he was unyielding. He was willing to admit of change in the law, but not by virtue of any external power.[61] It was merely part of that same rule that accorded weight to canon and civil law, the rule that held that no foreign law might be binding until "it be received and authoritatively engrafted into the Law of England."[62] Here was Hale at his best, recognizing the law at all times in "perpetual adaptation" and at all times evading the possessive hold of the king.

The appeal to historical fact afforded the monarchy its best instruments of legal control. The Conquest was there for all to see. The dispensing, suspending, and pardoning powers were parts of a prerogative derived from the early truth of a law belonging to the king. History was on the side of monarchy and should have been sufficient to consolidate the Stuarts' claim; but it was not. At every turn the Stuarts were challenged, and the attempts to qualify their legal dominion were meeting with some perceptible success. The most dramatic historical counter advanced by the opponents of the king's control was the argument of the ancient constitution. Vested beyond the limits of memory or extant written record, in the dim and polemically secure environment of pre-Conquest England, were the indestructible foundations of Anglo-Saxon liberty. It was of little consequence that these glorious beginnings could not be documented or that they never in fact existed. What was important was that the terms of the debate were eventually accepted by both sides and that king and Parliament, as institutions, each contended for origins of greater antiquity.[63] This in itself was a great victory for Parliament. It had summoned historical myth to redress the advantage to monarchy provided by historical fact. It had framed the debate to its own liking and in historical terms upon which it might prevail.

The most important feature of the ancient constitution had to be its static and inviolable condition. It would not be enough to cite an Anglo-Saxon legacy unless the integrity of that heritage was in some way guaranteed. If it could be shown that the constitution could be, and had been, altered, then whatever it once had been was of little consequence. Ancient liberties had to be more than immemorial; they had, of necessity, to be fundamental as well. This was the formula of the early seventeenth century, advocated so persuasively by Coke. Yet it was not to last. Only until the Civil War was there an epidemic acceptance of a law and constitution that were fixed and unalterable, of a fundamental and immutable jurisprudence that not only did not change but could not change, even as a result of the Conquest. All of this was severely undermined by the Interregnum.[64] By 1660 a good deal of constitutional thinking had experienced a noticeable turn. Although the legitimacy of Cromwell could be denied, his political imprint was not so easily to be eradicated. The aberrant upheaval of the Civil War was in the painfully immediate past and therefore much more difficult to manipulate than the effects of the remote and imperfectly understood Conquest. The period 1642–60 could be rendered a legal nullity, but the early work of the Long Parliament before, and the destruction of the remnants of feudalism after, bore witness to the radical constitutional changes that were possible.

Once it became apparent that the law could change, it was only a small step further to admit that it had changed. The evidence was everywhere to be found. As Hale was to record, the common law was continuously adapting to the relentless movement of circumstances and events. Clearly, this was a more sophisticated approach to the law, but one that was fraught with political danger. Once the law was recognized as alterable, its mystical properties would be severely impaired. No longer could it be so easily alleged that the law was sovereign. The result was that the older rhetoric yielded to a more realistic acceptance of the law's political place. Instead of the image of the law existing on a plane apart, awaiting the summons to arbitrate differences in the lives of men, there was, in the second half of the century, a narrowing focus upon the ways in which the law was to be both declared and applied. This, indeed, seems to be one of the more important intellectual advances taking place after 1660.

The claim for the law's supremacy did, of course, continue into the Restoration, although with far less effect. Polemicists still spoke of the king and all his subjects being in the law's debt, of the king's being obliged to the law for the crown on his head, and every Englishman being beholden to the law for the sum of his liberties.[65] Yet this was not quite the equal of thinking the law to be sovereign. There was always the recognition, if only implied, that the sovereignty of the law was a façade behind which the reality of control was to be found.[66] And with increasing frequency this recognition was being stated quite explicitly. Petyt, for example, was aware that the law as supreme was a comfortable refuge only so long as the premise could insure a desired result. That result was the transfer of control from king to Parliament. In the plainest language possible Petyt spoke of Parliament as having "Absolute Power in all Cases, both to make Laws, and Judicially to Determine Matters in Law."[67] As a statement of Parliament's constitutional position it was extreme because it denied to the king a critical judicial function; but as a piece of constitutional theory it was consistent with the second earl of Nottingham's similarly unmistakable appreciation of the law as totally without any life of its own, of the idea that "promulgacion is of the essence of the Law."[68]

To speak, in the seventeenth century, of men being ruled by the law is rhetorically the same as saying, in the nineteenth century, that men are governed by machines or, in the twentieth century, that their lives are directed by the computer. In each case the putative ruler is nothing more than an effective tool offering great benefits to any who can use and control it — a truth which, regarding the law, was coming increasingly to be admitted as the seventeenth century progressed. The direction of this intellectual current was thus toward a break between political reality and constitutional abstraction and therefore toward an uncomfortable separation between law and justice. Hale had suggested that the laws which were "made known by supreme power" ought to be the positive expression of natural justice, but he knew that that would not always be the case.[69] Justice might live in abstraction; but law, which was expressed in rules and forms, could not. The political problem, then, was to control the ways in which the law was to be made and, beyond that, the means by which it was to be interpreted. Ultimately, the political nation would have to agree to the location of sovereign power, to reach a consensus on the source from which the law would move. The king, in this regard, had a presumptive claim of right. He could draw support from history, religion, and a dependent judiciary. Hobbes had said as much, and Filmer, as well, had been unequivocal on this point. "It is not the law that is the *minister of God,* or that *carries the sword,"* argued *Patriarcha,* "but the ruler or magistrate.... [F]or the law is but the rule or instrument of the ruler."[70] A further example of this thinking translates the theoretical position into one more practical. In 1682, Sir William Smith, a justice of the peace at Middlesex Quarter Sessions, summed up much of the case for the king's legal advantage by first repeating the maxim that the king's authority was derived from God and then proceeding to note that, although the king was obliged to administer his realm according to law, "the best Law, and most useful that ever was made, would lye still for ever, if it was not acted and quickened by some Authority. This Authority is the King's, which he had from God, and his Majesty transmits it to us and others, who act by his Commission to put the Laws in

108   execution."[71] The law, in other words, was the king's to
interpret and therefore his to control.

A claim for the sovereignty of the law could also be used to
disguise the wish for a sovereign legal profession.[72] Coke, it
might be argued, had something like this in mind. In any
event, the aspirations of the common lawyers did suffice to
arouse the suspicions of the king and for James and Coke to
engage in a vigorous contest for the coveted jurisdictional
control. Coke's dismissal in 1616 signaled his defeat. But
even if he had been able to prevail, his victory would have
been short-lived. As long as judges sat at the king's pleasure
and as long as there were all too few who would venture to
challenge their king, the legal profession could not aspire to
the kind of custody of the law for which Coke had labored.
The king, for the most part, controlled his judges, and for
that reason alone he controlled the law. This, more than
anything else, explains why Parliament and the common
lawyer laid such great emphasis upon precedent and why, as
a corollary, they denied that judges were invested with
discretion. Only if the judiciary could be tied to rules was
there any hope of directing the law in opposition to the king.
It was thus that Parliament and the common lawyer were so
often to be found in common cause. Each had ample reason
to distrust the other; but when the common adversary was
the king, it was to their mutual advantage to cooperate.

Coke had symbolized the joining of political independence and judicial integrity. As a royal justice he had, in
fact, seemed to exercise greater zeal in the interests of the
"long robe" than in the interests of the king. But, by the
Restoration, Coke had been long gone, and there was none
to take his place. Hale, every bit the judicial equal of Coke,
directed his energies toward the creation of a stable jurisprudence. He placed less emphasis upon himself and more
upon the legal system that could be expected to outlive him.
Aware of the king's political control of the bench, Hale was
extremely wary of judge-made law. It was, he believed, for
the courts to expound the law and for Parliament alone to
alter it.[73] Hale's concern for the difference between judicial

and legislative powers led him to distinguish carefully between a "power to make a declarative law and a power to declare law." The former was the greater warrant because its application could extend to the entire people. Judicial authority, however, was much more limited because it "doth not extend *ultra partes litigantes.*" So suspicious was Hale of judge-made law that he was unwilling to commit himself to a total acceptance of *stare decisis.* "If all the judges of England deliver their opinion in a point of law, it weighs far as an authority in the like case; but yet it is not binding farther than the parties concerned in that case."[74] Judges were to be bound to a strictly regulated procedure. Where possible, litigation should be determined by the application of existing precedent. If, however, a case were one of novel impression, then the judiciary was to deduce a conclusion from the express law. Only if these two guides were unavailable should a judge endeavor to employ his natural reason and arrive at a rational construction of what the law should be.[75] As a formula it was more of an idealization than a reflection of the contemporary judicial process. It was evidence of a real and necessary concern for the dangers of an unregulated judiciary.

Hale had given more thought than most to the role of the judiciary, but he was not alone in his misgivings about his colleagues. Halifax expressed considerable anxiety over the imprisonment of the law by an incompetent bench,[76] and Petyt made no secret of similar fears. What troubled Petyt, and rightly so, was the specter of uncontrolled judicial discretion.[77] His view of the problem focused upon a contest for legal control between Parliament, representing the people, and a judiciary representing the king. In its way it was a perspective no less Whiggish than the earlier belief in the unshakable alliance between the common law and Parliament; yet it demonstrated a greater awareness of the law as a prized object rather than an active, self-generating performer in a relentless battle against Stuart evil. Petyt argued that judges, in interpreting acts of Parliament, were bound strictly to follow Parliament's legislative intent. There

110   could be no unnecessary expanding of statutes or anything
approximating judicial review.[78] For Petyt to adopt such a
strong position was, in this circumstance, easily understandable; but it clearly suggested a denial of fundamental law, a
tenet which, at other times, proved decidedly important to
the parliamentary cause. This reliance upon legal constructions which were often at variance with one another but
always consistent with the same political ends was remarkably characteristic of the time.

Throughout the period it was obvious to the politically
astute that control of the legislative process was necessary for
control of the law. The arguments for an immemorial and
inviolable common law, predating monarchy and changeless
through time, though still effective, were growing weaker. It
was increasingly difficult to deny that the law was susceptible of change, and, as a result, contemporary polemical
interests began to shift. Rather than perpetuate the case for
a fundamental and immutable law, a new line of parliamentary attack focused upon the contractual principle of
mutuality. This, after all, was what the constitutional
argument was all about. Were the king and his subjects in a
relationship characterized by reciprocal rights and obligations, or did the constitution unfortunately afford to the
king a stature so exalted that he was not, in fact, responsible
to the people? To maintain the latter position would be to
suggest that the king was indeed above the law, an argument
which in seventeenth-century England was patently extreme
and largely unacceptable. Despite the posturings of James I
in *The Trew Law of Free Monarchies,* none of the Stuarts
had seriously laid claim to an absolute rule. It was because
Charles II and James II so willingly and so often admitted
their reliance upon law that men like Hobbes and, to a lesser
degree, Filmer were of minimal political comfort to the later
Stuart cause. Hale was only stating widely accepted constitutional thought when he wrote that monarchical power in
England "is not absolute & unlimited, but bounded by rule
& law."[79] The issue was not whether the king would be
subject to law but whether, and how, he or Parliament

would control that law which both so freely acknowledged.

The view of legislation in contractual terms had distinct advantages for Parliament. First, and most important, was that it implied the consent of someone in addition to the king. There had to be at least two parties to any contract, a requirement which would effectively nullify the monarch's power to legislate unilaterally. Law, then, was not imposed; nor was it given. It was, instead, a matter for discussion and agreement. Petyt was clearly echoing popular attitudes when he wrote that the English people were bound only to the observance of those laws which they "have taken at their free liberty by their owne consent."[80] Hale's argument was much the same, although constructed with greater care and more legal precision. English constitutional monarchy could well be reduced to a relationship built upon contractual negotiation, and this quite aside from the dubious existence of an "original compact." Acts of Parliament were nothing more than "concessions wherein the Subject grants Some thinges to the King, as Aydes, Supplyes, Subsidyes, Tenths, or Fifteenths. And the King att their request grants them Laws, and Liberties."[81] The relationship between king and people was therefore one of legal, if not political, equality. It was a fact not to be minimized. The legal doctrine of mutuality accorded to Parliament a parity of status with the king that no amount of abstract political theorizing could otherwise achieve. Both king and Parliament were to enjoy the standing of contracting parties, and each would have the consequent right to demand and receive a quid pro quo.

Hale carried the analysis even further. He knew, on the basis of long experience, that for an agreement to be binding there had to be a "meeting of minds" and that, all too often, this was not achieved. This was true not only of misunderstandings eventually to be adjudicated in the private law but of constitutional altercations as well. And as the contractual circumstances were often the same, so too were the principles and remedies to be applied. On the important question of whether, in law, a contract had come into being, a fundamental examination of the offer and

112   acceptance had to be undertaken. It was a principle of the common law that an acceptance must be unqualified in order that a contract arise. If the purported acceptance deviated from the terms of the offer, then it was no acceptance at all but a counteroffer. At that point there was no meeting of minds and therefore no contract. Hale took this as a comprehensive guide and applied it to matters of legislation.

> Now concerning the king's answering of bills or petitions in parliament, without which they are no law, regularly the king by his answer cannot make any law, but where the answer agrees with the petition: for if the commons ask one thing and the king grant another there is no law made, there is not a full concurrence of assent.[82]

Hale's analysis of the issue demonstrated the useful application of legal reasoning to difficult political matters. It was a commonplace statement of the principle of offer and acceptance, made remarkable only by the appeal of constitutional analogy.

The real problem, however, was not the making of the legislative contract but the keeping of it. Was the king bound to honor his commitments? The question admitted of no easy answer unless the common law was held to apply. Then what seemed philosophically complicated became legally unmistakable. The king might renege on his obligations, but not because he had any legal right to do so. There could be no doubt that, once a contract had been created, it could not, without liability, be renounced unilaterally. A large part of the constitutional reaction of the late seventeenth century revolved about this very issue. Petyt criticized at length the thinking of Brady, Cowell, Mainwaring, and Filmer for implying that "It is for Marchants not for Kings to be bound by their Oaths."[83] Hale, too, spoke to this point: "for certainly Kings as well as others are bound to keep their faith and Promises."[84] As a constitutional proposition it was simple and persuasive, and it still commanded far greater currency than those modern theories of sovereignty which seemed to operate in total disregard of the common law. This is why Hale was, so much more than Hobbes, a representative of his age. Implicit in the Hobbesian view of legislation was the implied condition that the king might, whenever he deemed fit, suspend or abrogate any act of Parliament. This was politically unacceptable, and not the least because it was legally impossible. It was to suggest the existence of a contract without mutuality, which was no contract at all. It would oblige the people without obliging the king, a political circumstance quite tolerable to Hobbes but totally incompatible with the precepts of the common law. If the king was not bound to perform, then the agreement was illusory.

The calculated effect of binding the king to his legislative contracts was the undermining of his ability to employ the prerogative without restriction. If statutes of the realm were created by contract, then they could be modified or repealed only with the consent of all the contracting parties. It was another way of saying that a legislative change could not be effected without the consent of the king, Lords, and Commons. Each was indispensable to the process. An example of this approach was an anonymous tract of 1672 denying the monarch's right to dispense with the effect of any law. Those laws which are "the antient Common Lawes and Birthright of the nation" have "become in the nature of Covenants and Stipulations betweene the King and his people, nor was it ever allowed to any man that he had power to dispense with his promise and contract when he would judge it inconvenient to bee performed."[85] It was a convincing point, one that joined contract to the standard of the ancient constitution. Together they were to prove to be the best combined instruments of legal control available for challenging the power of the king.

There was yet one more weapon to be employed both by Parliament and by the king. It was the device of reason. As has already been noted, reason was an effective weapon of legal control largely because of its protean nature. Everyone

114   to some degree was possessed of it, a truth upon which James I
was quick to seize. He was equally quick to turn it to his
advantage. If reason were part of the equipment of all men,
it should be supposed that it belonged to the king as well,
and probably in greater degree than that enjoyed by most of
his subjects. Why, then, in disputed matters of law, if the
law be reason, should he yield to the interpretation of *his*
judges? It would, after all, be indecorous to think that the
natural intelligence of any jurist was in any way superior to
that of the king. The importance of the argument was that it
was eminently plausible and therefore politically dangerous.
If accepted, it would mean that whatever leverage Parliament might have in making the law, interpretation would
always be in the province of the king. This is what Coke
first, and then Hale, resisted, because both realized the
dire implications of allowing reason to "escape." The alternative, at least in theory, was remarkably simple: reject
the equivalence of reason and the law in the way that it was
understood to exist by the king. Coke spoke, therefore, of
the difference between "artificial" and "natural" reason,
while Hale spoke of the "reason of the law" and "reason at
large." The distinctions, however, were the same. The
availability of man's reason as a complete tool of legal
understanding was denied. Men could no more understand
the reason of the positive law than they could the reason of
divine law. The rationality of the law was viewed as a thing
apart, clouded in complexity and capable of understanding
only by a mind thoroughly trained in its mysteries.

Those disposed to political opposition recognized the
argument's sound practical appeal, although it could not
have been without some reservation. A lay society so much
involved in the joys of litigation could not be expected to
relinquish easily its vaunted claim to legal expertise; but it
was important to do so. Either "right reason" had to be kept
as the exclusive province of the legal profession, or the king's
opportunity for total control might never be countered.[86]
The point was often repeated, perhaps best by the anonymous author of the tract "Of the Alteration Amendment or

Reformation of the Lawes of England."[87] Written in 1665, that tract concentrated its argument on the problem of popular ignorance. Many people, it maintained, wonder why, if laws are "reasonable things," special study is needed to understand them. They are inclined to "thinke their Reason is much undervallued, if it be told them the Law is reason, and the law is thus."[88] That, of course, was exactly the point. Of the two varieties of reason, the one with which man was naturally endowed was, in this regard, of only marginal worth. Despite the seventeenth-century presence of an impulse toward rationalism, popular reason, in the important matter of the law and the constitution, did not count for very much at all. Law was not based upon reason. If anything, it was the converse that might be true. The law had become so fundamental to English society and its disposition of mind that it provided the most comprehensive base from which other thinking and other values could proceed. It was, for example, altogether in keeping with the broad middle range of contemporary political thought that a dictionary of law terms, dated 1681, should refer to legal maxims as not only the conclusion of reason but its *foundation* as well.[89] And Hale, in a somewhat different expression of the same point, was secure against rebuttal when he wrote that the application of natural reason and all the teachings of Plato and Aristotle would be of no help at all in understanding the English law of real property.[90] Custom and usage, the English experience embodied in statute and judicial decision, would, however, be something else.

The conclusion to which such argument logically led was that it was not moral and political philosophy, each built upon reason, that informed the law; rather, it was the other way round. And this, to the contemporary common-law mind, was as it should be. It was one thing to hold that man in his natural condition might best be guided by his natural endowments, of which reason was presumed to be the most effective. It was quite another thing to suppose that the same should be true in seventeenth-century England, where immemorial custom had for so long worked so well. It all seemed perfectly clear that, once man left his natural state for a political communion, he had entered upon an artificial creation. And for the regulation of an artificial society it was necessary to resort to artificial rules. "For as reason," argued Sir George Treby in the *quo warranto* proceedings against the City of London, "is given to the naturall body to governe it, So a politique body must have Lawes as its reason to governe it."[91] The argument was simple and direct, and it was well received. It washed easily over a political nation historically conditioned to the fundamental authority of its common law.[92]

None of this was to suggest that natural reason had no place in an English jurisprudence. Hale certainly recognized its value, even though he was careful to place it in a clearly subordinate position. In Hale's *Reflections* upon Hobbes he counseled judges to turn first to workable precedents, the "resolutions of precedent ages," and then, if that were not possible, to the standard of legal analogy. Only if these first two guides provided no answer was a judge to resort to "reason at large." And even then, Hale was careful to note, professional jurists would be better prepared than the layman to do this. It would be "their experience and observation and reading" that would give them

> a far greater advantage of judgment, than the airy spec-
> ulations, and notions, and consequences and deductions
> from certain preconceived systems of politicks and lawes
> of some that call themselves philosophers; which, though
> they may please the authors in the contemplation, yet,
> when they come to practice and use, vanish into smoak
> and nothing.[93]

This was the crux of Hale's concern. He feared natural reason because he mistrusted the undisciplined mind. To understand the law and its processes, it was necessary to avoid abstraction, however appealing, and focus attention upon the particular. That all natural men might have a common understanding of justice was of little utility if, when it came to the application of broad principles, there was no probability of "common consent." It was precisely to avoid the "unstable Reason of men" that Hale, and most of political England along with him, preferred to rely upon the law.[94]

The separation of law from reason provided the greatest assurance of keeping the law out of the hands of the amateur and, therefore, beyond his control. More important is that the king, himself an amateur in the eyes of the lawyer, could thereby be kept at bay. By making the law a thing apart, the agreeable gulf between lawyer and layman might be preserved. It was enough that every subject know what the law required him to do without understanding the evolution by which that obligation came to be. Distance would encourage respect and serve as an obstacle to interference, particularly from the king. It was thus, far in advance of Blackstone's making it an institutional truth, that the processes of the law were already regarded as a "mysterious science."[95] It was accepted by 1663 "that as soon as we understand the method of the law, we may understand the method of affronting the law."[96] It was also thus that an alliance was forged between lawyer and Parliament, the basis of which was the mutual desire for legal control and the consequent opposition to the Crown. Eventually it would have to be decided whether that control was to be exercised jointly. It was, even then, unrealistic to suppose that it would—that, once the king had been bested, control might continue to be shared. But the struggle for full parliamentary sovereignty was to be a battle for another day. For the present, what was paramount among the many concerns of lawyer and Parliament was that the king be denied. As long as that was accomplished, then, at least for the time, the interests of each would be served.

Part Three

the
political use
of the law

5   Retreat from Disorder

WHILE IT IS CERTAINLY TOO WHIGGISH TO IMAGINE THAT THE entire seventeenth century was mere preparation for 1688–89, it would not be wrong to argue that Restoration and Revolution make particular sense against the backdrop of constitutional disorder that preceded 1660. From 1642 to 1649 there was the growing uncertainty of where an unwanted rebellion would lead. Charles I could not be trusted, but until 30 January 1649 Charles I was king. Whatever else civil war may have resolved, it had not settled the relationship of a successfully rebellious Parliament to its chronically uncontrollable sovereign. In the end there appeared to be no choice but to yield to the unsettling realization that the king might be defeated ninety-nine times, yet still he would be king. But let the king claim victory only once, and those who had dared to oppose him would be hanged as traitors. Regicide, reluctantly and unconvincingly, seemed to be the only solution. Yet not only did it fail; in the attempt to end some seven years of political anxiety, another and more debilitating insecurity was born. An English commonwealth without a monarch became the subject of a highly questionable constitutional experiment.

In the long history of England there were ample precedents for kings without parliaments, but none the other way round. It is true that there had once been an acceptable hiatus between the death of one king and the coronation of a successor, a fact of some importance when it is recognized that accession and coronation had in the past been equated. The realm, therefore, might be without a nominal king for a few days or even weeks. Such interregna were, however, predictably terminable and created no constitutional problems. The rightful claimant in most instances began immediately to exercise royal authority. And not since the accession of Henry VIII in 1509, which had followed the death of his father by one day, had there even been any such technical interruption.[1] At the very moment of the king's death the title vested in his heir: "Le roi est mort, vive le roi." It was thus that the attempted abolition of kingship in 1649 ran against a well-developed constitutional tradition. To legislate kingship out of existence, particularly when the legislative process contemplated a partnership of king, Lords, and Commons, seemed almost to be an exercise in constitutional futility. Upon the authority of law and history there could be no lapse in monarchical continuity. For almost one hundred fifty years past it could be said with certainty that the king had never died.

Such were the unstable constitutional beginnings of England's Interregnum. For eleven years the Commonwealth and the Protectorate continued in a search for a legitimacy that was never realized. All that was or could be legitimate was Charles II, in whom kingship vested immediately and automatically on that day outside the Banqueting House in Whitehall when his father was "alive and dead." As long as the younger Stuart lived, as long as he was heir to his father's throne, the only choice open to the regicides was to pretend either the nonexistence of Charles II or the abolition of the monarchy. It was the latter option that was chosen; and perhaps because it meant such a violent rending of the constitution, it never really worked.[2] Monarchy had long since acquired the status of an estate in perpetuity, and the only arguable question remaining centered on the identity of the person who would be seised of that estate. In this regard there would be a presumption in favor of hereditary succession, but that presumption might still be overcome by conquest. Henry VII had done it and could be cited for his wisdom in grounding his claim upon seisin and for having Parliament acknowledge that seisin in the first year of his reign. He "did not press to have this as a Declaration or

Recognition of Ancient Right, but onely as an Establishment of the possession which he then had."[3] Cromwell, according to this formula, might have been a credible claimant to the throne, but ultimately he chose not to be. This presented what was to become an insoluble problem. However firm Cromwell's personal hold on the nation, he could not, without the legitimacy inherent in the Crown, create heritable institutions for rule.

Short of kingship there appeared to be no estate that could hope for constitutional or historical justification. Not that the attempt to pretend otherwise was not made. The argument could always be advanced that government by representative assembly without a king was enshrined in the ancient constitution. This is what Parliament suggested after Charles's execution. The *Act for the abolishing the Kingly Office* declared itself to be "a most happy way . . . for this Nation (if God see it good) to return to its just and ancient Right of being governed by its own Representatives."[4] Such, after all, was the value of the ancient constitution that it could be used whenever necessary to establish the conservative validity of any innovation. It was both undesirable and unnecessary to maintain that the state was moving into a constitutionally uncharted area so long as it could be argued convincingly that an English republic was not a departure but a restoration.

It was, by mid-century, a good formula, one that had been employed effectively throughout the Stuart period; but in this instance it did not work. However accommodating a refuge the ancient constitution was, it had its limits. Throughout the Interregnum it was never so expansive as to harbor safely and comfortably the idea of an England without a king. It would have been acceptable to argue that Parliament had antedated the king — provided the interval of time between the genesis of each was a matter of dispute — but only to establish which was entitled to legal and political control. The theory, at least until 1649, was never advanced in support of a republic.

Precedents for an elected monarchy could be found, but

they were precedents for kings and not for reigning lords protector. Ironically, then, it was here, where the ancient constitution might have been politically valuable, that it was never used. Pre-Conquest England had known elected monarchy on more than an occasional basis, and not really until the sixteenth century could inherited kingship based on primogeniture be thought of as firmly fixed in the constitution. This was Cromwell's tragedy. Republicanism deprived him of a crown, and by so doing it also deprived him of a legitimate base upon which to perpetuate his rule. If there was any mistake fundamental to the republican experiment, it was to be found in the belief that the Crown was the disposable capstone of the Commonwealth rather than its indispensable foundation.

With the death of Oliver in 1658 the value of legitimate monarchy became increasingly apparent. The Protector had been empowered to nominate his successor; but as the hapless Richard was soon to learn, a weak ruler was altogether powerless without the support of institutional validity. Richard's rule, therefore, was short-lived. On 22 April 1659 he dissolved his only Parliament and ceased effectively to be Protector. Oliver had managed the balance between Parliament and the army in a way that his son could not. The suggestion of disorder that had continuously haunted the nation from the execution of Charles I was now an almost certain prospect. While Parliament and the London army vied for control, Monck marched south from Scotland; and on 26 December, after one prior attempt had proved abortive, the Long Parliament was reconvened.

In circumstances of constitutional uncertainty the need to act "by colour of law" was accentuated. Monck would not admit to a plan for restored monarchy, but events were proceeding in that direction. A reassembled Long Parliament, including the survivors of those purged in 1648, was brought to bear upon this design. According to the legislation of 1641, the Long Parliament would have to be persuaded to dissolve itself before a "free parliament" could be summoned; and on 16 March 1660 that act of dissolution took place. Whether or not this afforced Rump had the authority to dissolve itself might prove to be another matter. But for the time being it was true that "by the month of March 1660 the position was this—a decayed remnant of parliament had been reinvigorated by a transfusion of Presbyterian blood in order to provide the energy for committing suicide."[5] Yet the Convention, when it met the following month, was not entirely sure that its predecessor had been properly interred. It acted, therefore, to legalize itself and to legislate the Long Parliament further out of existence. To be regular and certain, the Convention deemed it necessary to have "Declared and Enacted . . . That the Parliament begun and holden at Westminster the third day of November in the Sixteenth yeare of the Raigne of the late King Charles of Blessed Memory is fully dissolved and determined."[6]

The technical possibility of a revived Long Parliament had to be foreclosed. There were those who would reason that the members of the Long Parliament had been entrusted "to preserve their session, and establish their own authority against all means of their untimely dissolution" until that trust could be "honourably discharged."[7] If this were true, the Long Parliament might be denied the right to dissolve itself before the purpose of the trust had been accomplished. Legally, however, the argument was faulty. Even if a trust was irrevocable, the trustee might always return the corpus and resign his obligation. The grantor—in this case "the people"—could be divested of the right to terminate; but the trustee, in point of law, could not be so constrained. Against this it had been argued, by further analogy from the common law, that despite any efforts to the contrary the Long Parliament was automatically dissolved upon the death of Charles I. There was no question, William Prynne contended, that if a man, by will or deed, made an appointment of three persons to act jointly in the disposition of a parcel of land and one of the three died, the survivors would be deprived of all authority to continue under the terms of the appointment. What three parties

126   were empowered to do together could not, in law, be done
by two alone.[8] It was a familiar argument, made all the
more persuasive by the weight of precedent. Within the
context of Tudor and Stuart monarchy it could easily be
shown that those parliaments in existence in 1547, 1558, and
1625 were dissolved upon the death of the sovereign.

Nevertheless, there did exist the possibility of rebuttal. As
long as it might be said that the king in his "politic capacity"
never dies, it could, in this regard, be argued that the
"natural" death of Charles I was of no constitutional
consequence.[9] It was also here that the most basic of
constitutional issues was joined. Charles, after all, had
assented to the legislation of 1641; and if it could be
maintained that the king in Parliament was sovereign, any
contrary precedent might easily be denied. This was the
conflict between the supremacy of fundamental law on the
one hand and that of the king in Parliament on the other.
Consistent with the latter principle was the possibility that a
sovereign king in Parliament could, if it chose, cancel that
part of the prerogative which enabled the monarch to
dissolve Parliament at will. This explains in part why such
elaborate arrangements were undertaken to enable a recon-
stituted Long Parliament to dissolve itself. The theory of a
supreme king in Parliament having moved aggressively in
the direction of explicit recognition, there would be increasing difficulty in countering such sovereignty with arguments
based in fundamental law.[10] Nevertheless, the attempt was
frequently made. Applying, for example, the rule of indivis-
ible joint authority, Prynne could speak confidently of
Parliament as "a corporation compacted jointly of the king,
lords and commons house" which had been necessarily
dissolved at the death of Charles, notwithstanding any
legislation whatever to the contrary.[11] The notion of a
fundamental law, and particularly a fundamental common
law, was clearly still alive.

This was the great value of fundamental law. It could be
used to mean whatever was deemed convenient at any given
time, and there was always a great corpus of "basic"

jurisprudence from which to choose. Like the ancient constitution, with which it was often equated, fundamental law existed as an *a priori* assumption which had been dignified by age. In this case it also seemed profitable to maintain that whatever the Long Parliament had forced upon the king would have to be measured against the law of contract, specifically the doctrine of rescission. It could be argued generally from the private law that the breach by one party of his contractual obligation might have the effect of abrogating the agreement and returning the parties to the *status quo ante.* Such is the way that it was in the common law and in the civil law from which the doctrine derived. Even the feudal law could be called into service. "Bracton, Fleta, Horn, and Littleton agree, that if the Lord shall fail to protect his vassal, the vassal's oath is dissolved, for . . . the law intendeth a condition, and the law freeth him from his obedience." The same would also hold true of the defaulted obligation of Parliament "to protect the people from those frequent violations and outrages, irregularities and disorders that were daily committed upon the subject."[12] Once England had lapsed into such a condition, against which the Long Parliament was powerless to act, that Parliament could be said to have ceased to exist. It was clear, at least, from the law of contract, if only that law could be made to apply.

The process of providing for institutional regularity did not end with the demise of the Long Parliament. The Convention itself stood upon uncertain constitutional ground. Unlike the Long Parliament, its problem was one of legitimate birth rather than questionable death. It had not been summoned by a king and could not, therefore, claim to be a true Parliament. It was, at best, a "parliament by adoption" rather than one that had been "free-born."[13] Nevertheless, it sat for more than eight months, enacting with the king's assent a considerable part of the legislation upon which the Restoration was built.[14] This, for Charles, was the best of all worlds, a fact that was not lost upon his contemporaries. It was too great a risk, observed one

128   anonymous commentator, to "own it for a Parliament on Account of the Consequences. But on the other hand he would not deprive himself of the Benefit of the Resolutions of this Parliament, which restor'd him to the throne of his Ancestors."[15] But as soon as Charles II convened his first Parliament according to recognized constitutional procedures, that Parliament quite properly adopted a more circumspect approach. It sought immediately to ratify and confirm the work of its imperfect predecessor.[16] It was important to retreat as quickly, yet also as carefully, as possible from that unhappy interim of constitutional experiment.

The retreat was successful, albeit in some ways deceptively so. It suggested an initial conjoining of purpose between Charles and his Houses of Parliament that was not to last. The king and the political nation could agree to the precedent importance of a constitutional monarchy, but only as the context in which their continuing political struggle would be resolved. The seventeenth-century contest between king and Parliament was not itself to be so easily concluded. Only a temporary and vitally important pause had been achieved. No one doubted that the execution of the first Charles had brought disastrous consequences down upon the realm. For some the reasons were obvious: political disorder was the easily predictable result of a divine retribution. But to more sophisticated minds England was thought to have been removed from a legal and historical base fundamental to its ordered existence. The monarchy, which had not been disrupted in law, would still have to be restored in fact. It was therefore in the interest of both king and Parliament to have themselves, as the vitally constituent parts of the constitution, once again made whole. These interests had necessarily to merge, a legitimate framework had to be reconstructed, before the contestants for political power could resume their separate ways.

The year 1660, then, was a period of pause and constitutional rearrangement within the larger perspective of political continuity. Charles's "long" Parliament (1661–79) eventually drew away from him because it was concerned to renew the essential struggle only postponed by the Interregnum, the contest between king and Parliament for control of the law. To speak, therefore, of a "Cavalier Parliament" is at least connotatively inaccurate. This was a Parliament that reflected the mood of an entire nation in its desire to return from disorder. It appreciated, as did the parliaments of the first part of the century, the value of law and, more important, the security afforded by the rule of law. It was determined to exclude the possibility of another civil war. In this regard it repudiated, as did the king himself, the years immediately preceding Restoration. But to suggest that commitment to monarchy meant blind commitment to Charles II would be plainly incorrect.

Charles Stuart returned to an England that had been made only temporarily secure. Monck's work had been done well; but if the king had relied upon that alone, the Restoration might well have been short-lived. The attractiveness of Charles in 1660 was clearly something other than the attraction of force upon which Cromwell had largely based his power some eleven years earlier. In 1649 Cromwell was at the head of an army that was in effective control of the realm. Cromwell's appeal, therefore, was the unavoidable attractiveness of power, whereas that of Charles was the appeal of right. Both rulers, in their time, held out the hope and the promise of constitutional stability, but only Charles was possessed of the constitutional stature necessary to make it work.

Casting the Restoration in the familiar legal rhetoric of the century, Sir William Temple saw the event as the transformation of "usurped Powers" back to the "Ancient and Lawful Constitution,"[17] while another observer saw the state being restored after having been undone in 1641 "by fraud and deceit."[18] Whichever legal variant one preferred to use, it seemed clear that a wrong had been remedied in a manner that could best be understood by reference to legal forms. No specific writ was mentioned in a letter from Charles to Monck just prior to the Restoration, but the similarity between what was contemplated and an action in real property was readily apparent. Property which previously had been appropriated by force was now being recovered by right. The king having been "so long disposses'd" was now by operation of law to be rightfully seised of his throne.[19] The Declaration of Breda utilizes some of the same language, treating the Crown as equivalent to an estate in land. Charles expresses there his hope of being "put ... into a quiet and peaceable possession of that our Right."[20]

It is not surprising that so much emphasis should be laid upon legal form. The common-law disposition of mind had long been a part of the political culture and had worked its way deeply into the general fabric of society. This, in itself, was critically important, but there was also something more. Force and constitutional innovation as instruments of political change had been tried and found wanting. As a result, the king would be restored to his throne in a manner consistent with the precepts of law. He would be patient and forbearing rather than endeavoring "to come with a forein force to regain his right."[21] Every step would be measured carefully so that Charles might be rejoined to his people without further rupture to the constitution. It could no longer be attempted in any other way. The only alternative to the path of legal process had been proved a failure. Departure from legal respectability had led to regicide and republican disorder. It would not happen again. Constitutional conservatism was, therefore, to be the keynote of the Restoration and of the remainder of the century as well. Legal process, or at least its appearance "by colour of law," would serve as the constant guide to political action from 1660 on.

The tone set in 1660 did indeed remain the constant theme for the next thirty years, perhaps the most formative generation in England's modern constitutional development. The retreat from disorder rarely admitted of any deviation. For three decades it continued according to a strangely compelling orthodoxy until it arrived at the ultimate paradox — a revolution without impropriety. The

lesson of 1688–89 was that radical political change could be
effected without the appearance of constitutional disrup-
tion. A commitment to legal process and a common-law
disposition of mind had become so well perfected that even
revolution could be set within a framework of apparent
legitimacy.

The Revolution itself could not have been predicted; but
what did seem clear was that, if it were to occur, it would
somehow have to be countenanced by law. There could be
no repetition of the tragic and wanton mistakes of the 1640s.
Those errors were only too well remembered. The specter of
constitutional disorder never, therefore, disappeared, and
from time to time it took on a highly visible form. The year
1667 was one such time. After successfully guiding the
Restoration and rapidly assuming political hegemony as the
king's chief minister, the earl of Clarendon began to emerge
as something of an anachronism. His view was of a comprehensive society along the lines traced out by Elizabeth in the
previous century, but that idea had long since proved
unworkable. It may well have been that the king's father and
grandfather were too rigid or, indeed, simply too incompetent to achieve this goal; but, even if Charles II were better
adapted to the task, the time for comprehensiveness had
passed. The clearly recognizable moral of the civil wars, or
at least so it seemed to Parliament in the first decade of
Restoration, was that any relaxation of the principles of the
Anglican faith, "as by law established," afforded an opening
wedge of disorder that could not easily be closed. There
would be no concessions made to any dissenters from a
Church of England narrowly defined. It was this fear of a
comprehensive church, as well as the stated grounds of
bribery, corruption, and betrayal of the king, that brought
the House of Commons to revive once more the dangerous
precedent of impeachment.

After lying dormant for one hundred fifty years, impeachment had been restored to political vitality by the parliaments
of the 1620s. To foreclose the use of this formidable weapon
and to silence an otherwise insubordinate Parliament,

132   Charles I had opted for eleven years of personal rule,
during which Strafford and Laud, his principal ministers,
remained immune from any effective political assault. But
once reconvened out of necessity, the Long Parliament lost
no time in rising to the attack. Both Strafford and Laud
were impeached, and ultimately both were condemned.

Strafford's case was by far the more important proceeding.
By 1667 it had assumed the stature of allegory, the
revealed truth that conscious undermining of legal processes
leads to political disaster. The impeachment of Strafford
had been abandoned by Parliament once it became clear
that he could not be convicted of the crime with which he
had been charged. He had committed no act of treason.
Still, he would have to be destroyed; and for that purpose
Parliament was willing to pass an act of attainder. If
Strafford were not guilty of treason according to law, he
might yet be guilty according to Parliament. It was, at the
time, a necessary political maneuver, but twenty-six years
later Parliament was unwilling to attempt it again. To do so
would be to assert a parliamentary supremacy for which
England was even less prepared in 1667 than in 1641.
Although Parliament might assume the power to undermine
the rule of law, it could do so only at the price of subverting
constitutional stability. If political disaster had once followed
quickly upon legal abuse, it might do so again. There
was no evading the uncomfortable truth that civil war could
be traced, at least in part, to disregard of the law.

In the rush to be rid of Clarendon, the House of Commons
was prepared to impeach upon general and largely unsupportable
grounds. It was yet another tactic unpleasantly
reminiscent of 1641. Opposition within the House was
quickly mounted by those who recognized the dangerous
parallels to the proceedings against Strafford. Yet they were
not wholly successful. Many of the proposed articles of
impeachment were abandoned, but not all, and no specific
charge of treason was ever developed.

Originally, there were seventeen articles of accusation
against Clarendon. Among the more serious were the

charges that Clarendon had urged a standing army for the governing of the kingdom and that he had "advised the King to dissolve this present Parliament ... [and] to lay aside all thoughts of Parliaments for the future."[22] These were serious charges and were based upon real fears, but there was no available evidence by which they could be proved. Even the familiar employment of common-law paradigms, although obviously attractive, was not enough. John Vaughan admitted that Clarendon, as a minister of state, was privileged "to give Councell for the Kings Safety"; but, he continued, when "it comes to this that he breaks in upon the Laws invading the Contract between the King and his Subjects, It will be as if a man adviseth, That if the King wants money he may set up highway men to take it, and bring it to him."[23] It was a suggestion for which the nation was not yet ready: that there existed an original contract of government which could not, without serious repercussions, be breached by the king or his ministers. As a result, the impeachment had to be substantially trimmed. Ultimately, all but one of the seventeen articles were dropped.

The Commons finally compromised on the vague allegation that Clarendon "hath deluded and betrayed his Majesty and the nation in foreign treaties and negociations relating to the war; and discovered and betrayed his secret counsels to his enemies."[24] The Lords, however, would not go along. They would not have the earl sequestered from Parliament without the assignment of a particular treason.[25] This clearly was impossible. Clarendon, like Strafford before him, was guilty of no treachery which would allow for an action at law.

The positions advanced by those members who favored the impeachment reveal how close at times the Parliament might have come to a repetition of past mistakes; but the fear of what had happened before ultimately proved a sufficient brake upon any inclination to political expedience. The arguments of Sir Robert Howard and others who were strongly committed to the impeachment were eventually to fail of persuasion. It was Howard who believed

134   that the Parliament was not to be constrained by the common law. "Though common law has its proper sphere, 'tis not in this place — we are in a higher sphere. If impeachments of this nature be not allowed, we have no way left of impeaching a great person."[26] The logic was sound, but it had necessarily to proceed from a premise of full parliamentary sovereignty, the acceptance of Parliament's total and effective control of the law. The prospect was obviously attractive, but Parliament, still in the frightening shadow of republicanism, was not yet confidently ready to assert this claim.

Far more popular, even if patently disingenuous, was the implicit suggestion that, although the law was not to be disregarded, neither was it always necessary to pay it scrupulously close attention. Vaughan urged his colleagues to proceed with the business at hand — the impeachment of Clarendon — in the certainty that, if anyone's rights were thereby abridged, the ordinary process of the law would afford the requisite relief. Vaughan asserted that there would be no deleterious consequences of Parliament's proceeding in a somewhat unorthodox manner: any person injured could always seek his proper remedy. And, the argument continued, if there is no remedy afforded, it is a clear indication that there was no wrong done. "Our law has a remedy for all injury. — Where the law gives no remedy, there is no right. — *Damnum sine injuria*. — No injury where the law gives no remedy."[27] The reasoning may have been dishonest, but it had the advantage of pretending that at no time was the law being disregarded. It allowed the Commons to satisfy itself that what it was doing was not irregular and that Clarendon's impeachment conformed to legality, at least in its broad outlines.

As might be expected, the concept of precedent played a particularly important role in the proceedings. What most bothered many Members was that Clarendon was to be impeached upon "common fame," a controversial and dangerous practice which was bound to confirm an undesirable precedent.[28] A committee of the House was appointed to investigate this and to examine precedents for methods of impeachment. The result of their labors was uncertainty. The specter of 1641 was continually raised. Could they deny that a long list of articles of treason, all vague, was no substitute for a specific assignment of treason and that they were bordering perilously upon the cumulative treason which was used to condemn Strafford? And wasn't it true, as Sir Thomas Littleton reported, that in Strafford's case, too, the Commons was accused of proceeding merely upon common fame?[29] To what extent was Strafford's case a precedent, or, to be more precise, to what extent should it be *recognized* as a precedent? There was still, particularly on the level of politics, a good deal of confusion as to the binding effect of past actions. In the conference between the Commons and the Lords that followed upon the Peers' refusal to proceed with the Commons' impeachment, the issue was brought sharply into focus. In response to the Commons' citation of a number of cases that had occurred within the past fifty years, John Dolben, the recently consecrated bishop of Rochester, countered with the assertion that "these were recent, not ancient precedents"; and Strafford's, of course, was both recent and unhappily vivid.[30] The preference for antiquity was still very strong, although English jurisprudence on a nonpolitical level was evolving significantly toward the modern rule of *stare decisis*. This explains the rejoinder to Dolben that the newness of those recent cases "gives them, in some sense, the greater strength, as precedents in the Courts of Westminster."[31] Yet the case for "newness" was not historically ready to prevail even if one were to attempt to buttress it with familiar constitutional labels. In the constitutional mood prevalent throughout the century, the best one could do, said Edmund Waller, would be to suggest that "to ramble too much into antiquity is as dangerous as to innovate."[32] The warning may have been wise, but it was not heeded. The Lords would neither commit Clarendon nor proceed against him upon the Commons' impeachment. Whatever Strafford's case might have offered in support of an impeachment or an attainder,

136   it was not to be used. If it were a precedent, it was one to be
denied. It was eventually agreed that, as Bacon had said,
"the best precedents are in the quietest times";[33] and those
things, as another speaker went on to say, which have been
done in "barbarous times" are to be laid aside.[34] The two
houses seemed to be stalemated when the problem of what to
do with Clarendon was resolved by the earl himself. While
Parliament was debating procedure, Clarendon departed
the realm. This, however, did not end the split between the
Lords and the Commons. The Commons wanted the king to
issue a proclamation for Clarendon's apprehension and
return to trial. The Lords, however, prevailed. Their en-
grossed bill for banishing and disabling Clarendon was
eventually accepted by the Commons.[35]

In Clarendon's case the Lords refused to sacrifice the earl
on the altar of common fame for an end that the Commons
considered politically desirable. The result was that Parliament was able to hold intact its recently reconstructed
self-image of defender of the law. That image was one no
longer taken for granted the way it had been in the earlier
part of the century. Rebellion and regicide had seen to that.
In 1667, Parliament was still on probation. It may have been
a body of men vastly different from those who had served
under Cromwell, but a legislature that had once before
slipped into republican error might do so again. For-
tunately, in Clarendon's case, Parliament righted itself in
time. It opted for law rather than political advantage. And
again, in the struggle over Toleration, it could once more
reassert its familiar and comfortable dual role of royal
opponent and legal champion. In 1673 Parliament rejected
Charles's attempted Declaration of Indulgence on the
ground, as enunciated in the House of Commons, that penal
statutes on ecclesiastical matters could not be suspended
except by act of Parliament.[36] It was unnecessary for the
Commons to record that it did not trust the king's motives,
although that clearly was the case. It needed only to state
that Parliament was "bound in duty" to inform the king that
what he had proposed to do was not countenanced in law.[37]

There were, of course, more serious constitutional issues, not the least of which was the question of legal and political control. If the king were permitted to suspend any law *ex parte,* it would tend, as the Commons quickly noted, to a complete imbalance in sovereign power. It would mean that the king had usurped Parliament's function, a result which would lead, as Henry Powle feared, "to the overthrow of all things."[38] Mixed monarchy would have been supplanted by an absolute king. That was the basic long-term issue which Parliament realized had not yet been resolved. Yet Parliament, for the moment, could be content in the knowledge that it was successfully reestablishing its credentials as guardian of the law.

Two years later, in the 1675 debate over the "non-resisting test," the mood of the Parliament showed signs of shifting, even if only temporarily, from what it had been in the matter of Clarendon's impeachment. The change was evidenced by a bill that Danby had successfully guided through the House of Lords and which, if not for a subsequent diversion and prorogation, might have met with similar success in the Commons.[39] The measure proposed a test of allegiance for all officers of church and state in addition to all those in Parliament. It required a declaration "that it is not lawful upon any pretense whatsoever to take Arms against the King," and it cited particularly "the trayterous position of taking Arms by his Authority against his Person, or against those that are Commissioned by him."[40] The important change was not that the Lords could now be charged with adopting a particularly obsequious posture toward the king. Rather, it was that they were prepared, at least initially, to pass quietly over the importance of the king's "authority," which everyone understood to mean the king's "law." It would mean, if accepted, that the law might not be raised by Parliament as a bar to the king's will. The law, in matters of political conflict, would be totally abandoned to the king. As such, it would be for England a radically new policy of constitutional innovation. If this had been the prevailing sentiment three years earlier,

138   the Declaration of Indulgence would have passed through Parliament without complaint. The bill was therefore subjected to strenuous criticism, from the earl of Shaftesbury most notably in the Peers' own house, and from others outside it.[41] Shaftesbury maintained that the king's commission had necessarily to be limited by the law. In this he was persuaded by a line of argument of many years' standing. In the controversy over Indulgence and the Act of Uniformity twelve years earlier there had been concern that men might be called upon by an act of Parliament to submit to the king's arbitrary will as manifested in his illegal commissions.[42] Shaftesbury carried through with this theme. The king, he argued by way of example, should not be permitted to erect a standing army by his commission, for this would be opposed to the authority of the law. Here the sarcastic irony was easily transparent. The king *had* erected a standing army, and there seemed to be no effective way to bring the law to bear against this. But Shaftesbury was nonetheless troubled by the threatened implementation of a nonresisting test. He examined the possibility of a successful litigant's being put into possession of a house and lands and then being challenged by his disappointed adversary, perhaps a favorite of the sovereign, who, armed with the king's commission, would seek forcibly to effect a disseisin. "I conceive by the Law," said Shaftesbury, "the Man in Possession may justify the defending himself by Arms, and killing those who shall violently indeavour to enter his House, and yet in the Case the party whose House is invaded takes up Arms by the king's authority against those who are Commission'd by him."[43] It was a popular hypothesis used to demonstrate that, when the king's authority and the king's commission were in conflict, it was the latter that should be made to yield. Otherwise no man could hope to be secure in his property.

Yet it was not this narrow hypothesis that most interested those who were proposing the test. Nor were they, in their own estimation, threatening a shift from the law. They were, instead, thoroughly consistent in purpose. For them the constant thread from 1660 on was the avoidance of another lapse into political disorder. Theirs was the continuing fear of perverted legalism again precipitating constitutional crisis. If the "authority" of Charles I had been turned against him, the same thing could be done to his son. Even the regicides could and did claim that their acts were all pursuant to lawful authority.[44] The task, then, as it was perceived by those proposing the nonresisting test, was to foreclose all possibility of the law's being used as a justification for insurrection; and it was this perception which in turn accounted for the "Cavalier" Parliament's having moved so cautiously during the eighteen years of its life.

Caution, however, was not always appropriate to Parliament's task. There was the growing fear that the king's constitutional advantage might well proceed beyond the present Parliament's ability to cope. Reluctance to precipitate a constitutional crisis for fear of creating civil disorder was having the effect of surrendering too much political and legal initiative to the sovereign, and this at a time when the nation was being swept by the fever of the Popish Plot. It was thus that the Parliament in the last years of its life began to act with greater abandon. Of particular concern was the prospect of a Catholic king. James, duke of York, was the Catholic heir presumptive who in the fullness of time was expected to succeed to the throne. In addition, there was another attempt to revive impeachment upon uncertain grounds, this time directed against the earl of Danby, the king's chief minister since 1673. It was the second attempt to impeach Danby; and the proceedings, like those against Clarendon, promised to repeat the events of 1667, the Commons moving toward a judicial condemnation and the Lords refusing to commit. This time, however, a reprieve came in the form of a prorogation at the end of 1678, which was quickly followed by dissolution in January of the next year.

In dissolving Parliament the king was unquestionably acting in pursuit of his own interests, but he was not the only one eager to have this contentious body dismissed. The Long

140   Parliament of the Restoration had, by 1678-79, been in existence for eighteen years, and for some time there had been loud cries for its dissolution. A political nation deeply committed to the value of government by consent was beginning to think that such consent was being undermined by a House of Commons that had sat too long. There was also the suggestion that England's constitutional structure was in peril of total imbalance, the Commons taking on a condition of permanence to equal that of the Lords. The duke of Buckingham in 1677 alerted the Lords to what he believed was a dangerous innovation being introduced into the constitution, an alteration in the structure of government as established by "the Lawes of the Land, & the ancient constitution of Parliaments."[45] It was, he warned, "a dangerous thing to trye new experiments in a Government; Men doe not foresee the ill consequences that must happen when they goe about to alter those essentiall partes of it, uppon which the whole frame of Government depends."[46] The Parliament, therefore, was under attack from three sides—from the king, from those in the Peers' house who perceived a new threat to their constitutional position, and from those who felt that an England without a parliamentary election for almost two decades could no longer claim a constitution based upon the consent of the governed.

By the late 1670s there were men nearing forty who had never yet exercised their parliamentary franchise. As such, they claimed to have been deprived of their birthright, although they had committed no crime to warrant such a forfeiture. They even went so far as to question whether they could be bound to obey those laws of the realm which they had no representative part in making.[47] The issue being raised, if only implicitly, was that of "tacit consent." If government was based upon contract, how could anyone not a party to that contract be bound by its terms and conditions? It was a difficult question to answer, one that had proved particularly troublesome for contract theorists. It might be argued that, by accepting the benefits of a society, consent to the rules of that society was implied. This, of course, is what Locke tried to do, but the legal footing remained essentially weak. Nevertheless, it was clear that philosophical thinking was being very much informed by problems of legal interpretation and by the fact of a political generation that felt itself to be constitutionally deprived.

The end of the Restoration Long Parliament was followed immediately by writs of election for a new legislature, to meet in March 1678-79. The new group, however, proved to be very much like the old. It is true that the criticisms based upon lack of government by consent and upon the verging of a House of Commons toward permanence had now been laid to rest; but the new Parliament was no more receptive to the demands of the king than its predecessor had been in its last years. Most of the old problems remained, and the difficult question of what to do in the face of a Catholic successor began to assume a dimension larger than all others.

In 1678, shortly before the old Parliament was prorogued and subsequently dissolved, a campaign was mounted to force the duke of York from any remaining position of power. By virtue of the Test Act, James had already been deprived of the office of lord high admiral; yet he was still in position to exercise political influence in the counsels of the king. Consequently, on 1 November, Lord Russell "moved that an address be made to his Majestie to withdraw the Duke of York from his Majesties person & Councells."[48] In the search for precedents that followed, the case of the heir apparent during the reign of Henry IV was recalled. "Prince Harry . . . being got into the lewd company of Sir John Falstaff & others, Comitted outrages & Robberies upon the Highway, for which he was comitted to Prison by the Lord chief Justice."[49] The matter there was decidedly distinguishable from the instant case, but it did at least demonstrate that it was possible to withdraw the next in line of succession from the person of the king — and in March of the following year James left for Brussels.

Although the issue of exile was now resolved, the victory for the duke's opponents was necessarily small and temporary. Exile was not exclusion. James could be sent out of the

142   country; but unless some preventive action was taken by the nation, it now seemed certain that he would succeed his brother on the throne. Parliament was faced with an unsettling dilemma: to challenge the right of the legitimate heir presumptive to the throne smacked of the same kind of constitutional irresponsibility that had precipitated the hardships and misfortunes of the forties. Yet to allow for a popish king at a time when the fear of papist intrigue had reached new levels of intensity was to suggest with equal force a recurrence of the same kind of constitutional and civil disorder that everyone feared.

The simple truth was that there were a great many people who doubted seriously whether a Roman Catholic king could ever be trusted to honor and preserve England's liberties and "religion by law established." They questioned whether a papist in control of the law could be prevented from leading England back to Rome. How fragile and mutable was the law likely to become in the hands of a Catholic prince? It was a vital, even if somewhat misleading, question. Monarchical ability to manipulate the law had nothing whatever to do with the sovereign's religious predilections. A Protestant king, Charles I being the most recent notable example, was equally capable of channeling the law to his own advantage. But as the nation was less interested in constitutional theorizing than in the reality of a Catholic succession, it was an appropriate question to ask.[50] There was, after all, a disquieting precedent from the reign of Mary Tudor. It had been shown that law, by itself, could promise no defense against a committed monarch determined to alter the nation's faith. The concerns of the Exclusion parliaments were therefore well placed. They knew that whatever the trust they placed in the common law, it would not be sufficient to deter a Catholic monarch from using it effectively to Anglican disadvantage. "If," it was asserted, "we have no better security for our Religion than paper Lawes I doubt not but a popish successor will rescind them."[51] This, although somewhat dire in its prediction, seemed to be a fair appraisal of what James in the future would be equipped to do. By the last decade of Charles II's reign those instruments of legal control with which monarchy could consolidate its claim to sovereignty were already being very well developed. And where Charles was reluctant to press relentlessly for the dispensing and suspending power of the Crown, James might not be similarly restrained. Anxiety over a constitutionally insecure future was therefore for Parliament a critical concern.

The only shield that Parliament could raise in defense was the argument that its religion, like its liberties, was somehow fundamentally fixed in history and therefore inviolable.[52] To maintain this position, Protestantism and common law would have to become inextricably entwined. To the question, "is our Religion of no older date than the time of Edward 6?," the answer would have to be, " 'Tis as old as Christian Religion, and 'tis that we are now contending for, not a Statute Religion, but a common law Religion, a History of propriety in the Common Law of England."[53] The Reformation would have to disappear quietly or be construed as the sixteenth-century assertion of ancient rights. This, in fact, is what the Exclusion parliaments were imaginatively striving to do. It was not a new argument. The English tradition of imparting the color of regularity to every act of constitutional innovation was already well established. The same approach had been used before, most recently in the 1672-73 debate on Charles's proposed Declaration of Indulgence when Henry Powle, in the House of Commons, characterized the Henrician Reformation as the resumption by the king of his ancient hegemony over the English church. Powle noted happily that Henry's "being declared supreme head of the Church, in the Convocation, by instrument, . . . was nothing but the ancient Common Law restored, which was clearly expressed."[54] It was, to be sure, a tortured contrivance but an absolutely necessary one if political heresy were to succeed, if the religion of England for the first time were to be placed beyond the reach of the king. Despite all its protestations to the contrary, it was the Parliament and not the king that was once again beginning

144   to explore the uncharted limits of constitutional innovation.

The nation's fear of civil disorder was based upon something more than the simple prospect of a Catholic king. Romanism conjured up images beyond those of subjugation to an alien power. It meant, as well, a commitment to legal duplicity. Behind the common allegation that papists held the law in contempt there was the certain conviction that Jesuits had been supremely schooled to manipulate the law as effectively as any common lawyer. Indeed, the charge of "jesuitical equivocation" so often leveled against the Catholics could just as easily have been turned to suggest the quite acceptable, indeed complimentary, common-law art of careful distinguishing among cases apparently, but not actually, alike.[55]

A direct consequence of the equation of Catholicism and legal distortion was the constant fear of a popish plot to "execute" the king. To some who believed in the existence of the plot, it was considered to be so wide as to include as conspirators the queen and the duke of York. Especially frightening was the belief that to papists such a murder would constitute justifiable homicide. And if a mantle of legality could be cast over the contemplated murder of Charles II, the threat of its achievement seemed that much more real. Consistent with this approach was the revelation by the informant, David Morris, that Jesuits deemed it lawful to kill a man who had wronged their order; all the more, he suggested, would it be lawful for a wife to kill her husband if he had "wronged her bed."[56] That Charles had wronged the bed of Catherine of Braganza was open and notorious. No matter that the legal reasoning here was faulty, that the conclusion did not proceed necessarily from the premise. The fact that the king might be killed, and that for the killing a cause sufficient in law might be advanced, was enough to quicken the fear of regicide already alive in the nation's political consciousness.

Yet the fears were not to be found on one side alone. Those who opposed Exclusion shared equally in the general concern for the quiet of the nation. It was, they argued, precisely because of this concern, because they feared a repetition of civil disorder, that they would see nothing done to alter the succession. If Parliament were successful in barring the heir to the throne, it would be only one step further to depose a reigning king. "For they are sure, that by whatsoever Law, Power, or pretence, the Parliament can disinherit or depose the Heir, by the same they may likewise depose the Possessor of the Crown; as the Rump Parliament, de facto, has done."[57] Englishmen were to be alerted to the perils attendant upon any such constitutional innovation. The parallels to 1649 were demonstrably clear. Moreover, any attempt to deprive James of his "birthright" could only serve to undermine the general rule of law. If the heir to the throne of England could not rest assured in the predictable expectation of his inheritance, what possible "security of property or liberty" could any lesser subject ever enjoy?[58] It was the same argument that had been made in 1660 "for the restauration of the lawful heir to his right."[59] On both occasions the concern for the rule of law was that, if justice were denied to the sovereign, there was little chance that it might flourish among his subjects. Political anxieties were therefore to be found everywhere. Both Exclusion and non-Exclusion raised the awesome specter of the 1640s. Whatever the outcome of this new crisis proved to be, no one wanted a repetition of civil war. As a result, the most important restraining influence of the Exclusion years was at work from the start. Both sides were quite determined to avoid the precipitous mistakes of the past.[60]

Through the three Exclusion parliaments the effect of private-law patterns of thought was keenly felt. It was not that the private law itself was always made to apply. Rather, it was that the private law was used continually as the referential standard against which all constitutional departures had carefully to be measured. Most particularly, on the issue of the succession to the Crown, those who argued that the succession could not be changed were obliged to demonstrate that the rules were different from those which regulated private inheritance. The controverted rules of

146   monarchical succession thus became the deviations to be distinguished from the norms of the private law. It was, after all, the latter which were fixed and known, whereas the former were still in dispute.

Of singular importance was an equation of the Crown with an estate in land; and the most pressing constitutional issue of the period therefore seemed to be a determination of how, precisely, the Crown was held. For some ten years, beginning in 1679, the issue was hotly fought; but even when the question receded after the Revolution, a definitive answer was yet to be found. Was the Crown held in fee simple and therefore freely alienable? Or was it a determinable fee, an entail, or a life estate? Or might the king be deprived entirely of any beneficial estate, to be treated only as trustee of the Crown, with equitable title being reserved to the "people"? All these possibilities of tenure were considered at the time of Exclusion in order to establish whether James might be removed from the succession; and in varying degrees of persuasiveness, an argument could be made for each.

The most difficult position to support constitutionally was a Crown held in fee, for it implied that the king would be free to dispose of the succession in any way he might desire. Such an extreme position was at odds with the accepted view of a hereditary succession — a succession which many preferred to believe was indefeasible. It was understood, after all, on the authority of Coke "that the Dignity Royal is an Inherent inseparable to the Blood Royal of the King, and cannot be transferred to another"; and just as "None but God can make an Heir to a Crown [citing Coke on Littleton], surely None but the same Superintendent Power ... ought or can Dispossess or disinherit Princes."[61]

This seemed to suggest that monarchical succession could not be determined by the positive law, that, in the words of one publicist, "of necessity must Regal-Right and Inheritance be from the Law of Nature."[62] It was an obviously contentious position; and, not surprisingly, it was disavowed both by those who denied that there was any area of political concern beyond the reach of an act of Parliament and by those who recognized the existence of fundamental law but argued that it did not apply to the succession. It was, for example, urged by the author of "A Word without Doors Concerning the Bill for Exclusion" that government "did proceed of Nature" but might nonetheless "be altered or amended in any of its parts, by the mutual consent of the Governours and governed."[63]

Considerably more important than any theoretical support for tampering with the hereditary line were the formidable precedents drawn from the law and the history of the Crown. This was the position, based upon the sovereignty of king in Parliament, that most who favored Exclusion were prepared to defend. The deprivation of the duke of York was to be a venture in which Charles and his Parliament were to act conjointly. Henry VIII had been given statutory power to dispose of the Crown by his last will and testament. What the king might not do alone, king and Parliament might do together. And, once done, as was noted by Secretary of State Henry Coventry in 1679, the Tudor "might have given the Crown to his footman if he pleased, and made him King and by Law too."[64]

It was just this sort of appraisal that proved troublesome and confusing. Henry VIII's attitude toward the throne had shown itself at times to be near to arbitrary. He had spent years of his regnal life manipulating the succession in response to marital changes and political necessity, yet he had never acted on the authority of the prerogative alone. However compliant his parliaments may have been, it was always on the authority of Parliament that any alterations were made. Nevertheless, the appearance of a king who acted as if he were absolute was still a notorious image, one that the Exclusionists were anxious to avoid. They were at all times insistent that Exclusion would be neither an arbitrary nor an unconstitutional act. "We are," they maintained, "no ways concern'd in the Justification of our Bill to approve of the humorous Caprice of Henry the Eighth, and the arbitrary Laws that he made in his time about the Succession."[65]

148   No matter that Henry VIII was scrupulously attentive to the law. He still appeared to be capricious, whereas Exclusion, as proposed in the reign of Charles II, was to be a regular, legal, and constitutional procedure. It was to be consistent with the theory, not yet completely accepted, that what the king did in Parliament was supreme. This alone is how Parliament would be able to justify Exclusion upon constitutional grounds. No amount of political necessity would itself suffice. There would have to be the widespread conviction that "the Parliament of England had an unquestionable power to Limit, Restrain and Qualify the Succession as they pleased."[66]

For the scheme to succeed, then, there would have to be an acceptance, even if not the complete understanding, of king in Parliament as the sovereign power in England. It would mean that cherished notions of an indefeasible right of hereditary succession as part of a fundamental law would have to be abandoned. This was something that the nation as a whole was yet unprepared to do. Even the uncomfortable precedent of Henry VIII was of little assistance, because his will had had no effect whatever upon hereditary expectation. After his death, Henry was succeeded first by his only son and then, in turn, by his two daughters in order of birth. And when, in 1603, Elizabeth died, the crown descended to James, next in the hereditary succession, and not, as King Henry had intended, to the heirs of his younger sister Mary. It was even argued during the Exclusion years that such a descent of the Crown was exactly what Parliament had intended when it authorized Henry to dispose of the Crown by will and that it was never contemplated that the Crown would leave the hereditary line, except for the failure of heirs. As one anti-Exclusionist tract maintained, "it was never designed by him [Henry VIII] or any other, that a Lawful Heir should be excluded from succeeding."[67]

Most who were attracted to the political advantages of fundamental law were not content to ground their arguments in natural or divine abstractions alone, especially as the culture of the private law was so rich in relevant analogues. Some polemicists clung to the belief that the king had, at best, a life estate in the Crown and was forbidden by unalterable law to prejudice the expectations of those to whom the remainder of the estate had been left. It was agreed that the king could give away any number of things by devise[68] at his death so long as he did not compromise those things which were allegedly inalienable. He should not be permitted to dispose of "the Antient Crown and Jewels; much less can a King dispose of the Sovereignty itself."[69] It was, as Scottish legislation sought to confirm in 1681, the succession "according to the known degrees of Proximity in Blood, which cannot be interrupted, suspended, or diverted by any Act or Statute whatsoever."[70] This was firmly fixed in the common law and could in no way be changed.

The position in favor of the life estate was appealing. It was consistent with a legal incapacity to alter the succession and would therefore accommodate all those who desired a monarchy geared to known rules of inheritance; but on other grounds it was not totally satisfactory. The life tenant, it could be argued, still had the right to use the estate in any way he pleased so long as he handed it over to the remainderman intact. Life tenancy, therefore, would not be a sufficient brake upon a king with designs on arbitrary power. So long as the heir apparent — or heir presumptive, if there were no surviving son — could be assured of the Crown upon the death of the monarch, there might be no further restriction upon what the sovereign might do. This is why it would be better to contend in favor of a king without any beneficial estate in the Crown, a king who occupied an office in trust. To hold with this alternative position, that "Kings cannot alienate the Crown which doth not lie in Dominion, but in Trust, not in Property, but in care," was to have the advantage of insuring that any reigning king might always be called to account.[71]

Another possibility which found its genesis in the private law was that which was referred to as a "mortgage of the Crown." In its political application this would have had the same effect as a Crown held in trust. The idea was basically

150   one of compromise: there would be no interference with the hereditary succession, but the nation would have legal recourse against a Catholic king who attempted to subvert its rights. The Exclusionists were therefore urged to "grow a little kinder and treat for a Mortgage of the Crown, allowing equity of Redemption," on the theory that the king would be more sympathetic to their concerns if only they did not appear to be requesting a complete and irrevocable surrender of the hereditary principle.[72] There was even the lord chancellor's observation in 1679 that Charles might well be open to any reasonable suggestions from Parliament. The king, he said in his speech to both houses on 30 April, was willing to explore the possibility of constitutional safeguards in the event of a popish succession but would not do anything "to alter the Descent of the Crown in the Right Line, nor to defeat the Succession."[73] Yet the Exclusionists were not prepared to accept anything less than the removal of James from his future right to the throne.

Whether James actually had a future right was another matter. In law his was only a future interest, which would not and could not vest until his brother Charles died without issue. It was an important distinction to be drawn, because it helped to explain whether or not the oath of allegiance to the king, "his heirs, and successors," was to be construed as extending to the next in line to the throne. By one construction, based upon what was argued to be the "plain and common sense of the words," it did.[74] As a result, not only was Exclusion an illegal course of action; the mere attempt at it by way of a Parliament bill was a violation of the subject's oath.[75] But the plain and common sense of the words could be read another way as well. It was just as easily argued by Sir William Jones that any allegiance sworn to the king's probable successor while the king still lived was an act of treason,[76] so the oath must, of legal necessity, mean something else. It was, in fact, the better construction to interpret the words as an assurance of the continuity of allegiance to the Crown without any interruption at the death of the king: "That in Case of the Demise of the King, and the Devolving and Vesting of the Crown upon the Heir and Successor, the Oath that we took to the Predecessor, by virtue of those Words lays hold upon our Consciences, and obligeth us to him from the first minute of his Reign, but not before."[77] The result was that Exclusion might freely be considered without breach of allegiance at any time prior to the title vesting in the heir. Moreover, the matter was to be treated in its legal as well as its commonsense context, and in that perspective it was certain that no man had heirs or successors while he was still alive.[78] Here the private law was quite clear. To contend, therefore, for any present right in James was the equivalent of maintaining "that a Son hath a Right to his Fathers Estate before he is Dead: for the probable Successor can have no more Right to the effect of the Oath of Allegiance, than the Eldest Son to receive the Profits of his Fathers estate without his leave in his Fathers Life time."[79]

Short of a bill of Exclusion, there did not seem to be any legally effective way of keeping James from the throne. Even if he could be convicted on a charge of treason, this alone would not be sufficient to bar his accession. Here was one political area in which private-law paradigms could not be made to work. There was a clear distinction between the effect of a corruption of the blood upon an ordinary heir and upon one who would succeed to the throne; the effect upon the royal line would, according to good and accepted precedent, be absolutely nil. Many were to point out in Parliament, as did Mr. Foley on 11 May 1679, that "the case of Henry 7 is that he was attainted and by Act of Parliament but the Descent of the Crown upon Him did purge away that attainder, and that is good law."[80] For that reason, it was no matter if James could be impeached and convicted; so long as he survived his brother, the stain of treason, as Coke on Littleton made clear, would have no bearing on his capacity to ascend the throne.[81]

Whether any other infirmity might incapacitate the heir from assuming his inheritance was a more difficult question to answer. In this regard some members were persuaded to

152   look to the private law for cases of legal incapacity in the
hope that certain effective parallels might be drawn. It was
therefore suggested that, just as the law would prevent an
infant or a lunatic from assuming the immediate responsibility of his inheritance, whether it be Blackacre or the
Crown, so might it be with some other extraordinary
infirmity with which James might happen to be afflicted.[82] It
might be stretching the analogy much too far if James's
incapacity were found to be his Catholicism; yet in another
decade the nation would prove itself to be substantially more
receptive to just such an idea.

It was therefore clear that private-law rules might not
always be applied to constitutional issues. There were
definite distinctions between the two which for the most part
could be used effectively as an argument against Exclusion.
Where the opposite was true—where the difference tended
to support a more radical position—was at that point where
a particularly comprehensive explanation of the notable
differences could be offered:

> That there is one Rule for the Succession of the Crown,
> and another for the Succession of private Estates, is from
> these Reasons, that private Inheritances are disposed of
> in Succession, according to the presumed will of the
> Decedens, ... But the Discent and Succession of the
> Crown is governed and directed by the presumed will of
> the People; And that presumption of the Peoples Will
> is made by measuring and considering what is most
> expedient to the publick good, or by the express limitation
> of the People in their conferring the Royal Dignity.[83]

The radical implications of the argument were obvious. If
the rules of royal succession did not conform strictly to the
private law, it was only because the king was in a position
with unique responsibilities to his people. Here again was
the idea of a public trust, an idea that was growing in
currency and that would continue to do so into the Revolution. And if the monarch could be cast in this role of servant
of the common good, the question of the king's estate in the

Crown might no longer be apposite. Instead, as one polemicist maintained, the emphasis should be upon the collective "people" who had a property in the king. "Thus a King is not for's own but's Subjects sake only; and we have in truth rather title, &c. to Him than He to us."[84]

Nor did the attraction of rules of inheritance and real property end there. The concern for public order suggested further analogues. As long as the greatest fears were of a king who might abuse his inheritance, acceptable ways to bar him from that inheritance would continue to be sought. It was constantly tempting to remember that, in law, "if a man be like to ruine the Estate He may be Heir to wee disinherit every day."[85] This had long been the way to be rid of a profligate son. It was "well known in a private case, the Heir is usually thrown off and disinherited: if an entail, it may be destroyed: and if Law justifies it, the like in the Publick."[86] Particularly in the domain of public affairs should this be true, since the estate in question was the entire realm of England, carrying with it the vast responsibilities of rule. Even if private law could not be made to square precisely with normal patterns of monarchical succession, it seemed to many that some legal device would have to be found to avert the prospect of a potentially destructive king. Somehow there would have to be a way whereby it would not appear "an Act of Folly or Dishonesty to dispose of the Estate for the well-fare of . . . Posterity."[87]

The whole notion, then, of viewing the Crown in the terms of property could be molded by any political faction to meet its particular needs. The private law was of sufficient richness and malleability to be directed to almost any purpose. It was even suggested that, should the Exclusion bill become law, it would have the effect of "making the King himself for all ensuing ages to be Tenant at will to every prevailing Faction in Parliament."[88] The possibilities of application were almost without limit. Whether one opted for or against Exclusion or somewhere in between, there was always at hand a private-law principle to serve as guide.

The question of Exclusion was raised by three successive

154 parliaments, from 1679 to 1681. With each new Parliament, the opportunities for success seemed to grow; but the king, with the powers of prorogation and dissolution still at his exclusive command, could not be made to yield. It was a hollow victory for the House of Commons to produce an Exclusion bill in March 1681, as Charles quickly followed suit by informing Lords and Commons that they were dissolved. It was the last Parliament that Charles was to meet. Why the king refused to contemplate the advantages of Exclusion remains something of a puzzle. It was well known that he had little taste for his brother and a great store of affection for his natural son, Monmouth, the suggested Protestant alternative to the Catholic James. Shaftesbury, perhaps the most zealous champion of Monmouth's interest, observed in 1679 that the king hated his brother "perfectly and he [the duke of York] knows it."[89] Yet, despite the attempts to establish that Charles had in fact married Lucy Walter and that Monmouth was therefore the heir apparent,[90] Charles knew that such was not the case. A commitment to legitimacy, then, may well be one key to Charles's commitment to James. Another was the fear that passage of an Act of Exclusion would have led eventually, if not immediately, to civil war. James, it was thought, would not have accepted a parliamentary verdict and would instead have put his rightful claim to the sword.[91] Nor was Charles in any way eager to accept the implications inherent in Exclusion. He was not ready to admit Parliament to a position of constitutional equality, nor would he willingly allow it to gain any advantage which might threaten him in the same way as his father was threatened and eventually undone.

6

The Triumph of the Legal Mind

IN FEBRUARY 1685, UPON THE DEATH OF HIS BROTHER Charles, the duke of York succeeded to the English throne as James II. He was then fifty-two years of age, a confirmed Catholic, and the father of two Protestant daughters. No protest or resistance marred the accession, and the fact that James II was so well received could only be interpreted as a testimonial to the political acumen of Charles II in the last years of his reign. Had the late king expired after his illness of 1679, civil war might again have become imminent; but by 1685 the Crown could descend easily and without event.

Charles, by 1683, had done an extraordinarily effective job of recapturing the political initiative that had been surrendered temporarily to the Exclusionists. The Rye House Plot turned the tide completely against the militant Protestants, who had already lost substantial ground. The affair, still shrouded in uncertainty and reeking of some of the same noisome quality that characterized Oates's allegations, resulted in the discrediting of a number of the more prominent Whigs. The earl of Essex was moved to suicide in the Tower, while William, Lord Russell and Algernon Sydney perished on the scaffold. By this time Shaftesbury, already a broken man, had been driven into exile, where, early in 1683, he died. The purging of its leaders seemed for a time to have signaled the total collapse of the Whig cause. The attempt to wrest control of the law from the king, to change the accepted pattern of royal inheritance, had failed. Charles had asserted the still superior position of the Crown and, to cap his success, conveniently neglected to summon another Parliament, which, pursuant to the new

Triennial Act,[1] he was required to do no later than April 1684.

Charles had thus passed on the inheritance of the throne to his brother, and it would now be left to James to preserve that patrimony. From the start, despite an auspicious accession, the king's detractors were at work. Earlier rumors to the effect that James had been responsible for the Great Fire and the murder of Godfrey were now revived; added to them was the new allegation that Charles II's death was due to poisoning at his brother's command. Much more important, as a renewal of past complaints and an adumbration of things soon to come, was the charge that James was not England's lawful king because he had not been so proclaimed "by the Consent of the nation Esembled in parliament."[2] This might have been an oblique reference to the passage of more than three years without a Parliament having been convened, but it spoke with particular reference to the issue of government by consent. It was a corollary of the premise that king and Parliament, acting together, were beyond the reach of any constitutional limitation and of the further and much more radical assumption that no man could wear the Crown without Parliament's express approval. The hereditary succession, standing alone, would not be enough.

In 1685 this was still an extreme view. Much more acceptable was a conservative Tory position which viewed the succession to the throne as part of God's Providence, divine guidance which could be expressed in the familiar and happily compatible language of property. The Crown, according to Francis Turner, bishop of Ely, was firmly fixed in the right line of succession. This was not because of any passing of "title by God's immediate Designation." Rather, it was what Englishmen had come to expect from "ordinary Providence." Revelation, however, seemed more and more to be the unfolding of Truth from the ancient constitution. "Thè best Title to any inheritance of Ours," the bishop proclaimed in a sermon preached at James's coronation,

is from our Ancestors, and the best of that kind is from
Times beyond Memory. But who can pretend such a
Successive Title to his Estate, as his Majesty can show to
his Crown? How many Ages of our Ancestors have wanted
such a Title as this? How are some other Nations like to be
embroil'd with their Neighbours about their Succession to
the Crown, for want of this Blessing of a Clear Title?[3]

It was God, therefore, working through the positive law,
who assured James's succession, and it would have to be God
alone, presumably working in the same way, who could
divest the king of that inheritance if and when He so desired.
On that point the bishop was quite plain. If any king, no
matter how clear his title, were to evoke the wrath of God,
he could easily be deposed. "God is not obliged to stand by
the best Title: he may seize or dispose of the Goodliest
Inheritance as he pleases."[4]

James was aware of the residuum of mistrust that followed
him to the throne. Charles II, however successfully he
prepared the way, could provide only for his brother's
accession. He could not guarantee a peaceful reign, nor
could he remove the stigma of James's Catholicism and all
the fears that popery might arouse. The constitution was
only as strong as the commitment of the king to preserve it;
and if a Catholic king could not be trusted to honor that
commitment, the realm would come to a particularly critical pass. James sought to quiet these fears immediately. Very
soon after his brother's death he appeared at the Council
table, where he promised faithfully "to preserve Government
both in Church & State as it was by law established."[5] The
same promise was later made to Parliament.[6] The king
claimed to have no absolutist design. His trust in his ability
to govern within the laws of England was firm, for they were
laws which, he said, "were sufficient to make the King as
great a Monarch as he could wish." At the same time he
made it clear that he would "never depart from the Just
Rights & Prerogatives of the Crown."[7] The law provided him

158   with all that he would need, and he would use it to the fullest advantage.

The nation was not quite convinced. Suspicion had survived James's accession, and the attempt would now be made by the duke of Monmouth to convert that suspicion to his own use. Monmouth, with 150 men, left Holland in late May 1685. Landing at Lyme Regis, he met with some initial success, but in less than a month his force, swollen to about 4,500, was destroyed at Sedgemoor. Monmouth was captured, and this first, badly organized, attempt to depose James was at an end. Yet it is probable that, had Monmouth succeeded, he would not have claimed his throne by right of God's verdict. Such a basis of kingship had last been considered in 1485, when Henry Tudor defeated Richard III at Bosworth Field; even then, in the absence of any clear law of succession, all that was certain was that Henry was king because he had so described himself and because he had been able to make that description good.[8] Now, after two hundred years and the recent cataclysm of the Civil War, monarchy by conquest was no longer to be contemplated. Monmouth maintained, instead, that his mother, Lucy Walter, had in fact been married to Charles II and that James Stuart was therefore a usurper. Monmouth's bid for the Crown would be grounded in what was considered to be his heritable right. In the Taunton Declaration (20 June 1685) he was proclaimed king by his supporters upon no other ground than his right of descent.[9]

The failure of Monmouth's rebellion marked the height of English commitment to their Catholic king. James would not again be able to command the same allegiance. The rebellion was followed by Jeffrey's "bloody assizes" and, in the next session of Parliament, by James's pronouncement that, the Test Act notwithstanding, he intended to retain Catholic officers in a standing army. The Parliament objected and attempted to wean the king from his demands with a generous grant of £700,000. It was to no avail. James held his ground. Toward the end of November 1685 he prorogued

Parliament and eventually, in July 1687, dissolved it. He did not convene another for the remainder of his reign.

The king's popularity was now declining rapidly. Within another three years he would alienate the loyalty of the English nation, despite repeated assurances that he would preserve its rights and liberties. Borough charters were recalled, a peacetime army was maintained, and Catholics were to be found everywhere in positions of civil and military trust. There was even uncertainty of the degree to which one could be legally critical of the king's disregard of the Test. It was, for example, noted that loyal Protestants were in the uncomfortable position of courting treason should they speak out against popery. Catholicism was, after all, the king's religion, and anything said against that religion might at the same time be construed as an attack upon the king himself.[10]

But all this did not yet amount to a defense of resistance. Despite the fact that ancient liberties and the religion established by law were everywhere being subverted, the law was still very much on the side of the king and still very much within his control. If Parliament would not remove the legal incapacities of Catholics, James might still have his way by employing the powers of dispensation, suspension, and *quo warranto*. Those powers, of course, were considerable, but there was always the danger of exceeding the nation's political tolerance through their injudicious and unregulated use. James, then, might run the risk of straying into fatal political error even though, constitutionally, he would still be secure. How far the king could go in converting the law to his own use was a sensitive political question not easily susceptible of a precise response. The answer would necessarily depend upon the extent of the fear of a new civil war. There appeared to be no legal way to check the king in the far-ranging use of his constitutional powers save to label those powers as somehow in violation of the constitution. Yet to do that would join issue in a way frighteningly reminiscent of 1642. James, therefore, was politically safe only so long as

160

the fear of another civil war continued to outweigh the growing concern for England's being wrenched back toward Catholicism. Gilbert Burnet, later to be an apologist for the Revolution, wrote in 1687, on the occasion of James's first Declaration of Indulgence, that "the publick peace must always be more valued than any private oppressions or injustices whatsoever," and this despite the fact that a violation of "the trust that is given to the prince ... will putt men upon uneasy & dangerous inquiries."[11] This was the dilemma of the late 1680s, one that showed little hope of ever being resolved. It was, without acknowledgement, the high point in England of a Hobbesian view of the world.

Hope, however, was not abandoned. The king was old and, in the anticipated course of events, would be succeeded by his elder daughter, the Protestant Mary, wife of William of Orange. William himself was directly descended from Charles I and was therefore in his own right a part of the Stuart line. Moreover, he was the leading Protestant prince in Europe and had carefully maintained good relations with the English Crown. It was therefore unavoidable that, from 1685 on, he would be thought of as closely involved in the English succession and would be looked to as a possible, even likely, answer to the Catholic James. Should Mary succeed her father, she would share her throne with William, a prospect not altogether displeasing to those who prayed for a reversal of England's increasing inclination toward Rome. There might well be limitations placed upon William's rights as consort of an English queen, but they would not be prompted by the same fears of Catholic domination that over one hundred years earlier had characterized the response to Philip of Spain. William, in fact, had played his hand well. He had quickly dissociated himself from Monmouth and turned the duke out of Holland once it seemed that the United Provinces might be used as a base for an assault upon England. And after Monmouth landed in Devon, it was William who promptly dispatched three regiments in aid of his father-in-law's throne.

The hopes for a Protestant succession evaporated on 10

June 1688, when Mary of Modena, the king's second and Catholic wife, gave birth to a son; from that moment forward the course of events began to shift rapidly. The Protestant heiress presumptive was replaced by a Catholic heir apparent, and what had hopefully seemed a temporary popish aberration had now to be regarded as an irreversible commitment to a return to Rome. A rumor was quickly spread that the queen had not, in fact, been delivered of a son, that her putative pregnancy had terminated prematurely in a stillborn child, and that, to satisfy James and deceive the realm, an infant concealed in a warming pan had been smuggled into her chamber. No creditable evidence in support of the allegation was, however, available; and, notwithstanding the absence of a Protestant witness to the birth, the reality of James Francis Edward and a Catholic dynasty could not be avoided. There were still the formulaic addresses to the king, thanking him for securing "our natural Birth-right Liberty and Property both in Spirituals and Temporals,"[12] but these did not obscure the crippling blow to an Anglican succession. England's spiritual inheritance, as it was conceived by a Protestant majority, was now in danger of complete denial.

Twenty days later, Archbishop Sancroft and his six episcopal codefendants were acquitted of the charge of seditious libel in the Court of King's Bench. They had refused to read the king's second Declaration of Indulgence in their respective cathedrals and had petitioned against the king's use of the dispensing and suspending powers for the granting of toleration to Catholics. They believed that to read the Declaration, as directed, in every cathedral and parish church, would be an expression of at least tacit consent to the principle of indulgence, and this they would not countenance. Advanced as a counter to their reservations was the assertion that, in reading the Declaration, there was only a recognition of the king's authority and not an implied approval of the Declaration's content. It was a matter simply of the "King's Jurisdiction and the Duty of our Subjection."[13] By such a construction, proceeding in this argument

162   from the prescripts of the civil law, king and people were deemed to be in a master-servant relationship. The people were obliged to obey every command of their sovereign and for that reason might always claim that what they did was not necessarily indicative of what they believed. A "servant does not offend by obeying his Master's commands."[14] It was a question of what was and what was not to be construed as an act of consent. Yet the analogy, however valid, was not convincing to those who could easily associate civil law with popery and absolutism. The jury rejected all the arguments of the prosecution and returned a verdict in favor of the defendants. The seven bishops had received impressive support throughout the country; now they stood judicially vindicated.

The forces of opposition to "Jacobite despotism" were rapidly gaining momentum, and, on the same day as the acquittal of the bishops, an invitation signed by seven important men of the realm was dispatched to Prince William, urgently requesting him to save the English nation. Much of this, on both sides of the water, had been carefully laid out in advance. If the politics of the eighties were being guided in England by the memory of civil war, William's lesson from English history was somewhat more recent. His was the vision of Monmouth faltering in the west country. William would not risk the same failure of support that had brought Monmouth to ruin three years earlier at Sedge-moor. Unlike Monmouth, the Prince of Orange was a head of state and not a desperate adventurer. He would bide his time until he could be assured of a substantial force with which to invade and the hard promise of support from men of quality in England. He would wait until conditions under James warranted a move. The invitation of 30 June suggested the support that he demanded and conditions that were right.[15] Still, William could not be entirely sure how he would be received. There were others in England, men at least equal in importance to those who were signatories of the June invitation, who would not commit themselves to what clearly was an act of treason. On 27 July 1688 the earl of Nottingham wrote to William explaining why he had not joined in the invitation. Conditions, he admitted, were serious, but they were not so grave as to warrant precipitous action. "I cannot apprehend from them such ill consequences to our Religion or the just interests of Your Highness that a little time will not effectively remedy, nor," he went on, "can I imagine that the Papists are able to make any further considerable progresse."[16] Nottingham may well have been right, but William, by the end of the summer, was preparing to act.

James responded to the fear of invasion in several ways. He dissolved the Ecclesiastical Commission, and he restored the charter of the City of London; but he would not relinquish any more of his prerogative. He specifically refused to yield on the dispensing power and decided to recall the writs for a new Parliament which had been ordered at the end of August. None of this had any effect in forestalling William's move. On 10 October William closed out all speculation by announcing from The Hague that he was preparing a descent upon England. In his declaration he set forth a long and detailed indictment of the reign of James, a reign replete with evils which could be remedied only by the summoning of a free and lawful Parliament. Such an ideal could not, however, be realized so long as the "evil counsellors" of the king were in a position to control the elections by fraud and force. William therefore declared that

> since our dearest and most entirely beloved Consort the Princess, and likewise ourselves, have so great an interest in this matter, and such a right, as all the world knows to the Succession to the Crown; . . . [and since we have been] solicited by a great many lords, both spiritual and temporal, and by many gentlemen, and other subjects of all ranks . . . , we have thought fit to go over to England and to carry with us a force sufficient, by the blessing of God, to defend us from the violence of those evil Counsellors.[17]

164 William was now committed; and even before setting sail
for England, he would have to be considered a much more
formidable threat than Monmouth ever was. The prince was
not merely one more challenger in the long history of
pretenders to the English throne. He was, instead, like
William I some six hundred years earlier, a foreign prince, a
powerful and prestigious commander at the head of an
invading army.

No one doubted that William had an "interest" in the
English succession. Yet it was plain that the interest concerned was so far removed as to deny him any immediate
rights under English law. The prince, in 1688, did not have
the standing necessary to inquire into any English affairs, let
alone to raise questions about a future heir's right to the
throne. His interest in the Crown placed him behind the
infant Prince of Wales, the Princess Mary, and the Princess
Anne. Even if the legitimacy of the birth of James Edward
could successfully be disproved, a matter of some serious
doubt, William's present rights would not be advanced. His
proximity to the heiress presumptive would place him in a
position of considerable political influence, but legally that
would be all. This was the thrust of the objections raised to
William's declaration. He was, observed one publicist,
"neither heir apparent, nor presumptive; and if he were,
our laws know no such doctrine. Is this the way to preserve
the rights of the crown, to refer those of the present possessor
over his head?"[18] It seemed to be a crucial and inescapable
point: James II was still very much alive and very much the
king. And even if it were to be supposed that William was
next in line to the throne (an assertion that no one made), he
would still be without the necessary standing to assert the
authority that his declaration presumed. "The most immediate Right to Succeed," observed the anonymous author
of "Animadversions upon the Declaration of His Highness
the Prince of Orange,"

is no right to intermeddle before the Succession falls. I am
Successor to my Father, but cannot therefore dispose of

his Estate, chuse his Tenants for him, and appoint what
Covenants he shall make in his Leases, any more than a
stranger to his Bloud.[19]

These were the careful legal exceptions, based in large part
on the private law as well as the developing rules of
monarchical succession, that William would encounter and
would have in some way to overcome. Increasingly, it
seemed that the way would have to be by law. William might
mount a successful invasion, but if it were to appear to be
something other than what it was, the protective color of law
and legal right would have to be employed. Despite all
pretenses to the contrary, the situation in the autumn of
1688 was, at the very least, one of a foreign prince pre-
suming to supervise and insure the summoning of an English
Parliament. William, whatever his claim, did not have the
standing asserted in his declaration to refer to such a
Parliament an "inquiry into the Birth of the Pretended
Prince of Wales"[20] and all matters relating to the right of
succession.

   Time and again the question of William's standing would
be raised. It would be raised after the prince's successful
landing on English shores, after James's flight to France, and
after the de facto assumption by William of some of the
more vital prerogatives of the Crown. It was a question that
would not be quieted even by the completion of the Convention's work and the commencement, in law, of William
and Mary's reign. And always it would be the exacting mind
of the law that would be brought to bear upon the larger
questions of the constitution. Those who would continue to
raise well-settled and discomfiting principles from the private law could point in this instance to a familiar rule of
property: "For tho an Heir in Remainder at Common Law
may have a Verdict against his Father upon account of
Wastes; yet I never heard of a Total Ejectment in that Case.
Besides, it is well known that none but the next Heir can
bring that Action."[21] Not only, then, might it be argued that
the prince had no standing to "commence this suit"; even if

he did, it was in error to allow him the judgment, as the remedy sought and obtained was not properly contemplated in law.

The need to speak in the familiar language of political conservatism was readily understood by William, even if this necessary adherence to proper form was not in itself any guarantee of success. Like Monmouth before him, William asserted that he was coming to England to preserve, not to conquer. In Monmouth's case it was for "defence & vindication of the Protestant religion, & the Laws, rights, & Priviledges of England from the Invasion made upon them."[22] William's declaration was much the same. His "expedition" was being prompted by a desire "to preserve and maintain the established Laws, Liberties and Customs, and, above all, the Religion and Worship of God" as it was established by law.[23] Both, then, would have it that they were coming to the aid and defense of England. Monmouth, of course, also claimed that he was the rightful king, an allegation of standing which, in a curious way, made him infinitely more respectable. In this regard William was deficient, and he attempted to repair that deficiency by speaking boldly, even if falsely, of his "right, as all the world knows, to the Succession to the Crown."[24] Proper form had to be observed if William were to project the necessary image. He had no desire to be compared with Monmouth, but, like Monmouth, he knew that it was necessary to speak of "preservation." Both, then, were conservative insofar as their assaults, one abortive and one successful, were instituted, not to effect change, but to prevent it.

The competing themes of preservation and conquest were no less appreciated by the loyal adherents of the king. One such supporter noted cynically that, if William were successful, he would be nothing more than a conqueror. All that would then remain for him to preserve would be his own defective title, and that he would have to do by force.[25] William denied this, and in his Additional Declaration expressly rejected any "wicked attempt of Conquest."[26] On the assumption that a conquest would by definition be complete, over the people as well as over the existing king, he argued that it would not be reasonable to suppose that those who had invited him to England would have done so had the invitation suggested the voiding of "their own lawful Titles to their Honours, Estates and Interests."[27] Nevertheless, James's position in point of law, if not of fact, appeared by the end of October still to be secure. How valuable this was and how long it would continue to be so were another matter. James was by then politically unpalatable; but with the great weight of the law still on his side and under his nominal control, there seemed little that could legally be done to loosen his hold. No matter how desirable it might be to be rid of him, he remained the rightful king. William might well be the only practical solution; but how much William could do for the English would be an unanswerable question as long as enough people either believed or feared what might as well have been a maxim, that "He that hath the best right can make us the best title to what we have or want."[28]

Although William was without the standing necessary to intervene in the affairs of the realm, it might be argued that the English "nation" was not similarly constrained. Both government and law could be acceptably understood as the products of contractual negotiation; and the collective "people" represented in Parliament were, as much as the king, properly to be regarded as an interested party. It was this interest that William sought to represent. Repeatedly appearing in his declaration was that interpretation of the English constitution which repudiated any attempt by the king at unilateral control of the law. The objection to the dispensing and suspending powers was that, "as no laws can be made but by the joint concurrence of king and parliament, so likewise laws so enacted, which secure the public peace and safety of the nation, and the Lives and Liberties of every subject in it, cannot be repealed or suspended but by the same authority."[29] William's appeal to the English, and in particular to the political nation, was that he had struck the sensitive and responsive chord of Parliament's claim to control of the law. Not only did he deny the king's right to act *ex parte*, he also denied the power of a dependent judiciary to surrender to the king those rights of the people which it was in the jurisdiction of king in Parliament to protect.[30] William was palatable to the English because he was, on the surface, eschewing any ambition of his own; he was purporting only to aid the redress of a dangerous constitutional imbalance. "Our Expedition," he proclaimed, "is intended for no other design, but to have a free and lawful Parliament assembled as soon as is possible."[31]

Nor was William carelessly critical of the king himself. James was not to be characterized as a usurper. He was the duly constituted king of England and as such could "do no wrong." William, therefore, quite properly addressed his declaration to the wrongs which had been perpetrated by the king's "evil counselors," those who "did invent and set on foot the king's Dispensing Power"[32] and who, having "the chief credit with the king, have overturned the Religion, Laws and Liberties" of the realm.[33] It was, of course, a difficult fiction to maintain at a time when James was increasingly the personal focus of constitutional despair. Yet the maxim, at least for a little while longer, was to continue to regulate English affairs. One critic of William's declaration noted that it "seems very unreasonable, that while the counsellors commit the fault, the king and the innocent kingdom must pay the reckoning";[34] and another commentator was pleased to point out that the king, at all times, acted upon nothing less than *legal* counsel. What more, it was asked, could James do? Not himself having been "bred at the Inns of Court," he was both pleased and obliged to refer questions of the prerogative to the lawyers. And when they assured him that he was justified in his use of the dispensing power, and still there were complaints, he referred the matter to the courts.[35] Evil counsel, then, if one were inclined to see it this way, might well be equated with legal counsel, because every step of the way it was, in fact, upon legal counsel that James took careful pains to rely. The law could thus be seen to be operating on both sides of the political issue, a fact which to astute contemporaries seemed scarcely surprising.

On 5 November 1688, with the aid of a "protestant wind," William's "force sufficient," under the banner of the House of Orange, landed at Torbay on the Devonshire coast. James's reaction to the invasion and to William's declaration was well considered: he interpreted the act as an assault upon his throne despite every disclaimer by the Dutchman to the contrary. He characterized William's declaration as an attempted usurpation of royal authority. What possible standing did the prince have to require "the peers of the realm, both spiritual and temporal, and all other persons of all degrees, to obey and assist him in the execution of his designs, a prerogative inseparable from the imperial crown of this realm"?[36] It would be difficult for William's English supporters to deny the reality of the prince's *invasion*. For that reason the subject was, for the most part, conveniently avoided. It was much easier and wiser to repeat the language of William's declaration and to speak of "invitation" and "preservation." Sir George Treby, in his address to the prince on 20 December, went even further. He raised the unpleasant word "invasion" only to assert explicitly that it was James and his advisers, not William, who were the "true invaders"—those who, in the meaningful language of the law, had "broken the close" of the English constitution. "Reviewing our late Danger," he said,

> we remember our Church and State, over-run by Popery and Arbitrary Power, and brought to the point of Destruction, by the Conduct of Men (that were our *true* Invaders) that brake the Sacred Fences of our *Laws* and (which was worst) the very Constitution of our *Legislature*.[37]

It seemed that, in addition to its precise common-law meaning, *quare clausum fregit* could, as a cause of action, be rhetorically adapted to an effective political end. And

170   although it was reasonable to suppose that a complaint
           would hold much more easily against William—he who
           "with force and arms broke the close of the plaintiff"—such
           was not to be the case. The law, at least metaphorically, was
           falling away from the king's control. James, and not Wil-
           liam, was to be considered the trespasser, the defendant
           against whom an action should properly lie.

           Another defect noted in William's declaration was the
           illogicality of his assumption that a "free parliament" could
           ever exist contemporaneously with the presence of a foreign
           army on English soil. How, it might be asked, could any
           Parliament be expected to operate outside the context of
           that series of events set in motion by William's landing on 5
           November? The dual pressures of the armed force, on the
           one hand, and the demonstrations in support of the prince
           and in opposition to popery, on the other, created an atmo-
           sphere hardly conducive to free deliberation. It has even
           been suggested that it was the activites of the "mob" which
           underscored the need to turn the provisional government
           over to William.[38] Not only the loyalty, then, of the Con-
           vention, but its independence as well, was realistically called
           into question long before that assemblage ever met. Conse-
           quently, once the shift in actual power from James to
           William had taken place, it was not likely to suppose that
           the eventual convocation of a "parliament" would result in
           anything more than constitutional posturing. The hasty
           stamp of legal color would be applied to a foreign monarch
           whose claim to the English throne could be rooted only in
           the unacceptable alternative of conquest or election.

           The prophecy of ratification was eventually borne out,
           although the Convention's proceedings suggest that much
           more than constitutional posturing was involved and that
           the outcome was at least on several occasions in doubt. Yet,
           on 13 February 1689, only three weeks after the Convention
           first met, the Crown was offered jointly to William and Mary
           with the understanding that the exercise of monarchical
           power would, during William's lifetime, be vested in him

alone. If any glory was to be salvaged from this illegitimate
transfer of the throne, it would have to lie in conscientious
pretense and rigid adherence to the niceties and necessities
of constitutional form. Those who had defected from James
would have to go further yet to assure themselves

> that no rational and unbiased person would judge it
> Rebellion to defend their Laws and Religion, which all
> English princes have sworn at their coronation; . . . They
> indeed owned it rebellion to resist a king that governed by
> law; but he was always accounted a tyrant that made his
> will his law; and to resist such an one they justly esteemed
> no rebellion, but a necessary defense.[39]

In much the same tortuous spirit it was also suggested that
the Church of England, long nurtured on the political
principle of nonresistance, would endorse the Revolution
because it was necessary to save the king against his will.[40] It
would be argued that the oath of allegiance to the king was
binding only so long as James did nothing to endanger the
constitution. Once, however, he could be charged with the
attempt to destroy both law and religion, the obligation was
no longer in effect. Adopting a position well understood as a
principle of contract, some churchmen would posit that
"when the King did not govern by Law, he could not expect
our obedience; that the obligacion was mutuall; that upon
that supposition we were at Liberty."[41] Instead of interpreting the commitment to the king as one of absolute
nonresistance, they would argue that the common-law doctrine of mutuality relieved all men of their contractual
obligations of allegiance. Here would be the way for the
church to distinguish its earlier loyalty to Charles I from its
growing inclination to abandon James. The understandable
truth was that by 1688 no one was willing to compare the
present situation with that of 1641–42, let alone with the
tragedy of 1649. The retreat from disorder of a half-century
past continued to condition the nation's political thinking even

beyond the successful landing of William. As long as it could be believed that the present king might be a tyrant, while the late king of blessed memory quite clearly was not, there was no reason to suggest that the outcome of this new enterprise would be the same as the disastrous consequence of the ill-fated civil wars. Those Anglicans who would support the Revolution would also hold firmly to the stated belief that "King Charles the 1st governed by Law, & that saying the contrary of him was a Slander."[42] Ironically, it was true—but no more true of Charles I than of James II. Yet a distinguishing myth was necessary. In the face of the century's second monarchical threat to the constitution it would have to be maintained that the first threat had never in fact been there.

James's first attempt to flee the realm was on 11 December. The effort, however, was frustrated by his almost immediate capture off the Kent coast near Faversham; but twelve days later, on 23 December, a second escape from his confinement at Rochester was made good. William was now free to further the ends of his declaration. On Christmas Day he met with some 90 lords at Westminster and, on the day following, with approximately 160 members of the parliaments of Charles II's reign and the aldermen and deputies of the Common Council of London. The result of these meetings was the request that William temporarily assume the administration of public affairs and issue letters for the summoning of a Convention. The prince agreed to undertake this exercise of responsibility for a provisional government, and on 29 December letters signed by William were issued for the election of members to the Convention to meet at Westminster on 22 January 1689. It was a highly irregular procedure but one which appeared in the circumstances to allow of no practicable alternative. Even Nottingham, perhaps the most punctilious critic of much that would ensue shortly in the Convention, treated the arrangement as though it were perfectly reasonable and proper. As there had to be someone to exercise the power of the executive, once James had departed the realm, and "as [there is] none so fitt, because of his Relation to the Crowne, & his presence here, . . . as the Prince," it seemed almost a matter of course that he should be asked.[43]

IN THE REVOLUTION OF 1688–89 THE FACT OF GREATEST constitutional significance was that the English nation first deposed a duly constituted king and then pretended that nothing of the sort had happened at all. Other than this, little was done. The "Glorious Revolution," stripped to its barest essentials, therefore suggests an unavoidable paradox in English history, a patently unconstitutional act which stands as perhaps the greatest monument to the victory of English constitutionalism. There is, however, the possibility of reconciliation. It lies in the manner in which the Convention of 1689 "legitimized" the illegal and pretended that the Revolution was never there. In "reestablishing" the government, the risk that Nottingham apprehended — of undoing all of England's "old and Legall foundations" — was met, and, by elaborate and necessary pretense, overcome.[44] The triumph was not of substance but of form, not of law but of legal mind; and if any moral emerged, it may well have been that constitutionalism could be preserved as long as it was thought to have been preserved.

Much had changed since the time of the Exclusion parliaments. What was possible in 1689 was the result of circumstances that, ten years earlier, had not yet matured. An argument against Exclusion had been that it would violate an important guarantee of the criminal law, the assurance that no man may be punished in praesenti for a crime to be committed in futuro.[45] This objection, valid and effective in 1679–81, had fully evaporated within the next decade. By 1689 the political nation was seeking to rid itself of a king who had realized its worst fears. It was proceeding now upon more confident grounds, acting remedially rather than preventively and in a way much more conformable to the common law. James, as king, could be charged with that actual subversion of law, liberties, and religion that in 1679, while he was still duke of York, could with an uneasy

174 foreboding only be anticipated. This, in large measure, was why the Revolution could be justified in a manner necessarily denied to the attempts at Exclusion. It was the Revolution that was consistent with the common-law practice of redressing an injury already done, while Exclusion endeavored, in advance, to set forth general rules and guiding principles. What was feared most by the Exclusion parliaments was prospective harm, and what they were therefore requesting was in the nature of punishment before the illegal act had been done. Such relief the common law had not been designed to allow. Once a recognized wrong had been perpetrated, the remedial powers of the law could be employed, but not before. Whereas James's guilt might be proved in 1689, ten years earlier it could only be feared.

It was in this spirit of a legal mandate that the Convention came together on 22 January 1689; and it was in the same spirit that the critical imperfections in the Convention's very existence were eventually overcome. A Parliament could be summoned only by a king; otherwise its existence was an act of treason and its work nothing more than a legal nullity. This much was clear in the law; and, as if to add authority by way of prophecy, Watkin Owen recorded in his law dictionary in 1681 that "A rebellious assembly is an assembly of 12 persons or more intending, going about practicing or putting in use unlawfully of their owne authority to change any lawes or statutes of this realme."[46] A principal, however, might subsequently ratify the unauthorized acts of a self-appointed agent, and to this end Charles II, ascending the throne in the twelfth year of his reign, legitimized the work of the Convention of 1660 by duly convening a proper assemblage in 1661, a Parliament which could and did confirm the acts of its immediate and imperfect predecessor. No comparable salvation was available in 1689. The acts of an illegally assembled Convention could never be legitimized by a king and queen who owed their regal existence to the same body. Constitutional continuity then, if not obviously, was at least technically in danger of being severed irreparably.[47] This was the exact point to be made by Heneage Finch in his speech to the Commons house of the Convention. He would, he said, remind the Convention that "Parliaments that are Called by Kings, cannot make Kings, much less can a Convention not Called by a King. . . . It therefore seems to me a Sollicisme in Law That a meeting less in Authority than a Parliament Shoud presume to make a King."[48] The point was well taken and did not admit of any easy response.

The only path around the obstacle of the Convention's irregularity seemed to be by way of constitutional innovation, a route that very few were prepared publicly to take. Consequently, the issue of the Convention's critical defect was for the most part avoided, in much the same way as the equally vexing impediment of the birth of the Prince of Wales. Those who did take a stand in support of the Convention's legitimacy usually chose to argue that the authority of any Parliament derived not from the monarch but from the people, and for that reason it was of little substantive importance that the Convention was summoned by someone other than the king.[49] That, in fact, may have been true, and ultimately it was a position that was tacitly to be vindicated. Yet considerations of substance alone were not sufficient to justify the unorthodox proceedings at hand. English constitutionalism through 1688 had been characterized continuously by a commitment to form, a commitment which, through the brief life of the Convention, would be scrupulously maintained. Even the Whigs, who were intent upon setting William on the throne, were at the same time so closely bound to precedent that they could never readily accept their own often repeated slogan, *Salus populi suprema lex.*[50]

By the time the Convention met, England had been without the services of a monarch for more than four weeks. James, at Saint-Germain, was far removed from the political arena; and although he announced his readiness to reappear as soon as the nation returned to its senses, the focus of government was clearly upon William. The Convention therefore convened in an atmosphere of greater pressure

176   than that which confronted its 1660 prototype. Charles II, unlike William, was not in England at the time of the earlier Convention's deliberations; and although his claim to the throne was more firmly anchored in hereditary right, he had much less control of the situation.

With regard to the political composition of the Convention, it is not certain whether that body was essentially Tory, essentially Whig, or whether the balance was held by 183 new members, who had never before sat in a Parliament and who may have been guided more by necessity than by allegiance to party or principle.[51] This last suggestion is appealing because it accounts, at least in part, for the moderation of the Revolution settlement; but it is not the entire answer. Transcending all factional differences was a basic unanimity of purpose. Whigs, Tories, and independents alike were in common accord on the method for perpetuating the English Crown and for securing a lasting settlement: through indefectible parliamentary procedure the form, if not the substance, of constitutionalism would be preserved. Notwithstanding fundamental disagreement as to who should occupy the throne and the way in which the warrant of the executive should be exercised, there was no deviation from the common struggle to legitimize the illegal and to find a precedental mandate for anything they might do. That this attempt was successful is apparent, for England was to emerge from 1689 committed to the fiction that nothing irregular had been done.

When the Convention first met on 22 January, there was nothing to distinguish it in appearance from any previous Parliament duly summoned by the king's writ. This, in itself, was remarkable, as the unorthodox circumstances were obviously suggestive of urgency. Neither house, however, was to be hurried, and both took great pains to be meticulously observant of all parliamentary rules. The form of election and the seating of the speaker of the house of Commons, Henry Powle, was entirely regular. He even partook of the formality by which a newly elected speaker humbly declares his defects and urges the election of one more capable.[52] The same procedure was followed by the Lords, and in both houses there was the regular appointment of all necessary officers and clerks.[53]

The formalities were being observed, and the Convention was still a long way from entertaining any question of substantive importance. First, in the House of Commons, there was a detailed debate on the procedure by which vacancies were to be filled. On this note it was resolved as a general rule that an application be made to Prince William for a letter authorizing the filling of any unoccupied seat. This seemed to be as close as the Convention could come to acting with the appearance of legality, as the chancellor, now being without a seal, could not execute the orders of the House.[54] It was, to be sure, a technical impediment only, and it prompted one member, who would have preferred election warrants to issue from the speaker alone, to remark that "We are in so unfortunate an age, that it has improved precedents especially on mistaken grounds."[55] But, mistaken or not, the Convention neither ignored its precedents nor flouted its procedures. Sir Thomas Clarges, for example, believed that the speaker's warrant would be sufficient authority to send out a writ,[56] but he also conveyed accurately the mood of the Convention when he took careful note of the gravity of its task:

The matter before you is of the greatest weight; therefore I hope you will proceed with prudence and wariness. Whole counties, as yet, have no members: and, that there may be no imputations upon us, and that all exceptions may be taken away, I would have this great affair debated in a full house.[57]

The admonition was heeded. The first two days of the session were almost entirely absorbed by administrative detail; and, on Wednesday, 23 January, the House of Commons adjourned until the following Saturday morning with the understanding that, during the two intervening days, the Committee of Elections and Privileges would

178   continue to meet. On Saturday the House reconvened and agreed to adjourn again until Monday, the 28th, at which time it would proceed to consider, as per a resolution of the 22nd, the condition and state of the nation.[58] It was therefore that the substantive issues were not considered by the House of Commons for almost one week from the time that William had made known to both houses the necessity of a prompt resolution of the problems of the succession. "The dangerous condition of the Protestants in Ireland requiring a large and speedy succour, and the present state of things abroad, oblige me to tell you," he said, "that next to the danger of unreasonable divisions among ourselves, nothing can be so fatal as too great a delay in your consultations."[59] Yet no procedural shortcuts were countenanced. A petition to both houses to bestow the Crown upon the Prince and Princess of Orange was rejected by the Lords because it was not signed and by the Commons because "They would not be awed in their votes, nor be directed; for that they ought to be free."[60] Perhaps that was asking too much, perhaps they could not in these circumstances be absolutely free; but they could, by adhering always to proper form, create the necessary illusion of legality. "I am," said Nottingham during the course of the proceedings, "very desirous ... that every thing of this nature should be done in the ancient, usuall, legall Method."[61]

Of the numerous options for settling the Crown, not one was sufficient in law. Even if it could be agreed that James had abdicated, there would be, in the first instance, no choice but to consider the Crown as having passed to the heir apparent. So long as the rules of hereditary descent were to be followed strictly, there was no alternative. If, however, it were found desirable to circumvent the hereditary succession, the Convention would have to meet the same array of legal impediments that had faced the Exclusion parliaments a decade before. This it did in the manner of its predecessors, by the application of analogues from the private law. In the matter of Exclusion and Revolution, then, there was a demonstrable consistency in approach, even though the results in each case were remarkably different. In both cases those who would alter the succession found that the previous two hundred years could offer only the merest suggestion of constitutional authority, since from 1485 on there had been no break in the line of descent. Henry VIII had employed Parliament to void his first two marriages with the result that, by 1536, both Mary and Elizabeth had been made bastards.[62] Furthermore, he had sought and received a legislative grant of authority for the making of a testamentary disposition of the Crown. Neither of these devices, however, was to have any effect upon the succession. Henry, in fact, reversed himself by his third Act of Succession (1544). Mary and Elizabeth were returned in line for the throne behind their half-brother, Edward; and Henry, in the event of a default of heirs, was empowered to dispose of the Crown by letters patent or by will.[63] Henry did execute a will, in December 1546, whereby he confirmed the provisions of the 1544 act and further directed the Crown to the heirs of Mary, his younger sister, in the event of a failure of the lines of Edward, Mary, and Elizabeth. This attempt, if successful, would have bypassed the Stuart line. It did not succeed. Not only Mary and Elizabeth, but James as well, ascended the throne in a manner consistent with hereditary prescription. Whether Mary and Elizabeth would have been prevented from ascending the throne if there had been no will and if the act of 1544 had not placed them back in the succession, we can only speculate. In all probability they would have been barred, and the succession would have been diverted from the hereditary line. We cannot, however, be sure. We know only that Henry's full testamentary directions were not followed and that, from Henry's death in 1547, through James's accession, and up, indeed, until 1689, every monarch succeeded to the throne as of hereditary right. If there was any constitutional option, it had not been realized. The succession, if only in fact, was being clearly limited to the hereditary precept.

The task of the Convention was made much more difficult because of the earlier failures to effect Exclusion. The years

180   1679-81 might now be read as the confirmation of the indefeasible right of hereditary succession, a commitment to legitimacy rather than to the supremacy of king in Parliament. But even if a sovereign king in Parliament, as acceptable political theory, could be reinvigorated, it was, by 1689, an unusable alternative. James clearly was not inclined to accede to the undoing of himself and the alteration of his line. The truth, therefore, was unpleasant but nonetheless unavoidable: only the recall of James, without conditions, could comport with the injunctions of the constitution as it then stood. This the Convention was unprepared to do, even though it was this alone that everyone could agree the Convention might somehow be "authorized" to do. One line of contemporary argument was that the Convention could not give to William more than it had—which was considered to be very little indeed. Its power was deemed "too scanty to be able to make a new king, though it may call home that to whom we have most, if not all of us, sworn allegiance."[64] And if the Convention did nothing at all, there seemed little doubt but that James had a legal right to return. Among those who favored such a return there was the supportable belief that James had been made to leave under duress, that he was like the man who "by a violent Invader is made to swear to pay a sum of money, [for whom] it is acknowledged lawful ... to implead the thief to recover from him what in performance of that involuntary oath, he hath paid him."[65]

Despite its legal and constitutional appeal, the option of recalling the king to his full right and power was never seriously considered. As a consequence, each alternative possibility of settlement had to be considered alongside its concomitant degree of illegitimacy. The result was ironic and fraught with discomfort, for the color of legality of each proposed scheme of settlement seemed, without exception, to vary inversely with its appeal.

The suggestion most nearly approximating constitutional propriety favored the conditional recall of James. The proposal, however, was attractive only to those who were

unable to countenance any form of defiance of the king and
who were therefore out of touch with the accomplished fact
of revolution. Their solution, moreover, was incompatible
with their professed doctrine of nonresistance, an absolute
doctrine which did not admit of qualification. It would be
folly to assume that any attempt to strip James of his
prerogative could be more acceptable philosophically because it suggested resistance in a lesser degree. "If resistance
was unlawful, then the Tories had no business to be
imposing conditions upon an anointed king."[66]

Much more popular with those who were unprepared for
the permanent separation of James from his throne was the
idea of "regency." They believed that no king, however
malevolent, could ever forfeit his crown.[67] "But supposing,"
noted Sir Richard Temple in the Commons, "the case were
of an infant or lunatic, the nation may in that case provide
for the government."[68] Certainly, if the private law were to be
used as a guide, this was true. It was well settled that infants,
lunatics, and idiots were legally incompetent in the administration of their affairs and that those affairs should therefore be handled by others.[69] This might be the way out if the
government could be conceived as apart from the Crown
and if the former, without impairing the rights of the latter,
could be devolved upon Mary or William, or possibly both.
The scheme proposed would have deprived James of all
monarchical powers, which would, in turn, be vested in the
regent. And to insure the practical success of the plan, the
king, as one tract subsequently suggested, could have been
forbidden to come "within five hundred miles of any part of
his Dominions."[70] There was considerable appeal in the
regency proposal but, at the same time, a number of
apparent obstacles. Nottingham was one who was initially
troubled by the logical inconsistency of government continuing in the name of a discredited king. "It is," he had said
at the December meeting of the Lords Spiritual and Temporal at the Guildhall, "owning the King who hath forsaken the
Kingdom."[71] Then, too, although the concept of regency
was not unknown in the England of 1689, its application

might have to be, for James was neither infant nor lunatic. His incapacitating infirmity, if any, could be neither physical nor mental; it would have to be moral. James would be declared unfit for the exercise of government by virtue of his religion. The reasoning was strained, but for some it was nonetheless compelling. The bishop of Ely, much attracted to the regency solution, attempted to demonstrate that the king, although continuing to reign, might no longer be capable of exercising the powers of government. "As there is," he said,

> a Naturall Incapacity for the exercise, as Sickness, Lunacy, Infancy, doating old age, or an incurable disease rendring the party unfitt for human society, as Leprosy or the like, so I take it, there is a morall Incapacity, and that I conceive to be a full irremovable perswasion in a false Religion, contrary to the doctrine of Christianity.[72]

It was even argued at a later time that Roman Catholicism was much the same as those moral and perhaps mental infirmities that were more familiar to the law, drunkenness being the one example that most easily came to mind. A man might just as well, having imbibed an excess of papism as an excess of alcohol, lose control of his reason; and if, under the pernicious influence of either, he committed a crime, he would not be permitted to plead a want of intent. He would be "adjudged a wilful Criminal" and made to "suffer accordingly."[73] In this regard James's crime consisted in allowing the nation to slip into popery despite his expressed intention to preserve the realm in its religion as established by law. There was a confusion here of a number of legal principles, but that was hardly important. What did seem to matter was that an argument recognized in the private law could be employed to effect whatever changes might be considered necessary in the constitution. There was, for this purpose, little difference between one cause of action and another. An appeal of felony, alleging constructive intent, and a "peticion ... for the custody of a pretended Lunaticke" were of equal value. Each imparted the color of legality to "constitutional" options which had never been contemplated in law.

Support for a regency was almost sufficient to carry the House of Lords but in the end failed, although only barely, since it was deemed unworkable.[74] An exiled king in whom the right, if not the power, of kingship was never contested would be a continuing menace to the quiet of the nation. He would reasonably be expected to seize any opportunity to overthrow a settlement predicated upon a regency in which he had never acquiesced. The lawyers in the House of Commons were also quick to remark that no Parliament, by the laws of England, was authorized to consider a regency without the king's consent.[75] Such a compromise, said Henry Pollexfen, would be "a strange and unpracticable thing, and would be introductive of a new principle of government amongst us."[76] Regency was not feasible and therefore was unacceptable; even so, both its consideration and its rejection were couched in the vocabulary of the law. Even those who staunchly favored a regent indicated their readiness to pay allegiance to William should he become king, on the constitutional ground that a *de facto* king had a right to obedience. Such was the lesson to be derived "from the law and from the history of England."[77]

Once the regency proposal failed to carry, it was only a matter of time before the Crown would fall to one or both occupants of the throne of Orange; but the Convention was not yet finished with its struggle for a legitimate base. On 28 January the House of Commons had

RESOLVED, That King *James* the Second, having endeavoured to subvert the Constitution of the Kingdom, by breaking the Original Contract between King and People; and, by the Advice of Jesuits, and other wicked Persons, having violated the fundamental laws; and having withdrawn himself out of this Kingdom; has abdicated the Government; and that the Throne is thereby vacant.[78]

184   The Lords, however, were not prepared to accept the resolution in its entirety and on 2 February sent a message to the House of Commons to the effect that they concurred in the Commons' vote, with two amendments: there was to be a substitution of "deserted" for "abdicated," and the words, "and that the throne is thereby vacant," were to be omitted.[79] Issue was thereby joined and was not to be resolved until such time as both houses could meet together in a free conference, a meeting which took place on 6 February.[80]

The great fear was of an elective Crown; and although the settlement of 1689 could, in retrospect, easily be explained in those terms, both houses of the Convention expressly denied that an election was what, in fact, was taking place. This was not to suggest that there was no historical or constitutional authority for such a course or, indeed, that election could in no way be justified "legally." It could be argued that when a king forfeits his throne there is a reversion of the line to the people, who may then do with the throne what they will. The only restraint upon the sovereign people is that they do not violate the law of God. This was the position advanced in support of the monarchical choice that the Convention eventually made. It was consonant with the view, later to be expressed in the dispute over the oaths of allegiance and supremacy, that as "God has not made any law determining the succession of the crown ... the sovereign power is at absolute liberty to dispose of it to whom & as they please."[81] The idea was both attractive and dangerous. It had the advantage of being a position derived from an acceptable interpretation of Scripture, that if the Bible did not explicitly proscribe a course of procedure, in particular a mode of governance, then an elected monarch was theologically permissible. Elective monarchy could, in this manner, be respectably equated with Anglican episcopacy. The constitution of church and state might be justified and explained upon the basis of what conformed best to the needs of good government. The approach was therefore similar to one used at the time of Exclusion. Ten years earlier, in response to the contention

that the disinheriting of James would be a "sin against God," 185
it was maintained that "sin is the Transgression of the Law."
And, as God did not make such a law, we must consider the
other rule "written in another place, where there's no Law,
there is no Transgression."[82]

The argument was dangerous if it was to be predicated
upon sovereignty residing in the people. It might open the
way for a future heir to be denied the Crown because he was
wanting in popular favor. This was one reason why the
Lords balked at the idea of declaring the throne vacant. Yet
it was the dilemma haunting those who were afraid of
elective monarchy that many were, at the same time, eager
to be permanently rid of James and the threat of a Catholic
succession. There was a variety of ways for James to be
reasoned out of existence. Whether his flight was to be
regarded as an "abdication" or a "desertion" was of lesser
importance than the strongly held pretense that the king
had voluntarily and inexcusably "withdrawn himself" from
the realm. A Catholic succession, however, was another
matter. The Lords had difficulty in accepting the proposition
that an act of the king could "bar or destroy the Right of the
Heires to the Crown."[83] They believed in hereditary monarchy and preferred to think that the succession was fundamentally fixed in the constitution and therefore indefeasible.
To think otherwise, as one polemicist would observe
disapprovingly after the Revolution, was tantamount to
"docking the entail of the crown."[84] Yet that, in fact, might
have been the best metaphorical key to an understanding of
events. If the Crown were to be treated as an entail, it would
suggest a continuation of the heritable line, but a line
which, in certain circumstances, everyone knew might always legally be broken.

A compromise course was the one which ultimately
prevailed. The Commons pretended that it was meeting a
unique and distinguishable situation on its merits and was not
setting a dangerous precedent for the future succession of
the Crown. Eventually the Lords agreed, although they were
much harder to persuade. They had first to be satisfied that

186   all that was meant by the word "abdicate" was that James
had "renounced the government for himself"[85] and that
hereditary monarchy was to remain unimpaired. This was
the sought-after assurance from the Commons that Nottingham reported to his own house on 6 February. "They
disclame," he said, "the pretence of an elective kingdom."[86]
The result was that, despite the regrettable although necessary alteration in the Stuart line,[87] the fiction of hereditary
monarchy was permitted to continue. "It is not," said
Serjeant Maynard,

> that the Comons do say, the Crown of England is allways
> and perpetually Elective, but it is most necessary, that
> there be a Supply, where there is a defect, and the doing
> of that will be no alteration of the Monarchy from a
> Successive one to an elective.[88]

The default in the heritable line, specifically, and to a large
extent the disconcerting truth of revolution, generally, were
to be regarded as temporary aberrations requiring immediate attention; but once these unique conditions — the
latter real and the former imagined — were rectified, there
would be no reason to suppose that England and hereditary
monarchy would not be put back on their proper collective
course. It was, as Macaulay would observe more than one
hundred fifty years later, only "a slight deviation from the
ordinary course of succession."[89]

There was, of course, an obvious flaw. Even if it could be
allowed that "there be a Supply, where there is a defect," no
one had yet shown how the heritable line had failed.[90] The
Prince of Wales was very much alive, as were the Princess
Mary and the Princess Anne. No matter how determinedly
the Commons might resolve that the throne was vacant, it
would be difficult to overcome the hard constitutional objections of the Lords. It was, they pointed out, "a Maxim of our
Law that the king never dies."[91] But, if the throne was not
vacant, neither was its occupant or occupants known, as the
Lords refused to declare by whom if was filled. Repeatedly

the members of the House of Commons called upon the Lords to state clearly whom they believed the occupant to be, but to no avail.[92] No one was going to utter the ineffable: that by the processes of the constitution, if the king was legally dead, the Prince of Wales was his immediate and automatic successor.

From the beginning it was apparent that the legitimate existence of the infant James Edward would not be admitted. The tone of the Convention had been set one month before it met, on 24 December, in an exchange between Henry, second earl of Clarendon, and the aging Lord Wharton. Clarendon had urged upon the peers assembled at Westminster that an inquiry be made into the birth of the Prince of Wales. Wharton objected strongly. He thought it a grave mistake for anyone even to "mention that Child" and expressed his profound hope that "we shall hear no more of him."[93] And no more, indeed, was heard. The conspiracy was so successful and the pretense so complete that, when the work of the Convention was done, it could appear to many that the members had no choice but to supply the defect that was surely there. Certainly, said Paul Foley, member for Hereford, if the whole royal line should fail, it would be incumbent upon the Lords and the Commons to fill the throne. And that, he maintained, comes nearest to the Case in question, where the Successor is not knowne, for if he had been, we should have heard of him before now."[94] Foley's analysis epitomized the position of those in both houses of the Convention who needed a rationale of legal color for the move to an elected monarch. It may well have been disingenuous in the way that any pretense is a knowing distortion of truth. Yet the mistakes of the Civil War and Interregnum were so eagerly to be avoided that any pretense in keeping with monarchical continuity was, in the same degree, to be embraced. In 1649, after the execution of Charles I, the political nation had to choose between continuing the monarchy, on the one hand, and moving to a republic, on the other. It chose the latter. It opted for constitutional innovation as the alternative to a continuation of

188   the Stuart line in Charles II. It had not considered the extreme possibility of ignoring the existence of Charles and placing upon the throne a monarch who might be more responsive to what were considered to be the nation's needs. In 1689 this "mistake" was not to be made again. Circumstances and the memory of 1649 would impel the Convention to an elective monarchy while preserving the myth of a constitution that remained fundamentally untouched. The members of the Convention would do what they thought they must and would then pretend that what they had done was entirely regular and had involved no conscious choice at all.

For those who were unable to accept the fiction of a "nonexistent child" there was still another way to avoid the prospect of a Catholic succession. The private law would once more be consulted for persuasive, if not binding, authority. Reviving one of the arguments current at the time of Exclusion, Serjeant Maynard reminded the convention that, according to the rules of inheritance, there could be no such thing as a hereditary descent during the life of the king. "No man," he said, "can pretend to be king James' heir while he is living."[95] A man alive would have an heir apparent or presumptive; but, on the authority of Coke and others, until he was dead there could be no heir. For the purpose of Exclusion the argument was sound; but not even the considerable prestige of Coke could save the situation in 1689 from a posture inconsistent with what had already transpired. The maxim *Nemo est haeres viventis* would be rendered irrelevant by the acceptance of the premise that the king was legally dead. Since James II had laid down the government and had departed the realm, he was therefore to be regarded as demised in law.[96]

It could, however, be argued that the oath to the king, his heirs, and successors was "copulative" and that no allegiance was owed to anyone who was not both the king's heir *and* his successor. That much, of course, was true; but the contrivances of legal reasoning would have to be exploited somewhat further if a transfer of allegiance to William was legally to be justified. What would therefore be

urged during the later debates over the new oaths was that
the putative Prince of Wales could not claim to be his
father's heir because he was, as all the world could see,
clearly not his successor.[97]

In point of fact there was no way to seat William upon the
throne without undermining the principle of hereditary
monarchy. But the Convention was not to be diverted from
the attempt or from the pretense that it had succeeded.
James II was to be treated as dead and his infant son as never
having lived. Even though imperfect, it seemed to be the
only solution; its defects would have quietly to be ignored.
Such was the treatment accorded to the admonition of
Nottingham, who had warned that

> if you do once make it elective, I do not say that you are
> always bound to go to election, but it is enough to make it
> so, if by that precedent there be a breach in the hereditary
> succession; ... and I cannot see by what authority we
> can do that, or change our ancient constitution, without
> committing the same fault we have laid upon the king.[98]

The allegation was correct and clear, but it was not to be
considered: the Convention was in jeopardy of redressing the
illegal acts of an evil king by deeds of its own which were no
more lawful.

Notwithstanding its illegal course, the Convention never
deviated from a constitutional posture. At every turn and in
every decision there was the evident appeal to the direction
of the law. Sir Christopher Musgrave reflected the spirit of
the assembly when he contended that law and not expedience should be the judge of whether a king might be
deposed. Whether, in fact, the king had "forfeited his
inheritance to the crown" was not to be subject to a
consensual determination. Somewhere there had to be a
clear legal precedent for the guidance of political action,
and it was incumbent upon the "long robe" — the lawyers —
to find it.

It was not surprising that an age so immersed in the

190

intricacies of litigation should look naturally to the private law for guidance in public affairs. England in the seventeenth century was accustomed to thinking in legal and precedental terms; and when the Commons was resolved, and the Lords agreed, "that it hath been found by Experience, to be inconsistent with the Safety and Welfare of this Protestant Kingdom, to be governed by a Popish Prince,"[99] the emphasis was properly upon the word "experience." Here, and throughout the proceedings, there was little or no appeal to the dictates of reason. The Convention, like the common law, was to draw upon the wisdom and practice of the past; it was not to rely upon some ill-defined and abstract standard. Precedents in history were similarly sought and passionately argued despite the fact that historical authority, if any, was hopelessly confused. The Convention, however, was not to be dissuaded, even though the futility of its task was made painfully apparent. The earl of Pembroke reminded his colleagues that the existing precedents were unfortunately in conflict and that there was no hereditary line that had not, at some point, been interrupted. He urged them, therefore, to look elsewhere for counsel.[100] His exhortation notwithstanding, the search for precedents went on; and if they could not be found in the common law, the Convention was prepared to go the the civil law and the canon law as well. In the determination, for example, of the respective merits of "abdicated" and "deserted," it was soon agreed that neither word was known at common law.[101] This being the case, one member, John Somers, later to become lord chancellor, summoned such non–common-law authorities as Grotius, Calvin, and Bartolus to prove his point that "abdicate" was the proper choice.[102] Nottingham was one who was not convinced, and for a short while the debate centered more upon the standing frictions between common lawyers and civilians than upon the merits of the case at hand. Nottingham argued that neither word was derived from the common law, and for that reason he would use neither word. He would, instead, have a solution to the dilemma deduced exclusively from common-law rules alone.

"I am," he said, "so much in love with our own Law, that I would use noe words in a Case, that so much concerns our Legall Constitution, but what are fetcht from thence."[103] The problem, however, was that there were no applicable words to be drawn from the common-law experience, and, in the end, "abdicate" was accepted by both houses because it was a "legal word" and because it worked.[104]

The influence of the law was carried even further. The suggestion of an original contract implied above all else a bilateral agreement, to be executed by the king on the one hand and the people on the other, which released either side from its obligations in the event of the other's breach. This, in its most common acceptation, was the almost universal understanding of the way in which the contract was composed. Nowhere in the debates of the Convention or in the political disputation that surrounded those debates was the influence of Hobbes or Locke to be felt. The two great contractarian philosophers of the English seventeenth century had devised, each in his own way, a theory of government based upon an original contract to which the king was not a party. For Hobbes it was crucial that an absolute sovereign not be bound to any contractual obligation, and for Locke it was only after the people had contracted originally among themselves to leave the state of nature that a limited government was established by a "second contract" or, more to the point, by an instrument of trust. Hobbes's construction was unacceptable, and Locke's, if it was considered, was not nearly so appealing as a compact between king and people which placed the two on a level of legal parity. The appeal of James as a contracting party was in the strong attraction of the notion of a king who could not claim obedience as a matter of inherent right but whose claim would necessarily have to depend, rather, upon the exchange of a quid pro quo.

Even more basic than the identity of the parties to the original contract was the existence of the contract itself. On this point there seemed to be virtual unanimity. All could agree that somewhere in the unrecorded past a binding agreement had been reached which formed the basis of the present constitution.[105] To be sure, there were those who were troubled by the death of the original parties. How, it was asked, could the present king be bound by an obligation undertaken by a remote and unknown predecessor? It was more of a legal than a political problem, and the law would once more provide the answer. Each new king would become obligated to the terms of the contract by the process of novation. This was taken as the proper construction to be placed upon every new accession. "For when any prince succeeds, he must necessarily succeed only in the Rights & upon the terms of his predecessors."[106] The new king would merely be substituted for the old. And if novation were not enough, it could also be argued that, on the theory of ratification, each successive monarch would be held to the same commitments as his predecessor. "The very assuming of the Regal Authority" was to be regarded as "a vertual Ratification of the original contract."[107]

It was a more difficult problem to achieve a common understanding of the terms of the contract. Most agreed that the contract established the present form of monarchical government, hereditary in nature and grounded in law. Further clarification was difficult and, as expected, was attempted in a manner wholly consistent with the political beliefs of whoever was trying. Those on the side of James II were quick to allege that an unambiguous part of the contract was the maxim "The King can do no wrong" and that, as a logical corollary of that proposition, he is therefore unaccountable to the people.[108] Yet, if that were the case, it might prove to be no contract at all but an agreement that, in law, was illusory. Whether or not for that reason, the argument in favor of an unaccountable king had little persuasive effect. Still, there were other Jacobite tacks to be tried, including the rather straightforward assertion that, since a strict principle of hereditary monarchy was fixed in the contract, it would be a material breach for the people to turn away from James and his posterity.[109] By this construction the Crown could not be removed from the hereditary line, nor would the king be able, by his own acts, to destroy the succession.[110]

It was on the combined question of what constituted a breach of contract and what the political results of such a breach might be that the greatest controversy was aroused. It was attractive to suppose that the contract contemplated a set of circumstances like those which emerged in 1688–89 and that the Convention was doing only what the original terms required. This is what Sir Thomas Lee had in mind when he asked "whether upon the Originall Contract there was not power reserved in the Nation to provide for itself in Such exigencyes?"; [111] but that was extending the compass of the contract far beyond most people's reasonable expectations. It seemed more in keeping with the current situation to conceive of James as "having endeavoured to subvert the Constitution of the Kingdom, by breaking the Original Contract between King and People," and, having established that, to move to an examination of the consequences that would flow expectedly from the breach.

What was argued with the greatest force was that James, by breaching the original contract, had forfeited his throne for himself and his posterity.[112] This position enabled the Convention to move easily, and by color of law, from a Catholic to a Protestant sovereign. But, again, there was the unavoidable disadvantage of any approach that suggested a movement to elective monarchy. Maynard tried to steer the Convention clear of these larger troublesome questions by seeking to reduce the matter to legally manageable terms. It was, he said, quite simple. "If two of us make a mutuall agreement to help and defend each other from any one that shall assault us in a Journey, and he that is with me, turn upon me & break my head, he has undoubtedly abdicated my Assistance and renounced it."[113] Such a construction would admit of a much simpler approach to the matter of James's breach of the original contract, but it did not, and could not, quiet the fears of an elective monarchy. The king,

194   if Maynard was right, had by his actions clearly forfeited his subjects' allegiance, and those subjects might now proceed to place another on the throne.

In some ways the shift in control of the law was manifested most dramatically in the subtle transmutation of prerogative into trust. If executive power were no longer to be seen as the exclusive preserve of the king but instead as a bundle of responsibilities delegated to the king by the people, the constitutional balance would be completely reversed. This, of course, is what Locke was suggesting. It was also the frequent frame of reference during the course of the Convention's debates. If the king held the government by an instrument of trust, it could be argued that any act contrary to the terms of that trust constituted a forfeiture.[114] The analysis, however, was much too facile. It took into account the form but not the substance of the law. It was therefore for Nottingham once again to make a telling legal distinction. He remarked that it was, for a trustee,

> a violation of his trust to act contrary to it; and he is accountable for that violation, to answer what the trust suffers out of his own estate; but I deny it to be presently a renunciation of the trust, and that such a one is no longer a trustee.[115]

Just as every breach of the original contract was not properly to be regarded as a material breach, one that automatically dissolved the compact and every obligation flowing from it,[116] so too was a trust of government meant to withstand all but the most destructive acts of renunciation.[117] Therefore, said Nottingham, the nation must not allow itself to view every deed of malfeasance committed in the name of the king as an act of abdication, because by so doing there would be the implied abandonment of the ancient principle that "The king can do no wrong" and the substitution in its stead of the doctrine of *respondeat superior*.[118] Such a substitution, however, was inevitable, and the work of the Convention may in one sense be counted as the transition in fact from the king's inviolability to the proposition that, for the acts of an evil administration, the master must answer.

THE CONVENTION OF 1689 DID NOT REPRESENT A CONSTITU-tional achievement because of any dedication to the sub-stance of English law. It was, instead, something more subtle: not the victory of the law, but of its configurations and procedures. No arguments advanced during the few weeks of the Convention's life were to claim support unless they seemed in some way constitutionally plausible, unless they could at least pretend to conform to an established practice. The truimph was in the successful attempt to cloak the expedient in an aura of precedent; and although the lawyers were repeatedly called upon to put the Convention "in a way practicable," the hand of restraint was always in evidence.

Once again the unresolved questions of the Exclusion years had been raised, and once again they had gone unanswered. No one understood now, any better than he had before, the estate of a king in the English Crown or to what degree the prerogative had been impaired. Certainly the Revolution had succeeded in lessening the king's control of the law, but it was not yet known exactly how far the balance of that control had been shifted. It is true that James II and his posterity, as represented by his infant son, had been removed from the throne and from the succession. In this regard the Revolution had accomplished what Exclusion could not. But the progress of English constitutionalism was still best explained by the similarities between these two political watersheds rather than by their differences. In both instances the wedge of elective monarchy was denied and the myth, at least, of a hereditary succession was preserved. The pretense was, of course, infinitely more fragile in 1689 than it had ever been before. It could not sustain the burden of further definition without risk of shattering. This might explain why the constitutional results of the Revolution were never nearly so clear to contemporaries as they seemed to be to later generations of confident historians. The cost of

196   constitutional success was the continuation of political am-
            biguity. It appeared to be a price worth paying.

Conclusion

The language of politics in the seventeenth century was rich and expressive. Among its various strands were the vocabularies of theology, civil law, patriarchalism, the "public interest," and civic humanism; [1] but, for the most part, when it came to constitutional politics, educated Englishmen thought and spoke in the language of the common law. This was particularly true of the political generation after 1660, for whom republicanism and religious fundamentalism were no longer reliable guides to constitutional change. The emphasis of Restoration constitutional politics was upon England's religion "as by law established" and upon the institution of monarchy as legally unavailable to responsible challenge. "We will have a King," Roger Morrice recorded in 1688, "for the Lawes know nothing but the name of a King." [2] Morrice was in sympathy with William's cause, but his premise and conclusion were shared equally by those who opposed the Revolution.

Morrice's statement was constitutionally accurate as well as politically acceptable. With the restoration of the monarchy the republic had been consigned to legal oblivion. No act of the Long Parliament to which Charles had not assented, nor any act of later republican parliaments, had any standing in law. Morrice was therefore right to observe that the law contemplated monarchy alone. But he was also an apologist for the Revolution, and to justify that event was — or should have been — a wholly different matter. Yet it was not. Morrice, his contemporaries, and a subsequent historical tradition were eminently successful in translating revolution into constitutional regularity.

198   Necessary to this historical and historiographical achievement was the opportunity for constitutional pretense and self-delusion. That opportunity was provided by the legal dimension in English political culture. Legal rhetoric, moreover, was highly adaptive. When justification in law was impossible, justification "by colour of law" assumed the necessary burden of making proposed constitutional change appear regular. It was neither accidental nor insignificant that each important constitutional issue of the time was perceived as an extension of a private-law matter. The debate over the succession was formulated as an investigation into the right of inheritance and the ways in which an heir to an estate might be deprived of his patrimony. Similarly, the relationships between king and Parliament and king and people were consistently reduced to analyses based upon the lawyer's understanding of property, contracts, and trusts.

None of this was unique to this political generation or even to the entire Stuart era. For centuries political Englishmen had explored the limits of their constitution with the aid of paradigms drawn from the common law.[3] Yet from 1660 to 1689, and particularly after 1678, when James's suitability to the throne was called sharply into question, constitutional discourse relied more upon the language of the law than on any other political vocabulary. This language, moreover, was not the exclusive property of any one party. It was used with equal frequency and equal facility by king and Parliament, Whig and Tory, Catholic and Protestant, all drawing upon their common legal heritage. Yet in 1689 the Whigs and Protestants won, and they set themselves with renewed vigor to the extensive elaboration of constitutional myth. The historiographical result of that effort was that law, legal language, and a whole legal disposition of mind became in time more closely identified with Stuart parliaments than with Stuart kings.

The Revolution did not resolve all the outstanding problems of constitutional politics. The outline of a modified relationship between the new king and a yet unsettled political nation was suggested but not yet clearly defined. That curious document, the Declaration of Rights, stated publicly, although without legal effect, that monarchical control of the law by way of the dispensing and suspending powers ought no longer to be tolerated. And with the hope, more anxious than confident, that the Prince of Orange would honor the Declaration and its assertion of constitutional principles, the Convention proclaimed William and Mary king and queen.[4]

The new reign thus began on a note of constitutional uncertainty; but before the year was out, the Bill of Rights confirmed in law what the Declaration had only been able to pretend—that the drive toward absolutism had, at least for the moment, been arrested.[5] Yet what had happened was not that the law had triumphed but that once again, as in 1649—although this time without a violent rending of the constitution—the law had been wrested from the king's control. The Stuarts had exploited the law not wisely but too well. The legal past was theirs, but it was one of the several ironies of history that what should have been an indefeasible legacy was jeopardized and then lost through politically insensitive, even if constitutionally proper, use. At no time after 1660, however, did Parliament embrace any other political standard in order to win. Parliament opposed the king with its own interpretation of the law; and, when that failed, it assumed the burden of legal justification by recourse to the best, indeed the only, approximation of law it could find—the weapon of legal color. A Parliament without sufficient law and history on its side might have used its revolution as a means to overcome both. Instead, it appropriated both. With consummate rhetorical skill, Parliament took away the king's law and rewrote his constitutional history.

Notes

INTRODUCTION

1. The theme of the "ancient constitution" formed an indispensable part of the seventeenth-century legal and historical mind. This theme has been explored and developed in the major achievement of J. G. A. Pocock, *The Ancient Constitution and the Feudal Law* (1957).

2. On the subject of the Long Parliament's assault upon the Caroline judiciary, see W. J. Jones, *Politics and the Bench* (1971).

3. Donald Veall, *The Popular Movement for Law Reform* (1970), p. 161.

4. Ibid., pp. 226–27.

5. Gilbert Burnet, *A Sermon Preached In the Chappel of St. James, Before his Highness the Prince of Orange, the 23rd of December 1688* (1689), p. 1.

6. Of particular value for important detail on the Revolution and the several years preceding it are J. R. Western, *Monarchy and Revolution* (1972), and J. R. Jones, *The Revolution of 1688 in England* (1972).

CHAPTER 1. ATTITUDES

1. Reminiscence by Langton, a student of Hale, in Seward, *Anecdotes of Distinguished Persons;* cited by Serjeant Runnington in his introduction to Matthew Hale, *The History of the Common Law of England and an Analysis of the Civil Part of the Law* (1820), p. vii. Consistent with Hale's attitude is the preface to this small printed volume, "The ... Impeachment of ... Clarendon" (1700), which ends with this thought: "I shall only add that several of our greatest Men have highly valued it [this book] in Manuscript, and I doubt not but all who read it, will think of it, not only for a lawyer's, but every English Gentleman's Study."

2. Christopher Hill, *Intellectual Origins of the English Revolution* (1965), p. 256.

3. For an assessment of the Yorkist and Tudor periods see E. W. Ives, "The Reputation of the Common Lawyer in English Society,

202   1450-1550," *University of Birmingham Historical Journal* (1959-60), p. 157. Also see William J. Bouwsma, "Lawyers and Early Modern Culture," *American Historical Review* (1973).

4. Cited by J. W. Gough, *The Social Contract* (1957), p. 89.

5. "Concerning the Oaths of Allegiance and Supremacy ... " (c. 1700), BM, Stowe MS 293, fol. 4v.

6. Barbara J. Shapiro, "Law and Science in Seventeenth-Century England," *Stanford Law Review* (1969), p. 729.

7. Gilbert Burnett, *The Life and Death of Sir Matthew Hale* (1682), p. 120; W. S. Holdsworth, *A History of English Law* (1966), vol. 6, p. 581; Shapiro, "Law and Science in Seventeenth-Century England," pp. 740-49. Also see Serjeant Runnington's edition of Hale's *The History of the Common Law of England and an Analysis of the Civil Part of the Law* (1820). Runnington, on the title page of the *Analysis,* quotes Blackstone: "Of all the schemes hitherto made public for digesting the Laws of England, the most natural and scientifical of any, as well as the most comprehensive, appeared to be that of Sir Matthew Hale, in his posthumous 'Analysis of the Law.' "

8. William Petyt, "A letter, touching the Judicature of the House of Peers," BM, Hargrave MS 100, fol. 42.

9. Holdsworth, *History of English Law,* vol. 6, pp. 581-82.

10. This statement of Hale's attitude toward equity comes from someone unnamed by Burnett but identified as "one of the greatest Men of the Profession of the Law" (Burnett, *Life and Death of Sir Matthew Hale,* p. 176). It is probable that it was Nottingham. See Holdsworth, *History of English Law,* vol. 6, p. 574, n. 1.

11. Cited by Alan Harding, *A Social History of English Law* (1966), pp. 277-78.

12. "Reflections by the Lord Cheife Justice Hale on Mr. Hobbs his dialogue of the Law," BM, Hargrave MS 96, fol. 6.

13. Historians have occasionally been troubled by the ease of Hale's professional transition from the Protectorate to the restored monarchy. The fact that Hale functioned as a judge under Cromwell and later under Charles II might suggest that he was guilty of political time-serving. Charles Gray, however, thinks Hale's career can be explained as an allegiance to the continuity of the law and so relieves Hale of any implication of opportunism (Charles M. Gray, ed., introduction to Sir Matthew Hale, *The History of the Common Law of England* [1971], p. xiv). Hale's most recent biographer, Edmund Heward, agrees with this judgment but is disturbed by Hale's resignation from the Court of Common Pleas at Cromwell's death: "His scruples seem to have reappeared and he said he 'could act no longer under such

authority.' There does not appear to be any difference in principle
between serving under Oliver or Richard, but Hale may have
thought that as a matter of expedience it might not be wise to serve
under Richard" (Edmund Heward, *Matthew Hale* [1972], p. 56).

14. Matthew Hale, *The History and Analysis of the Common
Law of England* (1713), p. 72.

15. Runnington, in his introduction to Hale's *History and
Analysis,* pp. i-ii.

16. Hale, *History and Analysis,* p. 46. As an expression of the
law's place in society, Hale's ideas were in sympathetic keeping with
those of his contemporaries. On the same theme see Lord Halifax,
"The Character of a Trimmer," in *The Life and Letters of Sir
George Savile, Bart.,* ed. H. C. Foxcroft (1898), vol. 2, p. 282;
William Petyt, "Jus Parliamentarium," BM, Harley MS 7165, fol.
7v, and Inner Temple, Petyt MS 512/k, fol. 26v; and the
argument by Henry Pollexfen in the 1683 *quo warranto* proceedings against the City of London, BM, Hargrave MS 61, fol. 192v.

17. Halifax, "Trimmer," p. 282.

18. Torture, although not recognized under common law, was
still used in Westminster proceedings on the authority of the
prerogative; and, as there were no legal regulations for its control,
it could be, and was, irresponsibly employed. Nevertheless, as a
means of obtaining evidence and confessions, torture had been on
the decline. Under the Tudors it was used in political cases and in
cases involving murder, embezzlement, and theft. Under the early
Stuarts it was seemingly confined to matters involving political
offenses or witchcraft, and by 1660 (being one of the several law
reforms of the Interregnum not overturned by the Restoration) it
had altogether disappeared. See Donald Veall, *The Popular
Movement for Law Reform* (1970), pp. 25-27, 162, 227.

19. Maynard's presentation, at a conference with the Lords
(1671), of the Commons' position in *Skinner's Case* (Anchitell Grey,
Debates of the House of Commons, 1667-1694 [1763], vol. 1, p.
447). The case is discussed below, chap. 3, p. 81.

20. Hale, *History and Analysis,* p. 207.

21. See Michael Oakeshott's introductory essay to his edition of
Hobbes's *Leviathan,* p. xlv.

22. Halifax, "Trimmer," p. 301.

23. Runnington, perhaps betraying more of his own attitudes
than those of his subject, says that Hale's Protestantism was a
"religion which he most sincerely held to be part of the common
law of the country" (Runnington's edition of Hale's *History and
Analysis,* p. xliii).

24. Reference to the Humble Petition and Advice of 1657, in

204 "Observations in favour of Christian Liberty, drawn from ... Dr. Robert Saunderson, formerly Bishop of Lincoln," BM, Add. MS 5389.

25. Holdsworth, *History of English Law*, vol. 6, p. 138.

26. "Vox Populi, Vox Dei ..." (1681), BM, Egerton MS 2134, fol. 5v.

27. "The Misleading of the Common People ..." (c. 1683–85), BM, Sloane MS 2753/1, fol. 16v.

28. J. G. A. Pocock, *The Ancient Constitution and the Feudal Law* (1957), p. 156.

29. BM, Add. MS 5847, fol. 177.

30. "The Great and Weighty Considerations Relating to the Duke of York ... Considered" (1680), BM, Add. MS 22,589, p. 14.

31. "Concerning Papists & Protestants" (c. 1685), BM, Sloane MS 2903/2, fols. 22–22v. Halifax was another who distinguished between Catholic and Protestant in legal-property terms ("Trimmer," p. 317).

32. John Price, "The Designed Loyaltie of the Renowned Generall George Monck ... ," BM, Harley MS 4178, fol. 81.

33. BM, Hargrave MS 61, fol. 117.

34. "A Speech Intended to have been spoken, by a member of the house of Commons ..." (1675), BM, Sloane MS 664, fol. 219.

35. "The Dutchess of Yorks Reasons for her turning Roman Catholick" (1670), BM, Add. MS 6703, fol. 42.

36. Coke, *Tenth Reports,* p. 42. Halifax, echoing Coke (although relying on a somewhat dramatic metaphor) makes the same point at the end of the century. In his discussion "Of Fundamentals" he asks whether the common law "doth not hover in the clouds like the prerogative, and bolteth out like lightning, to be made use of for some particular occasion?" (Lord Halifax, "Political, Moral and Miscellaneous Thoughts and Reflections," in *The Life and Letters of Sir George Savile, Bart.,* vol. 2, p. 496).

37. Samuel E. Thorne, *Sir Edward Coke* (1957), p. 7.

38. The difficulty the seventeenth-century common-law mind had in perceiving the feudal origins of English law is carefully demonstrated by Pocock throughout *The Ancient Constitution and the Feudal Law.*

39. This was not the same thing as the limitation upon legal memory which was fixed at the beginning of the reign of Richard I (1189). See Hale, *History and Analysis,* p. 4.

40. PRO, SP 9/3. Commonplace books were alphabetically arranged legal notebooks, kept by practitioners and students, which set forth writs, statistics, precedents, and principles of law. The material in them was usually gathered from learning exercises

at the Inns of Court, notes taken during the progress of actual
cases, and private readings. See Wilfrid Prest, *The Inns of Court under Elizabeth I and the Early Stuarts, 1590-1640* (1972), pp. 131-32.

41. "Of the Alteration Amendment or Reformation of the Lawes of England" (1665), BM, Harley MS 711, fol. 373v.

42. "Reflections on Mr. Hobbs," BM, Hargrave MS 96, fols. 11, 55.

43. Hale, "Alteration . . . of the Lawes," BM, Harley MS 711, fols. 374-374v.

44. Reason (or, more precisely, "natural reason") as an alternative to experience is discussed in chapter 3, "Control of the Law," and in chapter 4, "The Instruments of Control."

45. "Alteration . . . of the Lawes," BM, Harley MS 711, fols. 373-373v.

46. Ibid., fol. 392.

47. Coke, *Fourth Institutes,* p. 25.

48. J. W. Gough, *Fundamental Law in English Constitutional History* (1955), pp. 42-43; Gray, introduction to Hale's *History of the Common Law,* pp. xxiii-xxvi; Veall, *The Popular Movement for Law Reform,* pp. 66-67; C. P. Gooch, *Political Thought in England: Bacon to Halifax* (1915), p. 44.

49. Veall, *The Popular Movement for Law Reform,* ix.

50. See Christopher Hill, "The Norman Yoke," in his *Puritanism and Revolution* (1958), in which it is demonstrated that the radical reformers regarded law, and the social order that the law supported, as part of the Norman yoke of oppression.

51. "A New Year's Gift for Parliament & Army" (1651), quoted by Veall, *The Popular Movement for Law Reform,* p. 78.

52. C. H. Firth, ed., *The Clarke Papers* (1894), vol. 2, p. 219.

53. Veall believes that the failure of the reform movement is attributable to the "insufficient will of those in authority" (*The Popular Movement for Law Reform,* p. 239).

54. See Brian Levack, *The Civil Lawyers in England* (1973).

55. Pocock, *The Ancient Constitution and the Feudal Law,* chaps. 2 and 7.

56. Sir Joseph Williamson, secretary of state and keeper of the state papers through most of this period, recorded in one of his many notebooks that "Acts of P. are either Declarative of the Common Law, or . . . Introductive of a New Law" (SP 9/22).

57. Halifax, "Trimmer," p. 322 n. (quoting Lord Delamere); see also ibid., p. 286.

58. "Alteration . . . of the Lawes," BM, Harley MS 711, fol. 375.

59. This may help to explain why Hale's interest in reform was

206   largely without effect after his elevation to the bench. Veall (*The Popular Movement for Law Reform,* pp. 98-99) asserts Hale's continuing interest in law reform after becoming a judge, but Gerald Hurst, writing earlier, is unconvinced (Gerald Hurst, "Sir Matthew Hale," *Law Quarterly Review* [1954], p. 345). Gray appears closest to the truth when he writes that after the Restoration "Hale tried to keep a cautious version of the reformist spirit alive" (Gray, introduction to Hale's *History of the Common Law,* p. xxx).

60. "Alteration . . . of the Lawes," BM, Harley MS 711, fols. 393v and 395v.

61. Hale, *The History of the Common Law of England,* ed. Gray (1971), p. 18.

62. "Alteration . . . of the Lawes," BM, Harley MS 711, fol. 396.

63. Ibid., fol. 397.

64. Gray would probably disagree. His investigation of Coke and Hale leads him to conclude that "Hale's bias was prolegislative, as Coke's was antilegislative" (Gray, introduction to Hale's *History of the Common Law,* p. xxix).

65. Coke, *Eighth Reports,* p. 118.

66. For the controversy over Coke and judicial review see T. F. T. Plucknett, "Bonham's Case and Judicial Review," *Harvard Law Review* (1926); S. E. Thorne, "Dr. Bonham's Case," *Law Quarterly Review* (1938); Gough, *Fundamental Law,* chap. 3; and Raoul Berger, "Doctor Bonham's Case," *University of Pennsylvania Law Review* (1969). Also note R. W. K. Hinton, "English Constitutional Theories from Sir John Fortescue to Sir John Eliot," *English Historical Review* (1960).

67. "Reasons why protestant dissenters aught to concurre for the legal establishment of the late liberty" (1687), PRO, SP 8/1, pt. 2, fols. 138-40.

68. From "A common place book of 'remarkable sentences' compiled by an unknown editor during the reign of Charles II," BM, Harley MS 4686, fol. 6v. The equation of law and contract was not new. The idea, if not this particular sentence, may be attributable to the Sophists of classical antiquity. See Gough, *Social Contract,* p. 12.

69. On the controversial relationship between Coke and economic liberalism see D. O. Wagner, "Coke and the Rise of Economic Liberalism," *Economic History Review* (1935); S. E. Thorne, *Sir Edward Coke* (1957); C. Hill, *Intellectual Origins of the English Revolution* (1965); and B. Malament, "The 'Economic Liberalism' of Sir Edward Coke," *Yale Law Journal* (1967).

70. Debate on new coronation oath, 25 March 1689, in Anchitell

Grey, *Debates of the House of Commons* (1763), vol. 9, p. 196. Also in B. Behrens, "The Whig Theory of the Constitution in the Reign of Charles II," *Cambridge Historical Journal* (1941), p. 45.

71. Cf. Pocock, "Burke and the Ancient Constitution," *Historical Journal* (1960), p. 141, n. 28, reversing his earlier suggestion (*The Ancient Constitution and the Feudal Law,* pp. 241-43) that Hale's adaptive common law had disappeared by the time of the Revolution.

72. Prest, *Inns of Court,* pp. 41, 115-16, 209.

73. Langton's reminiscences, cited by Runnington in his introduction to Hale's *History and Analysis,* p. viii.

74. Holdsworth, *History of English Law,* vol. 5, p. 425, n. 2, quoting *Coke on Littleton,* 235b.

75. BM, Hargrave MS 394.

76. Prest, "Legal Education of the Gentry at the Inns of Court, 1560-1640," *Past & Present* (1967), p. 39, quotes Prynne's complaint about "the declining diligent study and publicke exercises of the Common Law ... now overmuch neglected, discontinued or perfunctorily performed."

77. Prest, *Inns of Court,* especially chaps. 6 and 7; Holdsworth, *History of English Law,* vol. 6, pp. 481-93; and Holdsworth, *Some Lessons from Our Legal History* (1928), pp. 167-68.

78. Hale, "Reflections ... on Mr. Hobbs," BM, Hargrave MS 96, fol. 13.

79. Ibid., fol. 55v.

80. Prest, *Inns of Court,* p. 221.

81. Sir Peter Leicester, in his grand-jury charges at Quarter Sessions, frequently cited Coke in support of the powers of the Crown. See Elizabeth M. Halcrow, ed., *Charges to the Grand Jury ... by Sir Peter Leicester* (1953).

82. "The Protestant Admirer," BM, Add. MS 22,589, p. 2.

83. Some commentators went even further. In a commonplace book of "remarkable sentences" compiled by an unknown editor during the reign of Charles II, it is stated categorically that "Lawyers are not to be depended on" (BM, Harley MS 4636, fol. 20).

84. "Brief Reflections upon the Inconveniences attending wilful and malicious Forgery and Perjury ..." (1685), *Somers Tracts,* vol. 9, pp. 246-47.

85. John Kenyon, *The Popish Plot* (1972), pp. 256-57.

86. "Of the Alteration Amendment or Reformation of the Lawes of England" (1665), BM, Harley MS 711, fol. 391v.

87. "A Letter to Monsieur Van. B— — de M— — ..." (1675), PRO, PRO 30/24/6A/304.

88. PRO, SP 9/247/67.

208

89. "Fiat Justitia ... ," BM, Hargrave MS 401, fol. 63.

90. "Discourse on the Study of the Laws," BM, Hargrave MS 394, fol. 12v.

91. "The Last Speech and Carriage of the Lord Russel ..." (1683), PRO, SP 9/251/189, p. 4.

92. Burnett, *Life of Hale,* pp. 144-45.

93. Ibid., pp. 2-3.

94. Hale, *History and Analysis,* p. 176.

95. BM, Harley MS 4636, fol. 13v.

96. BM, Hargrave MS 149, fols. 2v-3.

97. "A Treatise about Government writ by John Lord Berkley," BM, Sloane MS 3828/9, fol. 89.

98. Delamere was being tried under a Lord Steward's commission because James II's first and only Parliament, having been prorogued, was not then in session and would, as it happened, never meet again.

99. PRO, SP 9/251/192, p. 13.

100. See E. W. Ives, "The Reputation of the Common Lawyer in English Society, 1450-1550," *University of Birmingham Historical Journal* (1959-60), in which the same point is made at some length for an earlier period.

CHAPTER 2. ANALOGUES AND METAPHORS

1. A draft work on "the rights of the Commons of England ... ," Inner Temple, Petyt MS 512/M, fols. 160-160v.

2. "Jus Parliamentarium," BM, Harley MS 7165, fol. 5; Inner Temple, Petyt MS 512/K, fols. 4v-5.

3. Inner Temple, Petyt MS 512/K, fol. 7v.

4. Inner Temple, Petyt MS 512/M, fol. 160v.

5. The case is discussed in greater detail in chapter 3, "Control of the Law."

6. PRO, PRO 30/24/6A/306; BM, Stowe MS 182/13, fol. 46.

7. In December 1682, upon the death of his father, Daniel became the second earl of Nottingham.

8. "Treatise on Parliaments," BM, Add. MS 36,087, fols. 64v and 67.

9. PRO, SP 9/22, fol. 263.

10. PRO, SP 9/251/184, p. 2.

11. "A dictionary of law terms ... ," compiled by Watkin Owen (1681), BM, Add. MS 19,762, p. 70.

12. Ibid.

13. "Fiat Justitia ... ," BM, Hargrave MS 401, fol. 63.

14. Address to the House of Lords, 5 February 1672, PRO, PRO 30/24/4/238. As another example of the same, see the king's

speech to both houses of Parliament in the following year, PRO, PRO 30/24/5/265.

15. A draft work "on the successive governments in England," Inner Temple, Petyt MS 512/H, fol. 257.

16. "Treatise of the Nature of Lawes in Generall ... ," BM, Hargrave MS 485, fol. 36.

17. Anchitell Grey, *Debates of the House of Commons* (1763), vol. 2, p. 21.

18. PRO, PRO 30/24/5/292, p. 13.

19. "Some Memoirs on a Sober Essay for a Just Vindication of ... Shaftesbury" (1681), PRO, PRO 30/24/6A/375, p. 11.

20. BM, Stowe MS 305, fol. 44v.

21. "The Use of the Lawe," BM, Harley MS 1201, fol. 1.

22. John Locke, *The Second Treatise of Government,* ed. J. W. Gough (1966), §§ 25-51.

23. Ibid., § 45.

24. Ibid., § 27.

25. In this respect see Locke, chap. 2, "Of the State of Nature," § 6, in which he speaks of each man's "life, health, liberty, or possessions" as part of God's property. Also see Richard McKeon, "The Development of the Concept of Property in Political Philosophy," *International Journal of Ethics* (1938).

26. Locke, *Second Treatise,* § 28.

27. See J. G. A. Pocock, "Machiavelli, Harrington, and English Political Ideologies in the Eighteenth Century," *William and Mary Quarterly* (1965).

28. "A Letter to Monsieur Van. B— — de M— — at Amsterdam ... " (1675), PRO, PRO 30/24/6A/304.

29. "A Specimen of the State of the Nation ... ," PRO, SP/9/52, p. 2.

30. As an example of property as an almost universal metaphor, Petyt, in his "Jus Parliamentarium," spoke of the law itself as "the hedge and fence about the liberty of the subjects" (BM, Harley MS 7165, fol. 6).

31. "Concerning the Oaths of Allegiance and Supremacy ... " (c. 1700), BM, Stowe MS 293, p. 5.

32. Elizabeth M. Halcrow, ed., *Charges to the Grand Jury at Quarter Sessions, 1660-1677, by Sir Peter Leicester* (Northwich Quarter Sessions, 19 April 1670), p. 62.

33. "Concerning the Oaths of Allegiance and Supremacy ... " (c. 1700), BM, Stowe MS 293, p. 7.

34. "Observations in favour of Christian Liberty, drawn from ... Dr. Robert Saunderson ... ," BM, Add. MS 5389, fol. 28.

35. "Concerning the Oaths of Allegiance and Supremacy ... " (c. 1700), BM, Stowe MS 293, fol. 4v.

210

36. Contract law in the seventeenth century was not yet fully developed. It was being put together from a variety of strands, although from *Slade's Case* (1602) the dominant strand was that of *assumpsit*.

37. PRO, PRO 30/24/238.

38. This was the argument advanced by Anthony Ascham in his *Tract on Marriage* (1647). On this point see Quentin Skinner, "The Ideological Context of Hobbes's Political Thought," *Historical Journal* (1966), p. 309.

39. "Concerning the Oaths of Allegiance and Supremacy ..." (c. 1700), BM, Stowe MS 293, fol. 19.

40. Ibid., fol. 20.

41. For a completely different interpretation, one that holds that it was Locke's political rationalism rather than the common-law mind which serves to explain 1688-89, see Pocock, *The Ancient Constitution and the Feudal Law* (1957), chap. 9.

42. For a discussion of the sixteenth- and seventeenth-century understanding of these "correspondences" see E. M. W. Tillyard, *The Elizabethan World Picture* (1943).

43. G. R. Elton, in a concise and well-stated notice of the debate, argues that the early parliaments were both judicial and political in nature. See his *"The Body of the Whole Realm"* (1969), pp. 1-12.

44. Matthew Hale, *History and Analysis,* p. 14.

45. "That the King hath power in his own Person to hear, and determine all kind of causes ... ," BM, Harley MS 4892/2, fol. 10.

46. "Humanum est Errare ... ," (1688), BM, Harley MS 6274, fol. 106v.

47. Alan Harding, *A Social History of English Law* (1966), p. 253.

48. B. Behrens, "The Whig Theory of the Constitution in the Reign of Charles II," *Cambridge Historical Journal* (1941), p. 58.

49. "A Discourse ... setting forth the jurisdiction of the Lords and the power of the Commons ..." (1671), BM, Stowe MS 299, fol. 41v.

50. Hale, *History and Analysis,* p. 2.

51. BM, Harley MS 1243, fol. 233v.

52. Instructions for the "Parliament to be holden at Oxford the 21st of March" (1680), PRO, PRO 30/24/7/499.

53. Lord Halifax, "The Character of a Trimmer," in *The Life and Letters of Sir George Savile, Bart.,* ed. H. C. Foxcroft (1898), vol. 2, p. 342.

54. Ibid., p. 296.

55. PRO, SP 9/32.

56. J. P. Kenyon, ed., *The Stuart Constitution* (1966), pp. 62-63.

57. The earl of Salisbury, reporting the king's response to Cowell's assertions (1610) (quoted ibid., p. 12).

58. Ibid., p. 109.

59. G. R. Elton argues persuasively that the claims for an unregulated prerogative in the first part of the seventeenth century were aberrations and that the Tudors fully recognized the prerogative "as a department of common law" (G. R. Elton, "The Rule of Law in Sixteenth-Century England," in *Tudor Men and Institutions,* ed. A. J. Slavin [1972], p. 272).

60. "Jus Parliamentarium," BM, Harley MS 7165, fol. 7v.

61. BM, Hargrave MS 149, fol. 72v.

62. Hale, *History and Analysis,* p. 26.

63. BM, Add. MS 28,043, fol. 102.

64. PRO, PRO 30/24/5/242.

65. "The Third Part of No Protestant Plot ..." (1682), PRO, PRO 30/24/6A/382.

66. Inner Temple, Petyt MS 512/K, fols. 209-209v. See also Francis D. Wormuth, *The Royal Prerogative, 1603-1649* (1939), esp. chap. 4.

67. BM, Add. MS 15,623, fols. 70v-71.

68. "Some Considerations upon the Question whether the Parliament is dissolved by its prorogation for 15 months" (1673), BM, Harley MS 6810/6, fol. 103v.

69. BM, Harley MS 7165, fol. 14.

70. "The Third Part of the No Protestant Plot ..." (1682), PRO, PRO 30/24/6A/382. Also see remarks of Sergeant Maynard (1671) (Grey, *Debates of the House of Commons,* vol. 1, p. 446).

71. "... Shaftesbury in the courte of the Kings Bench ..." (1677), PRO 30/24/40/45. Also see "Lord Shaftesbury's Speech in the House of Lords upon the debate of Appointing a day for hearing Dr. Shirly's Cause. November 20, 1675," BM, Hargrave MS 149, fols. 2v-3.

72. Hale, *History and Analysis,* p. 46.

73. From a draft of *Reflections by the Lord Cheife Justice Hale on Mr. Hobbs his dialogue of the Law,* in which Hale goes on to say: "The Next age may as lightly depart from the Decisions of this Age, as this Age recedes from the Decisions of former Ages. And by this meanes the great use and advantage of Laws will be disappointed, namely Certaintie, Consonance to it Selfe, whereby Men may know how to demeane themselves or advice others in things to be don or omitted" (BM, Hargrave MS 96, fols. 37v-38).

74. PRO, SP 9/22.

75. G. R. Elton, introduction to John Neville Figgis, *The Divine*

212   *Right of Kings* (1965), p. xxi; Franklin Le Van Baumer, *The Early Tudor Theory of Kingship* (1940), p. 93.

76. James I, *The Political Works,* ed. C. H. McIlwain (1918), vol. 1, pp. 61, 63, 69.

77. Margaret Atwood Judson, *The Crisis of the Constitution* (1949), p. 20.

78. Further to this point see J. W. Gough, *The Social Contract* (1957), p. 51.

79. BM, Sloane MS 664, fol. 215v.

80. PRO, PRO 30/24/5/292, pp. 10-11.

81. *Somers Tracts,* vol. 7, p. 451.

82. BM, Add. MS 5847, fol. 177.

83. *Somers Tracts,* vol. 7, p. 452.

84. "A Letter to Monsieur Van. B— — de M— — ... by Denzell Lord Holles concerning the Government of England" (1676), PRO, PRO 30/24/6A/304; BM, Sloane MS 3828/22, fol. 218.

85. "The Price of Abdication," BM, Harley MS 6495/15, fol. 234.

86. "A Letter from a Freeholder ... ," PRO, SP 9/250/141.

87. Shaftesbury's speech in the House of Lords, 20 October 1675, PRO, PRO 30/24/5/292, p. 10; BM, Hargrave MS 149, fol. 6.

88. BM, Add. MS 27,989/3, fol. 18. Petty also made the point that it was kingship alone, the office and not the man, which was immune from wrongdoing.

89. Quoted in "Old Englands legal Constitution," PRO, PRO 30/24/47/6.

90. "A Vindication of the Revolution ... ," BM, Stowe MS 291, fol. 4; BM, Harley MS 6810/6, fol. 102.

91. "Reflections by the Lord Cheife Justice Hale on Mr. Hobbs his dialogue of the Law," BM, Hargrave MS 96, fol. 18.

92. Halifax, "Trimmer," p. 289.

93. "Jus Parliamentarium," Inner Temple, Petyt MS 512/K, fol. 220.

CHAPTER 3. CONTROL OF THE LAW

1. Lord Macaulay, *History of England,* ed. C. H. Firth, vol. 3, p. 1234.

2. G. M. Trevelyan, *The English Revolution* (1965), p. 71. Also see Michael Landon, *The Triumph of the Lawyers* (1970).

3. See George L. Cherry, "The Legal and Philosophical Position of the Jacobites, 1688-1689," *Journal of Modern History* (1950).

4. G. R. Elton might well be one to reject this distinction because of his belief in a Tudor commitment to constitutionalism.

Yet he has also suggested that the Tudor opportunity to control the law might be a more important issue (G. R. Elton, "The Rule of Law in Sixteenth-Century England," in *Tudor Men and Institutions,* ed. A. J. Slavin [1972], p. 283). Joel Hurstfield, on the other hand, has long believed in the existence of a Tudor despotism. See his "Was There a Tudor Despotism after All?," *Transactions of the Royal Historical Society* (1967). Also note the mediate view of William H. Dunham, Jr., "Regal Power and the Rule of Law," *Journal of British Studies* (1964).

5. See, for example, "Jus Parliamentarium," in which Petyt records some of the effusive obeisances to the law made by James I and Charles I (Inner Temple, Petyt MS 512/K, fol. 7).

6. BM, Harley MS 4636, fol. 27.

7. "Proceedings ... by a Writt of Quo Warranto against the City of London," BM, Hargrave MS 61, fol. 152v. Also see Jennifer Levin, *The Charter Controversy in the City of London* (1969).

8. See chap. 2, pp. 48-52.

9. BM, Stowe MS 305, fol. 46.

10. BM, Egerton MS 2543, fol. 264.

11. Inner Temple, Petyt MS 512/N, particularly fol. 43.

12. *Incepta de Juribus Coronae,* Lincoln's Inn, Hargrave MS 4, p. 36.

13. James I, *The Political Works,* ed. C. H. McIlwain (1918), vol.1, p. 63.

14. "Speech of [Heneage] Finch to the Convention ..." (1688), BM, Stowe MS 364, fols. 139v-140.

15. Lord Halifax, "The Character of a Trimmer," in *The Life and Letters of Sir George Savile, Bart.,* ed. H. C. Foxcroft (1898), vol. 2, p. 285.

16. BM, Add. MS 36,087, fol. 128.

17. "Some Reflections upon his Highness the Prince of Orange's Declaration," *Somers Tracts,* vol. 9, p. 288.

18. "Preparatory Notes Touching the Rights of the Crown," Lincoln's Inn, Hargrave MS 9, chap. 2, pp. 13-14.

19. *The Proceedings in the House of Commons, Touching the Impeachment of Edward, Late Earl of Clarendon, Lord High-Chancellour of England, Anno 1667* (1700), pp. 88-89.

20. On this point see Corinne Comstock Weston, "The Theory of Mixed Monarchy under Charles I and After," *English Historical Review* (1960).

21. Sir Edward Coke, *Fourth Institutes.*

22. BM, Add. MS 28,043, fol. 102.

23. See, for example, Inner Temple, Petyt MS 538/4, and Burnet, BM, Stowe MS 305, fol. 46.

24. BM, Harley MS 1234, fol. 246v.

214

25. BM, Hargrave MS 492, fol. 12.

26. Hale, "Preparatory notes touching the Rights of the Crown," Lincoln's Inn, Hargrave MS 9, chap. 9, p. 7 (also chap. 7, p. 2).

27. Description by Conway Davis in the "Summary List of Petyt Collection" (typescript) at the Inner Temple.

28. Inner Temple, Petyt MS 512/N, fols. 6v and 132.

29. Inner Temple, Petyt MS 512/K, fol. 8v.

30. Lincoln's Inn, Hargrave MS 9, chap. 9, p. 6.

31. Roland G. Usher, "James I and Sir Edward Coke," *English Historical Review* (1903), p. 673, citing Sir Julius Caesar's notes in Lansdowne MS 160, fols. 425, 426, and 428.

32. Usher, p. 664, citing Coke, *Twelfth Reports,* p. 65.

33. Usher, p. 669, citing Caesar's notes in Lansdowne MS 160, fols. 423-24.

34. Cf. Hale, who believed that "by the constitution of this kingdom, all jurisdiction is derived from the king" ("Narrative of the Jurisdiction of the Lords House in Point of Reversal of Judgments Sentences or Decrees," Lincoln's Inn, Hargrave MS 6, p. 1).

35. William Cobbett et al., eds., *Collection of State Trials . . .* (1809), vol. 5, pp. 1085-86.

36. BM, Add. MS 27,989/3, fol. 17.

37. BM, Add. MS 10,118, p. 22.

38. Alfred F. Havighurst, "The Judiciary and Politics in the Reign of Charles II," *Law Quarterly Review* (1950), p. 250. Also see Havighurst, "James II and the Twelve Men in Scarlet," *Law Quarterly Review* (1953).

39. BM, Add. MS 27,989/3, fol. 17v.

40. W. S. Holdsworth, *The Influence of the Legal Profession on the Growth of the English Constitution* (1924), p. 15.

41. Committed along with Shaftesbury were three other peers, Buckingham, Salisbury, and Wharton.

42. BM, Stowe MS 182/13, fol. 46.

43. PRO, PRO 30/24/6A/306.

44. Ibid.

45. BM, Stowe MS 182/13, fol. 46v.

46. *Journals of the House of Lords,* vol. 12, p. 680.

47. BM, Hargrave MS 149, fol. 2v.

48. BM, Hargrave MS 115. See also Hargrave MS 100, a letter rejecting the thesis of *The Case Stated Concerning the Judicature of the House of Peers in the Point of Appeals,* another of Petyt's efforts.

49. William Cobbett, ed., *Parliamentary History of England* (1809), vol. 4, pp. 422-23.

50. ". . . Concerning the Powers of Judicature on the King's

Council and in Parliament," BM, Hargrave MS 492, fol. 42v.

51. The dispute over control of money bills raged outside Parliament as well as within. Two short tracts illustrating the debate are to be found in the Stowe MSS. One (BM, Stowe MS 299) argues that "the Lords are Partners (or at least ought to be) in the Gifts of Aids to the King" (fol. 46). Another (BM, Stowe MS 300) suggests that "it is the Commons grant in all ayds and not the Lords" (fol. 2). Hale, too, was interested in the question, but only in the larger sense of Parliament's control of finance. He wrote that it was "most certaine and unquestionable by the Law of England no common ayde or Tax can be imposed uppon the Subjects without consent in Parliament." Beyond that, provided the king did not use his dispensing power to get round the prohibition, the question of Commons versus Lords, on this issue, was a matter indifferent to the law (BM, Hargrave MS 96, fol. 42v).

52. *The Proceedings in the House of Commons, Touching the Impeachment of Edward, Late Earl of Clarendon, Lord High-Chancellour of England, Anno 1667* (1700), p. 93.

53. See Clayton Roberts, *The Growth of Responsible Government in Stuart England* (1966), p. 170.

54. Later Sir John, chief justice of the Common Pleas, the same who presided in *Thomas* v. *Sorrell.* See chapter 4, "The Instruments of Control."

55. BM, Stowe MS 368, fol. 75.

56. *Proceedings ... Touching the Impeachment of ... Clarendon,* p. 82; BM, Stowe MS 368, 75v.

57. Inner Temple, Petyt MS 512/L, fols. 78-78v.

58. Ibid., fol. 33.

59. Inner Temple, Petyt MS 512/M, fol. 4v.

CHAPTER 4. THE INSTRUMENTS OF CONTROL

1. 1 Gul. and Mar., sess. 2, c. 2 (*Statutes of the Realm,* vol. 6, pp. 142 ff.).

2. Not all of the relevant penal laws were suspended. The Test Acts of 1673 and 1678 were still to apply.

3. Toleration did not extend to all Protestant Dissenters from the Church of England. It was proffered only to those who would admit to the doctrine of the Trinity. Unitarians were therefore denied relief.

4. BM, Harley MS 4139, fol. 106v; Add. MS 5540, fol. 45.

5. BM, Stowe MS 307, fol. 4.

6. Ibid.

7. Ibid.

8. Charles II is sometimes credited with two declarations of

216   indulgence, one in 1662 and the other in 1672; but, as J. P. Kenyon has properly noted, only the second was an actual attempt to suspend the execution of the penal laws: "The first was a request to Parliament to pass a bill; the second was a suspension by proclamation of existing legislation" (J. P. Kenyon, ed., *The Stuart Constitution* [1966], p. 402a). James II issued two declarations, the first in April 1687, the second a year later.

9. James's Declaration of Indulgence, 4 April 1687 (cited in Kenyon, ed., *The Stuart Constitution,* p. 411).

10. "William Penn's Speech to the King at Windsor May 24th 1687 . . . ," BM, Add. MS 5540, fol. 43.

11. "Preparatory Notes touching the Rights of the Crown," Lincoln's Inn, Hargrave MS 9, chap. 12, p. 95.

12. Ibid. See also PRO, PRO 30/24/6B/425.

13. Lincoln's Inn, Hargrave MS 9, chap. 12, p. 95. The king's pardon, when properly used, was of so purgative a nature that it cured the guilt as well as the punishment. Hale notes that "it hath been held, that to call a man *thief* after his pardon of theft is actionable" (ibid.).

14. BM, Stowe MS 307, fol. 13.

15. PRO, SP 9/52, p. 19. Danby maintained that the "King may pardon any parliamentary attainder" (*BM,* Add. MS 28,043, fol. 102v). Strictly speaking, this was a different matter. The king had greater control of attainder, since no bill could pass without his consent.

16. PRO, PRO 30/24/6B/425.

17. As a matter of practice, convicted traitors were not pardoned, but the pardoning of a specific part of the sentence of a peer convicted of treason was a commonplace. Hale, citing Selden, wrote that the king "cannot alter the sentence or Judgment upon a person condemned but he may pardon any part of it & does pardon usualy all the Sentence upon a Noble Man being a Traitor but the beheading" (BM, Hargrave MS 136).

18. PRO, PRO 30/24/6B/425.

19. Matthew Hale, "Preparatory Notes touching the Rights of the Crown," Lincoln's Inn, Hargrave MS 9, chap. 9, p. 4.

20. BM, Stowe MS 304, fol. 171; Harley MS 1200, fol. 193; Harley MS 4139, fol. 98.

21. William Cobbett, ed., *Parliamentary History* (1808-20), vol. 4, pp. 261-62.

22. Historical Manuscripts Commission, *Seventh Report* (1879), Appendix, pp. 167-68.

23. *Journals of the House of Commons,* vol. 9, p. 758.

24. *Inner Temple,* Petyt MS 512/K, fol. 154v. See also the remarks in February 1689 of the common-law judges Dolben and

Levinz (Historical Manuscripts Commission, *Twelfth Report* [1890], Appendix, pt. 6, p. 29).

25. Holt, shortly thereafter (17 April 1689), was appointed lord chief justice of the King's Bench.

26. Historical Manuscripts Commission, *Seventh Report*, Appendix, p. 759.

27. "A Letter to a Bishop concerning the present Settlement . . . ," *Somers Tracts,* vol. 9, p. 375.

28. PRO, SP 9/6.

29. "Some Considerations upon the Question whether the Parliament is dissolved by its prorogation for 15 months," BM, Harley MS 6810/6, fol. 104.

30. Lincoln's Inn, Hargrave MS 4, pp. 85-86.

31. "A Letter from a Freeholder, to . . . [those] who have Votes in the Choice of Parliament-Men," PRO, SP 9/250/141.

32. BM, Harley MS 6810/6, fol. 104.

33. See the discussion in Paul Birdsall, " 'Non-Obstante' — A Study of the Dispensing Power of English Kings," *Essays in History and Political Theory in Honor of Charles Howard McIlwain* (1936), pp. 60-61.

34. "An Argument for the Kings Dispensing power in K-James the 2ds time," BM, Stowe MS 304, fol. 171v.

35. *Thomas* v. *Sorrell,* Exchequer Chamber [1674].

36. BM, Hargrave MS 339/3, fol. 35.

37. Ibid., fol. 37v.

38. Ibid., fol. 33.

39. Ibid., fol. 31.

40. BM, Hargrave MS 339/3, fol. 35.

41. Lincoln's Inn, Hargrave MS 4, p. 85.

42. BM, Hargrave MS 339/3, fol. 38.

43. "A short discourse in defence of the King's power of Dispensation . . . ," BM, Sloane MS 2753/5.

44. Ibid., fol. 53.

45. BM, Hargrave MS 339/3. fols. 31v-32.

46. BM, Sloane MS 2753/5, fol. 61.

47. Ibid., fol. 60. See also BM, Stowe MS 304, fols. 171-171v, which makes the same argument.

48. BM, Hargrave MS 339/3, fol. 32.

49. *Journals of the House of Commons,* vol. 9, p. 257.

50. Ibid., p. 252.

51. Ibid., p. 256.

52. On the general use of the prerogative in ecclesiastical matters, see E. F. Churchill, "The Dispensing Power of the Crown in Ecclesiastical Affairs," *Law Quarterly Review* (1922).

53. BM, Add. MS 5540, fol. 45; Harley MS 4139, fol. 106v.

218

54. "A draft work ... on the successive governments in England," Inner Temple, Petyt MS 512/H, fol. 12.

55. Lincoln's Inn, Hargrave MS 2, p. 10; Hargrave MS 9, chap. 2, p. 12.

56. Matthew Hale, *Common Law* (1820), pp. 72, 73, 91–92.

57. Ibid., pp. 83–84.

58. BM, Add. MS 10,118, p. 16.

59. Christopher Hill, "The Norman Yoke," in his *Puritanism and Revolution* (1958).

60. "A draft work ... on the successive governments in England," Inner Temple, Petyt MS 512/H, fol. 60v.

61. Lincoln's Inn, Hargrave MS 2, p. 13.

62. Hale, *Common Law,* p. 112.

63. J. G. A. Pocock, *The Ancient Constitution and the Feudal Law* (1957).

64. Donald Veall, *The Popular Movement for Law Reform* (1970).

65. See, for example, "Jus Parliamentarium," Inner Temple, Petyt MS 512/K, fol. 3v.

66. W. S. Holdsworth speaks to this point in *Some Lessons from Our Legal History* (1928), p. 71.

67. Inner Temple, "Jus Parliamentarium," Petyt MS 512/K, fol. 73v.

68. "Treatise on Parliament," BM, Add. MS 36,087, fol. 125.

69. "A Tract on the Leading Principles of the Law of Nature," Lincoln's Inn, Hargrave MS 13, Lib. 1, p. 1.

70. Sir Robert Filmer, *Patriarcha,* ed. Peter Laslett (1949), p. 101.

71. PRO, SP 9/251/184, p. 6.

72. See, for example, S. R. Gardiner, *History of England* (1883–84), vol. 2, p. 39; C. P. Gooch, *Political Thought in England: Bacon to Halifax* (1915), p. 46; D. L. Keir, *The Constitutional History of Modern Britain* (1938), p. 198. See also BM, Add. MS 17,022.

73. Hale, *Common Law,* pp. 27, 68.

74. "Preparatory Notes touching the Rights of the Crown," Lincoln's Inn, Hargrave MS 9, chap. 9, p. 3.

75. Hale, *Common Law,* pp. 69–70.

76. Lord Halifax, "The Character of a Trimmer," in *The Life and Letters of Sir George Savile, Bart.,* ed. H. C. Foxcroft (1898), vol. 2, p. 285.

77. Inner Temple, "Jus Parliamentarium," Petyt MS 512/K, fols. 72v, 116.

78. Ibid., fols. 72v, 116, chap. 2, passim, and fol. 135. The opposite view, in a circumstance of practical necessity, was adopted

by counsel in the earl of Shaftesbury's case. There it was argued
that "the construction of all acts of Parliament is given to the
Courts at Westminster and accordingly they have Judged of the
validity of acts of Parliament" (PRO, PRO 30/24/6A/306).

79. Lincoln's Inn, Hargrave MS 9, chap. 13, p. 1; also chap. 7,
pp. 1-2.

80. "A draft work . . . on the successive governments in England," Inner Temple, Petyt MS 512/H, fol. 194; see also "A draft
work . . . correcting . . . recent English historians and writers on
Parliament," Petyt MS 512/N, fol. 143.

81. "Reflections . . . on Mr. Hobbs his dialogue of the law,"
BM, Hargrave MS 96, fol. 24.

82. "Preparatory Notes touching the Rights of the Crown,"
Lincoln's Inn, Hargrave MS 9, chap. 9, p. 10.

83. "A draft work . . . on the successive governments in England," Inner Temple, Petyt MS 512/H, fol. 12v. See also BM,
Add. MS 5540, fol. 45v.

84. "Reflections . . . on Mr. Hobbs his dialogue of the Law,"
BM, Hargrave MS 96, fol. 24.

85. BM, Harley MS 6810/6, fol. 104.

86. See "Londons Liberties: or, A Learned Argument of Law
and Reason . . ." (1682), BM, Hargrave MS 179, fol. 227v, wherein Coke's equation of right reason and the common law is cited
and approved.

87. BM, Harley MS 711 (second tract). It is quite possible that
the tract was written by Hale.

88. Ibid., fol. 382.

89. BM, Add. MS 19,762, p. 75.

90. "Reflections . . . on Mr. Hobbs his dialogue of the Law,"
BM, Hargrave MS 96, fol. 12; also fols. 31v-32.

91. BM, Hargrave MS 61, fols. 100-100v.

92. See H. F. Jolowicz, *Lectures on Jurisprudence* (1963), p. 99.

93. BM, Hargrave MS 96, fols. 46v-47.

94. Ibid., fols. 5v-8.

95. See Daniel J. Boorstin, *The Mysterious Science of the Law*
(1941).

96. "Cabala, or an Impartial Account of the Non-Conformists'
Private Designs . . ." (1663), *Somers Tracts,* vol. 7, p. 580.

CHAPTER 5. RETREAT FROM DISORDER

1. Although the practice of beginning a reign at the exact
moment of termination of its immediate predecessor was not
regularized until the sixteenth century, it was known as early as
1483. Edward V began his brief reign on the same day as his father,

220   Edward IV, died (9 April 1483). And if one allows for a new reign beginning on the day following its predecessor, the custom of continuity can be dated back to 1307. See F. M. Powicke and E. B. Fryde, eds., *Handbook of British Chronology* (1961), pp. 2 ff.

2. The preamble to the "Act for abolishing the Kingly Office" declared Charles "to be Attainted of High Treason, whereby his Issue and Posterity, and all others pretending Title under him, are become uncapable ... of being King" (17 March 1648-49) (C. H. Firth and R. S. Rait, eds., *Acts and Ordinances of the Interregnum* [1911], vol. 2, p. 18). This, too, ran against the current of custom. In the private law, treason was sufficient to corrupt the blood and thus to bar an inheritance. The same rule had not, however, applied to the succession. Once the king was upon the throne, the corrupting effect of any attainder was automatically cured.

3. "A Brief History of the Succession ... ," BM, Add. MS 22,589, p. 10.

4. Firth and Rait, *Acts and Ordinances of the Interregnum,* vol. 2, pp. 19-20.

5. David Ogg, *England in the Reign of Charles II* (1963), vol. 1, p. 25.

6. 12 Car. II, c. 1 (*Statutes of the Realm,* vol. 5, p. 179).

7. Thomas Philips, "The Long Parliament Revived ... " (1661), *Somers Tracts,* vol. 7, p. 478.

8. Ibid.

9. Ibid., p. 479. The Convention's proclamation of the king, in May 1660, supports the theory of continuous kingship. It holds that "immediately upon the decease of our late sovereign Lord King Charles, the imperial crown of the realm of England, and of all the kingdoms, dominions, and rights belonging to the same, did by inherent birth-right, and lawful and undoubted succession, descend and come to his most excellent majesty Charles the Second, as being lineally, justly and lawfully, next heir of the blood-royal of this realm" (ibid., p. 430; William Cobbett, ed., *Parliamentary History* [1808-20], vol. 4, p. 34).

10. J. W. Gough, *Fundamental Law in English Constitutional History* (1955), pp. 145-58.

11. "The Long Parliament Revived ... " (1661), *Somers Tracts,* vol. 7, p. 478.

12. "A scandalous ... Pamphlet, entitled, The Valley of Baca" (1660), ibid., p. 399.

13. "The Several Speaches of Sir Edward Turner ... the tenth of May, 1661," ibid., p. 540.

14. Sir Joseph Williamson's Notebook records that the Convention was mindful of its precarious constitutional position and was therefore ready to offer Charles, immediately upon his arrival in England, "a Bill declaring the Continuance of this present parliament &c" (PRO, SP 9/22).

15. BM, Stowe MS 354, fol. 150.

16. 13 Car. II, c. 7 (*Statutes of the Realm,* vol. 5, pp. 309 ff.).

17. Sir William Temple, *An Essay Upon the Original and Nature of Government* (1680), pp. 92-93.

18. BM, Sloane MS 2753/1, fol. 2v.

19. PRO, PRO 30/24/34/15; *Somers Tracts,* vol. 7, p. 396.

20. BM, Add. MS 27,402, fol. 134; *Somers Tracts,* vol. 7, p. 395.

21. "Alderman Bunce ... to the Lord Mayor, Aldermen, and Common Council of London ... " (1660), *Somers Tracts,* vol. 7, p. 409.

22. Anchitell Grey, *Debates of the House of Commons* (1763), vol. 1, p. 16. On this point see also *The Proceedings in the House of Commons, Touching the Impeachment of Edward, Late Earl of Clarendon, Lord High-Chancellour of England, Anno 1667* (1700), pp. 1-2.

23. BM, Stowe MS 368, fols. 26v-27.

24. Grey, *Debates of the House of Commons,* vol. 1, p. 36.

25. Ibid., p. 41. A conference between the two houses failed to change the Lords' position. They held firm to their initial resolve (ibid., p. 52; *Proceedings ... Touching the Impeachment ... of Clarendon,* p. 79).

26. Grey, *Debates of the House of Commons,* vol. 1, p. 21.

27. Ibid., p. 42.

28. "Common fame" suggested something more than mere ·rumor; but, as Serjeant Maynard pointed out in the debates, it fell substantially short of provable fact. "Common fame is no ground to accuse a Man where matter of Fact is not clear; To say an Evil is done, therefore this man hath done it, is strange in Morality, more in Logick" (*Proceedings ... Touching the Impeachment ... of Clarendon,* p.12). The House, nevertheless, was prepared to proceed. Number eight of those articles originally proposed is perhaps the best example of what many members found objectionable: "That he hath, in short time, gained to himself a greater estate than can be imagined to be lawfully gained in so short a time" (Grey, *Debates of the House of Commons,* vol. 1, p. 16).

29. Grey, *Debates of the House of Commons,* vol. 1, p. 8.

30. Ibid., p. 49.

31. Ibid.

32. Ibid., p. 41.

33. Ibid., p. 12.

34. Ibid., p. 49.

35. Ibid., p. 67.

36. The Commons' resolution to that effect was passed by a vote of 168 to 116 (ibid., vol. 2, p. 26).

37. Ibid.

38. Ibid., p. 61.

39. The diversion was the case of *Shirley* v. *Fagg.*

40. PRO, PRO 30/24/5/294.

41. Contemporary tracts made public many of the same arguments that were employed in the Lords. See, for example, "A Letter from a Person of Quality to his Friend in the Country" (1675), PRO, SP 9/247/53.

42. BM, Stowe MS 293, p. 18.

43. "Reasons against the Bill for the Test by the Earl of Shaftesbury (1675)," PRO, PRO 30/24/5/294.

44. See, for example, the protestation of Major General Harrison, PRO, SP 9/246/40.

45. BM, Stowe MS 182/5, fols. 18v–19. On this point see also the earlier protestation of several Lords for a dissolution of Parliament dated 22 November 1675 (PRO, PRO 30/24/5/292).

46. BM, Stowe MS 182/5, fols. 18v–19.

47. *The Young Man's plea, or the Arguments of all those English men that are between the age of 21 & 37 years for the dissolution of this present parliament, who by reason of their non-age were not capable of giving their votes in the Election* (BM, Stowe MS 354, especially fol. 133).

48. BM, Hargrave MS 149, fol. 35.

49. Ibid., fol. 36.

50. For a survey of much of this constitutional theorizing as it appeared in the contemporary pamphlet literature, see Carolyn Edie, "Succession and Monarchy," *American Historical Review* (1965), and O. W. Furley, "The Whig Exclusionists," *Cambridge Historical Journal* (1957). Both Edie and Furley, however, pay limited attention to the use of analogues and metaphors drawn from the private law.

51. Remarks by Major Beake in the House of Commons, 11 May 1679, BM, Harley MS 4053, fols. 22–22v. The same sentiment was expressed in "The Third Part of No Protestant Plot . . . " (1682), PRO, PRO 30/24/6A/382, p. 14.

52. It could also be argued that it was the obligation of Englishmen to "transmit" Protestantism "as an inheritance to their posterity" (PRO, PRO 30/24/6A/382, p. 48).

53. Major Beake, 11 May 1679, BM, Harley MS 4053, fols. 22–22v.

54. Grey, *Debates of the House of Commons,* vol. 2, p. 16.

55. It had also become something of a commonplace to label as "jesuitical equivocation" any kind of specious reasoning or, indeed, any sort of unacceptable conclusion. The charge was not limited to Catholics. It held with equal force when leveled against Protestants. See, for example, "Great and Weighty Considerations Relating to the D, or Successor of the Crown, Humbly offer'd to the Kings most Excellent Majesty, And Both Houses of Parliament," BM, Add. MS 22,589.

56. From the proceedings of the Oxford Parliament, March 1680-81, PRO, SP 9/251/159.

57. "Great and Weighty Considerations ... ," BM, Add. MS 22,589, p. 2.

58. Ibid., p. 6.

59. "Alderman Bunce his Speech to the Lord Mayor, Aldermen, and Common Council of London ... " (1660), *Somers Tracts,* vol. 7, p. 410.

60. Further to this point see the excellent article by B. Behrens, "The Whig Theory of the Constitution in the Reign of Charles II," *Cambridge Historical Journal,* vol. 7 (1941).

61. "The White Rose ... ," BM, Add. MS 22,589, pp. 3 and 9. See also "Of Government. Mr. B. 1679," BM, Harley MS 6495/15, in which it is argued further, on the authority of Coke's *Fourth Institutes,* that "the Lords and Commons cannot assent in Parliament to any thing that tends to the Destruction of the King and his Crown to which they are sworne" (fol. 232v).

62. "The White Rose ... ," BM, Add. MS 22,589, p. 8.

63. Ibid., p. 4. See also "The Great and Weighty Considerations ... Considered ... ," BM, Add. MS 27,589, p. 4.

64. BM, Harley MS 4053, fol. 6v.

65. "Answer To a Letter, from a Gentleman of Quality in the Country to his Friend, relating to the point of Succession to the Crown," BM, Add. MS 22,589, p. 32.

66. "A Brief History of the Succession," ibid., p. 15. See also the supporting parliamentary arguments of Sir John Trevor, Paul Foley, and Secretary Jenkins in BM, Harley MS 4053, fols. 11 and 30v; and Hargrave MS 149, fols. 64v-65, respectively.

67. "Fiat Justitia ... ," BM, Hargrave MS 401, fol. 63.

68. "Devise" in the late seventeenth century was used to mean any kind of testamentary disposition of property. In a dictionary of law terms compiled by Watkin Owen in 1681, "devise" is defined as "where a man in his Testament giveth or bequeatheth his goods or his lands to an other after his decease" (BM, Add. MS 19,762, p. 32).

69. "The White Rose ... ," BM, Add. MS 22,589, p. 3.

70. From *An Act acknowledging and asserting the Right of Succession to the Imperial Crown of Scotland* (1681), PRO, SP 9/251/175.

71. "Answer To a Letter ... ," BM, Add. MS 22,589, p. 31.

72. *Observations Upon a late Libel* ... (1681), ed. Hugh MacDonald (1940), p. 33:

73. PRO, SP 9/247/56.

74. "Great and Weighty Considerations ... ," BM, Add. MS 22,589, p. 5.

75. Ibid.

224

76. "Sir Wm. Jones' Speech against the Duke of York, Nov. 1680," BM, Birch MS 4159, fol. 79.

77. "Great and Weighty Considerations ... Considered ... ," BM, Add. MS 22,589, p. 15.

78. "Of Government Mr. B. 1679," BM, Harley MS 6495/15.

79. Ibid., pp. 13 and 14.

80. BM, Harley MS 4053, fol. 30v. See also the similar remarks of Mr. Bennett on 27 April 1679, ibid.. fol. 3.

81. Sir William Jones spoke to this point in November 1680 (BM, Birch MS 4159, fol. 79). See, too, "Great and Weighty Considerations ... ," BM, Add. MS 22,589, p. 2.

82. Sir Hugh Cholmundely on 27 April 1679, BM, Harley MS 4053, fol. 4. Also see "Pereat Papa: or Reasons why a Presumptive Heir, or Popish Successor should not Inherit the Crown," BM, Add. MS 22,589, which combines the principle of incapacity with that of trust: "For 'tis presumable that he that succeeds in the Office of the Crown, should be Legally Adopted to execute so great a Trust" (p. 1).

83. "Answer To a Letter ... ," BM, Add. MS 22,589, p. 33.

84. "A Plea to the Duke's Answers," ibid., p. 3. See also "Answer To a Letter ... ," where it is alleged that "the succession of the Crown is the People's Right" (ibid., p. 32).

85. Mr. Hamden on 11 May 1679, BM, Harley MS 4053, fol. 21.

86. "Pereat Papa ... ," BM, Add. MS 22,589, pp. 2-3.

87. "The Protestant Admirer or, An Answer to the Vindication of a Popish Successor," ibid., p. 3.

88. "Great and Weighty Considerations ... ," ibid., p. 7.

89. PRO, PRO 30/24/7/498.

90. A letter in 1680 from Will Lawrence to Shaftesbury purports to establish that the king's eldest son is the lineal and lawful heir (PRO, PRO 30/24/6A/355).

91. J. P. Kenyon, "The Exclusion Crisis," *History Today* (1964).

CHAPTER 6. THE TRIUMPH OF THE LEGAL MIND

1. 16 Car. II, c. 1 (1664) (*Statutes of the Realm,* vol. 5, p. 513). Unlike the first Triennial Act (1641), this one had no provision for enforcement.

2. *Calendar of State Papers (Domestic),* 1685, p. 283.

3. BM, Add. MS 10,118, p. 23.

4. Ibid., p. 22. God was also at times referred to as the "Supreme Legislator." See Matthew Hale's "Treatise of the Nature of Lawes in Generall and touching the Law of Nature," BM, Harley MS 7159, fol. 6v.

5. BM, Add. MS 5540, fol. 45.

6. BM, Sloane MS 2281, fol. 71.

7. BM, Add. MS 5540, fol. 45.

8. See S. B. Chrimes, *English Constitutional Ideas in the Fifteenth Century* (1936), pp. 32–34; G. R. Elton, *The Tudor Constitution* (1962), p. 1; Mortimer Levine, *Tudor Dynastic Problems, 1460–1571* (1973), p. 34.

9. BM, Harley MS 7006, fol. 186.

10. "A Letter from a Freeholder to ... [those] who have Votes in the Choice of Parliament-Men," PRO, SP 9/250/141.

11. BM, Stowe MS 305, fol. 46.

12. Address from the Borough of Leominster, County of Hereford, *The London Gazette,* no. 2357, from Monday, 18 June, to Thursday, 21 June 1688.

13. "A Country Clergie-Man's Answer to the Reasons of the City Clergie-Man for not Reading the Declaration" (1688), BM, Add. MS 11,268, fol. 89.

14. Ibid., fol. 89v.

15. PRO, SP 8/1, pt. 2, fols. 224–27.

16. Ibid., fol. 246.

17. William Cobbett, ed., *Parliamentary History of England* (1809), vol. 5, pp. 9–10.

18. "Some Reflections upon his Highness the Prince of Orange's Declaration," *Somers Tracts,* vol. 9, p. 293.

19. BM, Add. MS 10,118, p. 21.

20. Cobbett, *Parliamentary History,* p. 10.

21. "A Letter to the Bishop of Sarum ... ," (1689), PRO, SP 9/247/70, p. 22.

22. "The Declaration of the Duke of Monmouth," PRO, PRO 30/24/44/76.

23. Cobbett, *Parliamentary History,* p. 1.

24. Ibid., p. 9.

25. "Some Reflections upon his Highness the Prince of Orange's Declaration," *Somers Tracts,* vol. 9, p. 294.

26. BM, Add. MS 10,118, p. 16.

27. Ibid. As to the effect of a conquest upon England, it may have been that William was more realistic, even if not as legally sophisticated, as Matthew Hale, who argued that the original Conquest did not injure the people in their rights. See chapter 4, above.

28. "Some Reflections upon his Highness the Prince of Orange's Declaration," *Somers Tracts,* vol. 9, p. 293.

29. Cobbett, *Parliamentary History,* p. 2; BM, Stowe MS 370, fol. 48.

30. Cobbett, *Parliamentary History,* p. 2.

31. Ibid., p. 10.

226

32. Ibid., p. 2; BM, Stowe MS 370, fol. 48.

33. Cobbett, *Parliamentary History*, p. 1.

34. "Some Reflections upon his Highness the Prince of Orange's Declaration," *Somers Tracts*, vol. 9, p. 291.

35. "Animadversions upon the Declaration of His Highness the Prince of Orange," BM, Add. MS 10,118, p. 22.

36. "Declaration by the King . . ." (1688), *Somers Tracts*, vol. 9, p. 269.

37. PRO, SP 9/52.

38. William Sachse, "The Mob and the Revolution of 1688," *Journal of British Studies* (1964). For a contemporary view, see "Some Account of the Revolution," BM, Add. MS 9363, fols. 13v-14, and Roger Morrice, "Entring Book," vol. 2, Dr. Williams' Library, MS 31. Q.

39. "The Nottingham Paper," Cobbett, *Parliamentary History*, p. 18.

40. Diary of Thomas Smith, D.D., a senior fellow at Magdalen College, Oxford, BM, Hargrave MS 401, fol. 35.

41. Ibid., fol. 37. This was the reported position of Thomas Barlow, bishop of Lincoln.

42. Ibid.

43. BM, Stowe MS 371, fol. 75v.

44. Ibid., fol. 116v.

45. The charge by Sir William Smith at Middlesex Quarter Sessions (24 April 1682), PRO, SP 9/251/184.

46. BM, Add. MS 19,762, fol. 51v.

47. On this point see F. W. Maitland, *The Constitutional History of England* (1961), pp. 283-85, and James Macpherson, *The History of Great Britain from the Restoration to the Accession of the House of Hanover* (London, 1775), vol. 1, p. 557.

48. BM, Stowe MS 364, fol. 68v; *Somers Tracts*, vol. 9, p. 305.

49. "A Vindication of the Revolution . . . ," BM, Stowe MS 291, fol. 14; "A Speech to Prove this Convention a Parliament," BM, Stowe MS 180/22, fol. 67.

50. B. Behrens, "The Whig Theory of the Constitution in the Reign of Charles II," *Cambridge Historical Journal* (1941), p. 53.

51. See J. R. Tanner, *English Constitutional Conflicts of the Seventeenth Century* (1928), p. 262, for the argument that the Tories constituted a majority of both houses but were divided into three factions and were thereby outweighed by the unanimous front of the Whig minority. For further data and commentary on the 1689 elections and the composition of the Convention there is James II's 1688 *Memorandum for those that go into the Country to dispose the Corporations to a good Election for Members of Parliament* (PRO, SP 9/247/66); see also J. H. Plumb, "The

Election to the Convention Parliament of 1689," *Cambridge*   227
Historical Journal (1937); George L. Cherry's compilation, *The
Convention Parliament 1689: A Biographical Study of Its Mem-
bers* (1966); David Ogg, *England in the Reigns of James II and
William III* (1957), pp. 224-25; Baron Dover, ed., *The Ellis
Correspondence* (1829), vol. 2, p. 56; Sir John Reresby, *Memoirs*
(1734), p. 269; Narcissus Luttrell, *A Brief Historical Relation of
State Affairs from September 1678 to April 1714* (1857), vol. 1, p.
494; and the recent analysis by Henry Horwitz, "Parliament and
the Glorious Revolution," *Bulletin of the Institute of Historical
Research* (1974), pp. 40-42.

52. Cobbett, *Parliamentary History*, p. 32. Lois G. Schwoerer,
"Press and Parliament in the Revolution of 1689," forthcoming in
The Historical Journal, discusses a contemporary newssheet
entitled *An Account of the Proceedings of the Lords and Commons, In the Parliament-House, upon their first Convention: With
the several Debates and Speeches relating thereunto.* In that
Account there is an apparently contrived speech which has Powle
delivering himself, not of the traditional disclaimer, but of a
partisan harangue in support of William's interests.

53. Ibid., p. 26.

54. The disappearance of the seal had occasioned considerable
consternation after James, fleeing the realm the first time, was
reported to have thrown the seal into the Thames. On 15 December the Peers who had assembled in London to meet with William
sent a delegation to examine Jeffreys in the Tower in an attempt to
discover "1. What he hath done with the Great Seal of England?
2. Whether he did seal all the Writts for the Parliament, & what he
hath done with them?" (BM, Stowe MS 370, fol. 38v).

55. Henry Seymour, member for St. Mawes (Cobbett, *Parliamentary History*, p. 35).

56. Ibid.

57. Ibid., p. 34.

58. *Journals of the House of Commons,* vol. 10, pp. 13-14.

59. Cobbett, *Parliamentary History*, p. 32.

60. Reresby, *Memoirs,* p. 310.

61. BM, Stowe MS 371, fol. 111v.

62. Henry's first Act of Succession (1534), 25 Henry VIII, c. 22
(*Statutes of the Realm,* vol. 3, pp. 471 ff.), voided his marriage to
Catherine but made no mention of their daughter, Mary. The net
effect was to create Elizabeth heiress presumptive and to leave
Mary's place in the succession ambiguous. It was not until Henry's
second Act of Succession (1536), 28 Henry VIII, c. 7, (*Statutes of
the Realm,* vol. 3, pp. 655 ff.), that Mary, along with Elizabeth,
was declared illegitimate and that both daughters were explicitly

removed from the succession. Only the issue of Henry's marriage to Jane Seymour (and any subsequent marriage) were to stand in line for the throne. For a discussion of this issue see Mortimer Levine, *Tudor Dynastic Problems: 1460–1571* (1973), chap. 3.

63. 35 Henry VIII, c. 1 (*Statutes of the Realm,* vol. 3, pp. 955 ff.).

64. "A Speech of a Commoner of England to his Fellow Commoner of the Convention," *Somers Tracts,* vol. 9, p. 305. See also the remarks of Heneage Finch, BM, Stowe MS 364, fols. 67–67v.

65. "Dr. Sandersons Paper and Censure," BM, Stowe MS 746, fol. 147.

66. Tanner, *English Constitutional Conflicts,* p. 263.

67. Historical Manuscripts Commission, *Twelfth Report* (1890), Appendix, pt. 6, p. 14 (29 January 1688–89).

68. Cobbett, *Parliamentary History,* p. 39.

69. An important difference between lunacy, which was deemed to be a temporary condition, and idiocy, which was, by definition, chronic, was that "custos of a lunaticke is subject to account, of an Idiot not so" (Sir Joseph Williamson's Notebook, PRO, SP 9/25).

70. "A Vindication of the Revolution . . . ," BM, Stowe MS 291, fols. 16v–17.

71. BM, Stowe MS 370, fol. 70v.

72. BM, Stowe MS 371, fol. 32. Turner's embracing of the regency solution may, on the basis of his later statements, have been merely a play for time while the more sincere attempt was being made to reinstate James. See Horwitz, "Parliament and the Glorious Revolution," p. 44, and Robert Beddard, "The Loyalist Opposition in the Interregnum," *Bulletin of the Institute of Historical Research* (May 1967).

73. *Reflections upon a Late Book, entitled, The Case of Allegiance considered* (1689), PRO, SP 9/247/69.

74. There is no dispute about the closeness of the vote, although the sources are at odds on the exact division. The manuscript minutes of the Lords suggest that the motion for a regency was defeated by a vote of 51 to 48 (Historical Manuscripts Commission, *Twelfth Report,* Appendix, pt. 6, p. 15). Clarendon's diary records 51 for and 49 against (Samuel W. Singer, ed., *Clarendon Correspondence,* vol. 2, p. 256), while Evelyn says it was 54 to 51. Horwitz ("Parliament and the Glorious Revolution," p. 44, n. 3) attempts to reconcile some of the differences.

75. Remarks by William Sacheveral, member for Heytesbury, Wiltshire (Cobbett, *Parliamentary History,* p. 86). It is interesting that the more legally impressive argument was not made. In law a lunatic and an infant are both incapable of consent, and it is for that reason that custody becomes necessary.

76. Cobbett, *Parliamentary History,* p. 88.

77. Gilbert Burnet, *The History of My Own Times* (1833), vol. 3, p. 378.

78. *Journals of the House of Commons,* p. 14.

79. *The History and Proceedings of the House of Lords* (1742), vol. 1, p. 341; *Journals of the House of Commons,* p. 17.

80. *Journals of the House of Commons,* p. 20.

81. "Concerning the Oaths of Allegiance and Supremacy," BM, Stowe MS 293, p. 25.

82. "The Protestant Admirer or, An Answer to the Vindication of a Popish Successor," BM, Add. MS 22,589, p. 3.

83. BM, Stowe MS 371, fol. 11v.

84. "A true and impartial Narrative of the Dissenters' New Plot" (1690), *Somers Tracts,* vol. 9, p. 462.

85. The point was raised by the earl of Rochester (Cobbett, *Parliamentary History,* p. 84).

86. Historical Manuscripts Commission, *Twelfth Report,* Appendix, pt. 6, p. 18.

87. Halifax called it "the pretence of Necessity" (BM, Add. MS 31,956, fols. 12v-13).

88. BM, Stowe MS 371, fol. 27v. Robert Filmer had in his *Patriarcha* anticipated something of this nature as a remote possibility. His solution, not surprisingly, was somewhat different. "It may be demanded what becomes of fatherhood in case the Crown does escheat for want of an heir, whether it doth not then devolve to the people.... No: the Kingly power escheats in such cases to the prime and independent heads of families, for every kingdom is resolved into those principles whereof at first it was made" (Robert Filmer, *Patriarcha,* ed. Peter Laslett [1949], p. 51).

89. Lord Macaulay, *The History of England,* ed. C. H. Firth (1914), vol. 3, p. 1310.

90. The question of proof, or the absence thereof, could be properly regarded as very important. In a later criticism of the proceedings of the Convention it was noted that, on the issue of the birth of the Prince of Wales, allegations were easily enough made but faltered when "call'd upon to descend to the Proof of Particulars" ("A Letter to the Bishop of Sarum: Being an Answer to his Lordships Pastoral Letter. From a Minister in the Countrey" [30 August 1689], PRO, SP 9/247/70, p. 23).

91. *The History and Proceedings of the House of Lords,* p. 340.

92. BM, Stowe MS 371, fols. 15v and 70.

93. "Diary of Henry Hyde, 2d Earl of Clarendon, for the year 1688," BM, Stowe MS 770, fols. 162-63.

94. BM, Stowe MS 371, fol. 117.

95. Cobbett, *Parliamentary History,* p. 89; BM, Stowe MS 371,

fols. 70–70v. Also revived was the sophistic contention that any oath sworn to the king's heir while the king still lived would be treason. That part of the oath was therefore to be treated as null and void ("Concerning the Oaths of Allegiance and Supremacy... ," BM, Stowe MS 293, p. 26).

96. BM, Stowe MS 371, fol. 71.

97. "A Vindication of the Revolution ... ," BM, Stowe MS 291, fol. 12.

98. Cobbett, *Parliamentary History*, p. 92. Similar concerns were voiced by Clarendon; see BM, Stowe MS 371, fol. 38.

99. *Journals of the House of Commons*, p. 15. Leopold von Ranke observed of this usage that the "word ['experience'] was to serve as an excuse for those who, before the experiment had been tried, had declared themselves against the exclusion of a Catholic from the throne of England" (*A History of England, Principally in the Seventeenth Century* [1875], vol. 4, p. 500). This fits perfectly with the common-law distinctions between punishment *in praesenti* and punishment *in futuro* noted on pp. 173–74, above.

100. Cobbett, *Parliamentary History*, p. 102; BM, Stowe MS 371, fol. 105v.

101. BM, Stowe MS 371, fols. 10–10v. The issue continued into the reign of William and Mary; see "The English-Mans Allegiance ... ," BM, Add. MS 32,095, fol. 389v.

102. Cobbett, *Parliamentary History*, p. 69; BM, Stowe MS 371, fols. 17–20.

103. BM, Stowe MS 371, fols. 39v–40.

104. On the further implication of the choice of words see J. P. Kenyon, "The Revolution of 1688: Resistance and Contract," in *Historical Perspectives: Studies in English Thought and Society in Honour of J. H. Plumb,* edited by Neil McKendrick (1974).

105. BM, Stowe MS 291, fol. 12v.

106. BM, Stowe MS 293, pp. 8–9.

107. Ibid.

108. "A Letter formerly sent to Dr. Tillotson ... ," *Somers Tracts,* vol. 9, p. 370.

109. BM, Stowe MS 371, fols. 105v–106.

110. See Nottingham's remarks in Cobbett, *Parliamentary History*, p. 66.

111. BM, Stowe MS 371, fol. 99.

112. BM, Stowe MS 293, pp. 25–26.

113. BM, Stowe MS 371, fol. 29.

114. Ibid., fol. 25.

115. Cobbett, *Parliamentary History*, p. 78; BM, Stowe MS 371, fol. 42.

116. BM, Stowe MS 291, fol. 12v; Stowe MS 371, fol. 34v.

117. It has been only since the middle of the nineteenth century that the dishonest trustee could be treated as a criminal. Only since then has there been an action for criminal breach of trust. The obstacle to this much-needed reform was that "at law" the trustee was regarded as the owner of the corpus of the trust, and a "man cannot be guilty of stealing what he both owns and possesses" (F. W. Maitland, "Trust and Corporation," *Collected Papers* [1911], vol. 3, p. 352).

118. Cobbett, *Parliamentary History,* p. 83; BM, Stowe MS 371, fols. 53-53v. In addition to the relation of king to minister, that of king to subject could also be viewed in the legal terms of master-servant. In this regard it was argued that a servant who has sworn himself to a master is nevertheless relieved of his allegiance "if through misfortunes he [the master] be render'd incapable of keeping a Servant" or if the master "shall usurp the Power of a Lord over him, to make him a slave, which he never swore to" (BM, Stowe MS 291, fols. 15v-16).

CONCLUSION

1. Ernst H. Kantorowicz, *The King's Two Bodies* (1957); Brian P. Levack, *The Civil Lawyers in England, 1603-1641* (1973); Gordon J. Schochet, *Patriarchalism in Political Thought* (1975); J. A. W. Gunn, *Politics and the Public Interest in the Seventeenth Century* (1969); J. G. A. Pocock, *The Machiavellian Moment: Florentine Political Thought and the Atlantic Republican Tradition* (1975).

2. "Entring Book," Dr. Williams' Library, MS 31. Q, vol. 2, p. 393.

3. See, for example, Margaret Judson, *The Crisis of the Constitution* (1949); S. B. Chrimes, *English Constitutional Ideas in the Fifteenth Century* (1936).

4. In 1954 Lucille Pinkham challenged the prevalent view of the Declaration of Rights, asserting that "at no time was the offer of the crown made directly or explicitly contingent upon acceptance of the declaration by William and Mary" (*William III and the Respectable Revolution,* p. 234). Since then the point has been examined and endorsed by Howard A. Nenner, "The Convention of 1689: A Triumph of Constitutional Form," *American Journal of Legal History* (1966), pp. 295-96; Robert J. Frankle, "The Formulation of the Declaration of Rights," *Historical Journal* (1974), p. 270; and J. P. Kenyon, "The Revolution of 1688: Resistance and Contract," *Historical Perspectives* (1974), pp. 49-50. See, however, Henry Horwitz, "Parliament and the Glorious Revolution," *Bulletin of the Institute of Historical Research*

232   (1974), pp. 47–49, for a strong argument in support of a conditional connection between the Declaration and the Crown.

5. For an understanding of the Revolution in the context of a developing Stuart absolutism see J. H. Plumb, *The Growth of Political Stability in England, 1675–1725* (1967); J. R. Jones, *The Revolution of 1688 in England* (1972); and J. R. Western, *Monarchy and Revolution* (1972). A full-length study of the Bill of Rights by Lois Schwoerer is forthcoming.

Bibliography

1. MANUSCRIPTS

Public Record Office

Shaftesbury Papers. PRO 30/24

These proved to be the most useful manuscripts in the Public Record Office. In addition to the large number of papers belonging to the first earl, relevant to much of his political life and thought, there are included in this collection some important letters and papers of John Locke.

State Papers Miscellaneous. SP 9

This large assortment of records and notes put together by Sir Joseph Williamson during his tenure as keeper of the state papers (1661–1702) were of considerable value, particularly his collections and comments on law and the prerogative during the period under examination.

King William's Chest. SP 8

Private papers of William III.

State Papers Domestic. Charles II. SP 29 and 30

State Papers Domestic. James II. SP 31

State Papers Domestic. William and Mary. SP 32

British Museum (now British Library)

Sloane MSS, Birch MSS, and Additional MSS

In and among the letters, diaries, tracts, essays, and pamphlets are extremely valuable discussions of every major political, constitutional, and legal issue of the period 1660–89. Many of the papers were authored anonymously, but a large number are by, to, or about such important figures as Charles II, James II, the Prince of Orange, Monmouth, Danby, Temple, Halifax, Petty, Hale, Penn, Locke, Somers, Hobbes, Clarendon (both first and second earls), Burnet, Evelyn, and Nottingham. The subjects, as well, are extensive and diverse. They range over a

234

wide variety of interests, touching on matters of law, prerogative, toleration, Exclusion, succession, revolution, oaths, and the dispensing and suspending powers.

Stowe MSS

Papers and tracts relating to affairs of state, the jurisdiction of Parliament, and legal procedure.

Harley MSS

Legal and political tracts and treatises, speeches in the House of Commons, and copies of several works by Matthew Hale.

Hargrave MSS

More copies of Hale's works, including his *Reflections on Hobbes's Dialogue of the Law,* materials on the case of *Thomas v. Sorrel,* and papers of the North family.

Lansdowne MSS

Dr. Williams' Library

MS 31. Q.

Roger Morrice, "The Entring Book: Being an Historical Register of Occurrences from April An: 1677 to April 1691," vol. 2.

Inner Temple

Petyt MSS

The Inner Temple Library houses the extensive collection of Petyt MSS, the work of an indefatigable antiquary and polemicist. Of the many volumes in this collection, the following were of the greatest utility in this study. Their description is taken from the "Summary List of Petyt Collection" compiled by Conway Davis (typescript).

512. A group of twenty-six volumes consisting of transcripts made by or for William Petyt from Public Records or other manuscript sources and from English and Continental printed books in his researches into English history, especially parliamentary history, mainly for his controversies with Dr. Robert Brady, and draft works on the same subjects.

512/H. A draft work composed and corrected by William Petyt in his controversies with Dr. Robert Brady on the successive governments in England.

512/K. Manuscript of William Petyt's "Jus Parliamentarium," posthumously published in 1739.

512/L. A draft work composed and corrected by William   235
Petyt in his controversies with Dr. Robert Brady, mainly on
the rights of the Commons.

512/M. A similar draft work composed and corrected by
William Petyt on "the rights of the Commons of England
asserted against Dr. Brady."

512/N. A draft work by William Petyt correcting what he
considered to be errors of recent English historians and
writers on Parliament.

512/P. Draft of a treatise, probably by William Petyt, on the
manner of succession of the Crown of England.

538. A group of fifty-six volumes, including collections relating to
Parliament, parliamentary diaries.

538/4. A corrected draft treatise and notes on "The Manner
of Proceeding in Parliament," with marginal notes by Petyt.

538/5. A collection concerning transactions in Parliament
between the Lords and Commons as to their rights, with
precedents, Edward I to Charles II.

Lincoln's Inn

Hargrave MSS

Much of Matthew Hale's work is in the Hargrave MSS at Lincoln's
Inn. The following manuscript copies were of particular value
(the descriptions are quoted from the typescript supplement to the
Hunter Catalogue).

8. Principles of the Law of Nature elicited through ratiocination
after the manner of the Mathematicians, including the
Demonstration of a Supreme Being and of a Future State,
by Lord Chief Justice Hale, copied from the original manuscript by Mr. Hargrave.

9. Preparatory Notes touching the Rights of the Crown, by Lord
Chief Justice Hale, copied from the original manuscript, the
greater part by Mr. Hargrave, the remainder under his
direction.

11. Treatise on the Judicature of the King's Council and Parliament. The original manuscript by Lord Chief Justice Hale.

12. The Jurisdiction of the Lords' House of Parliament considered according to Antient Records. The original manuscript by Lord Chief Justice Hale.

13. A Tract on the Leading Principles of the Law of Nature.
Original manuscript by Lord Chief Justice Hale.

236   2. PRINTED WORKS

Primary Sources

Burnet, Gilbert. *The History of My Own Times.* 6 vols. Oxford, 1833.

———. *A sermon Preached In the Chappel of St. James, Before his Highness the Prince of Orange, the 23rd of December 1688.* London, 1689.

Burnett, Gilbert. *The Life and Death of Sir Matthew Hale, Kt., Sometime Lord Chief Justice of His Majesties Court of Kings Bench.* London, 1682.

Calendar of State Papers (Domestic Series) of the Reign of James II, 1685. London, 1960.

Cobbett, William, ed. *Parliamentary History of England.* 36 vols. London, 1808-20.

———, and Howell, T. B., eds. *Collection of State Trials and Proceedings for High Treason and Other Crimes and Misdemeanors from the Earliest Period to the Present Time.* 33 vols. London, 1809-26.

Coke, Sir Edward. *The Fourth Part of the Institutes of the Laws of England: Concerning the Jurisdiction of Courts.* London, 1671.

———. *The Reports of Sir Edward Coke.* London, 1777.

Dover, Baron, ed. *The Ellis Correspondence.* 2 vols. London, 1829.

Filmer, Sir Robert. *Patriarcha and Other Political Works.* Edited by Peter Laslett. Oxford, 1949.

Firth, C. H., ed. *The Clarke Papers,* vol. 2. Camden Society, n.s., vol. 54. Westminster, 1894.

———, and Rait, R. S., eds. *Acts and Ordinances of the Interregnum, 1642-1660.* 3 vols. London, 1911.

Grey, Anchitell. *Debates of the House of Commons, 1667-1694.* 10 vols. London, 1763.

Halcrow, Elizabeth M., ed. *Charges to the Grand Jury at Quarter Sessions, 1660-1677, by Sir Peter Leicester.* Chetham Society, 3d ser., vol. 5. Manchester, 1953.

Hale, Matthew. *The Analysis of the Law: Being a Scheme or Abstract of the several Titles and Partitions of the Law of England. Digested into Method.* London, 1713.

———. *The History and Analysis of the Common Law of England.* London, 1713.

———. *The History of the Common Law of England and an Analysis of the Civil Part of the Law.* 6th ed. Edited by Charles Runnington, Serjeant at Law. London, 1820.

Halifax, Lord. "The Character of a Trimmer." In *The Life and*

Letters of Sir George Savile, Bart., vol. 2. Edited by H. C.   237
Foxcroft. London, 1898.

———. "Political, Moral and Miscellaneous Thoughts and Reflections." Ibid.

Historical Manuscripts Commission. *Seventh Report.* London, 1879.

———. *Twelfth Report.* London, 1890.

The History and Proceedings of the House of Commons from the Restoration to the Present Time. Vol. 1. London, 1742.

The History and Proceedings of the House of Lords. Vol. 1. London, 1742.

Hobbes, Thomas. *Leviathan, or the Matter, Forme and Power of a Commonwealth Ecclesiasticall and Civil.* Edited by Michael Oakeshott. Oxford, n.d.

James I. "The Trew Law of Free Monarchies." *The Political Works,* vol. 1. Edited by C. H. McIlwain. Cambridge, Mass., 1918.

Journals of the House of Commons, vol. 10.

Journals of the House of Lords, vol. 12.

Locke, John. *The Second Treatise of Government and A Letter Concerning Toleration.* Edited by J. W. Gough. Oxford, 1966.

The London Gazette, no. 2357, 18–21 June 1688.

Luttrell, Narcissus. *A Brief Historical Relation of State Affairs from September 1678 to April 1714,* vol. 1. Oxford, 1857.

MacDonald, Hugh, ed. *Observations Upon a late Libel, called A Letter from a Person of Quality to his Friend, concerning the King's Declaration, &c.* 1681. Cambridge, 1940.

The Proceedings in the House of Commons, Touching the Impeachment of Edward, Late Earl of Clarendon, Lord High-Chancellour of England, Anno 1667. 1700.

Reresby, Sir John. *Memoirs of Sir John Reresby.* London, 1734.

Singer, Samuel W., ed. *The Correspondence of Henry Hyde, earl of Clarendon, and of his brother Laurence Hyde, earl of Rochester, with the diary of Lord Clarendon from 1687 to 1690.* 2 vols. London, 1828.

Somers Tracts. 2d ed., vols. 7–9. London, 1813.

Statutes of the Realm. 9 vols. London, 1810–28.

Temple, Sir William. *An Essay upon the Original and Nature of Government* (1680). Augustan Reprint Society, no. 109. Los Angeles, 1964.

Secondary Sources

Aaron, Richard I. *John Locke.* 2d ed. Oxford, 1955.

Allen, C. K. *Law in the Making.* 7th ed. Oxford, 1964.

238   Baumer, Franklin Le Van. *The Early Tudor Theory of Kingship.* New Haven, 1940.

Beddard, Robert. "The Loyalist Opposition in the Interregnum: A Letter of Dr. Francis Turner, Bishop of Ely, on the Revolution of 1688." *Bulletin of the Institute of Historical Research,* vol. 40 (1967).

Behrens, B. "The Whig Theory of the Constitution in the Reign of Charles II." *Cambridge Historical Journal,* vol. 7 (1941).

Berger, Raoul. "*Doctor Bonham's Case:* Statutory Construction or Constitutional Theory?" *University of Pennsylvania Law Review,* vol. 117 (1969).

Birdsall, Paul. " 'Non-Obstante'—A Study in the Dispensing Power of English Kings." In *Essays in History and Political Theory in Honor of Charles Howard McIlwain,* edited by Carl Wittke. Cambridge, Mass., 1936.

Boorstin, Daniel J. *The Mysterious Science of the Law.* Cambridge, Mass., 1941.

Bouwsma, William J. "Lawyers and Early Modern Culture." *American Historical Review,* vol. 78 (1973).

Cherry, George L. *The Convention Parliament 1689: A Biographical Study of Its Members.* New York, 1966.

————. "The Legal and Philosophical Position of the Jacobites, 1688-1689." *Journal of Modern History,* vol. 22 (1950).

Chrimes, S. B. *English Constitutional Ideas in the Fifteenth Century.* Cambridge, Eng., 1936.

Churchill, E. F. "The Dispensing Power of the Crown in Ecclesiastical Affairs." *Law Quarterly Review,* vol. 38 (1922).

Churchill, Sir Winston. *Marlborough, His Life and Times.* 4 vols. London, 1967.

Clark, Sir George. *The Later Stuarts, 1660-1714.* 2d ed. Oxford, 1955.

Dalrymple, Sir John. *Memoirs of Great Britain and Ireland (1681-92).* 2 vols. London, 1771-73.

Dunham, William H., Jr. "Regal Power and the Rule of Law." *Journal of British Studies,* vol. 3 (1964).

Edie, Carolyn Andervont. "Succession and Monarchy: The Controversy of 1679-1681." *American Historical Review,* vol. 70 (1965).

Elton, G. R. "*The Body of the Whole Realm": Parliament and Representation in Medieval and Tudor England.* Charlottesville, 1969.

————. "The Rule of Law in Sixteenth-Century England." In *Tudor Men and Institutions,* edited by Arthur J. Slavin. Baton Rouge, 1972.

————, ed. *The Tudor Constitution.* Cambridge, Eng., 1962.

Figgis, John Neville. *The Divine Right of Kings.* Introduction by   239
G. R. Elton. New York, 1965.

Frankle, Robert J. "The Formulation of the Declaration of
Rights." *Historical Journal,* vol. 17 (1974).

Furley, O. W. "The Whig Exclusionists: Pamphlet Literature in
the Exclusion Campaign, 1679-81." *Cambridge Historical
Journal,* vol. 13 (1957).

Gardiner, S. R. *History of England, 1603-1642.* 10 vols. London,
1883-84.

Gooch, C. P. *Political Thought in England: Bacon to Halifax.*
London, 1915.

Gough, J. W. *Fundamental Law in English Constitutional History.*
Oxford, 1955.

——. *John Locke's Political Philosophy.* Oxford, 1950.

——. *The Social Contract: A Critical Study of Its Development.*
2d ed. Oxford, 1957.

Gray, Charles M., ed. Sir Matthew Hale, *The History of the
Common Law of England.* Chicago, 1971.

Gunn, J. A. W. *Politics and the Public Interest in the Seventeenth
Century.* London and Toronto, 1969.

Harding, Alan. *A Social History of English Law.* London, 1966.

Havighurst, Alfred F. "James II and the Twelve Men in Scarlet."
Law Quarterly Review, vol. 69 (1953).

——. "The Judiciary and Politics in the Reign of Charles II."
Law Quarterly Review, vol. 66 (1950) (pt. 1, 1660-76, January
1950; pt. 2, 1676-85, April 1950).

Heward, Edmund. *Matthew Hale.* London, 1972.

Hill, Christopher. *Intellectual Origins of the English Revolution.*
Oxford, 1965.

——. *Puritanism and Revolution.* London, 1958.

Hinton, R. W. K. "English Constitutional Theories from Sir John
Fortescue to Sir John Eliot." *English Historical Review,* vol. 75
(1960).

Holdsworth, W. S. *A History of English Law.* Reprint ed., vols. 5
and 6. London, 1966.

——. *The Influence of the Legal Profession on the Growth of the
English Constitution.* Oxford, 1924.

——. *Some Lessons from Our Legal History.* New York, 1928.

Horwitz, Henry. "Parliament and the Glorious Revolution." *Bulletin of the Institute of Historical Research,* vol. 47 (1974).

——. *Revolution Politicks.* Cambridge, Eng., 1968.

Hurst, Gerald. "Sir Matthew Hale." *Law Quarterly Review,* vol.
70 (1954).

Hurstfield, Joel. "Was There a Tudor Despotism after All?" *Transactions of the Royal Historical Society,* 5th ser., vol. 17 (1967).

240   Ives, E. W. "The Reputation of the Common Lawyer in English Society, 1450-1550." *University of Birmingham Historical Journal,* vol. 3 (1959-60).

Jolowicz, H. F. *Lectures on Jurisprudence.* Edited by J. A. Jolowicz. London, 1963.

Jones, J. R. *The First Whigs: The Politics of the Exclusion Crisis, 1678-1683.* London, 1961.

————. *The Revolution of 1688 in England.* London, 1972.

Jones, W. J. *Politics and the Bench: The Judges and the Origins of the English Civil War.* London, 1971.

Judson, Margaret Atwood. *The Crisis of the Constitution.* New York, 1949.

Kantorowicz, Ernst H. *The King's Two Bodies: A Study in Medieval Political Theology.* Princeton, 1957.

Keir, D. L. *The Constitutional History of Modern Britain.* London, 1938.

Kenyon, J. P. "The Exclusion Crisis." *History Today,* vol. 14 (1964).

————. *The Popish Plot.* London, 1972.

————. "The Revolution of 1688: Resistance and Contract." In *Historical Perspectives: Studies in English Thought and Society in Honour of J. H. Plumb,* edited by Neil McKendrick. London, 1974.

————, ed. *The Stuart Constitution.* Cambridge, Eng., 1966.

Landon, Michael. *The Triumph of the Lawyers.* University, Alabama, 1970.

Levack, Brian P. *The Civil Lawyers in England, 1603-1641.* Oxford, 1973.

Levin, Jennifer. *The Charter Controversy in the City of London, 1660-1688, and Its Consequences.* London, 1969.

Levine, Mortimer. *Tudor Dynastic Problems, 1460-1571.* London and New York, 1973.

Macaulay, Lord. *The History of England from the Accession of James the Second.* Edited by Charles Harding Firth. 6 vols. London, 1914.

MacPherson, C. B. *The Political Theory of Possessive Individualism.* Oxford, 1962.

MacPherson, James. *The History of Great Britain from the Restoration to the Accession of the House of Hanover.* Vol. 1. London, 1775.

Maitland, F. W. *The Constitutional History of England.* Cambridge, Eng., 1961.

————. "Trust and Corporation." *Collected Papers,* vol. 3. Cambridge, Eng., 1911.

Malament, Barbara. "The 'Economic Liberalism' of Sir Edward Coke." *Yale Law Journal,* vol. 76 (1967).

McKeon, Richard. "The Development of the Concept of Property in Political Philosophy: A Study of the Background of the Constitution." *International Journal of Ethics,* vol. 48 (1938).

Nenner, Howard A. "The Convention of 1689: A Triumph of Constitutional Form." *American Journal of Legal History,* vol. 10 (1966).

Ogg, David. *England in the Reign of Charles II.* 2d ed. 2 vols. London, 1963.

——. *England in the Reigns of James II and William III.* Oxford, 1957.

Pinkham, Lucille. *William III and the Respectable Revolution.* Cambridge, Mass., 1954.

Plucknett, Theodore F. T. "Bonham's Case and Judicial Review." *Harvard Law Review,* vol. 40 (1926).

Plumb, J. H. "The Election to the Convention Parliament of 1689." *Cambridge Historical Journal,* vol. 5 (1937).

——. *The Growth of Political Stability in England, 1675–1725.* London, 1967.

Pocock, J. G. A. *The Ancient Constitution and the Feudal Law.* Cambridge, Eng., 1957.

——. "Burke and the Ancient Constitution—A Problem in the History of Ideas." *Historical Journal,* vol. 3 (1960).

——. "Machiavelli, Harrington, and English Political Ideologies in the Eighteenth Century." *William and Mary Quarterly,* 3d ser., vol. 22 (1965).

——. *The Machiavellian Moment: Florentine Political Thought and the Atlantic Republican Tradition.* Princeton, 1975.

Powicke, F. M., and Fryde, E. B., eds. *Handbook of British Chronology.* 2d ed. London, 1961.

Prest, Wilfrid R. "Legal Education of the Gentry at the Inns of Court, 1560–1640." *Past and Present,* no. 38 (1967).

——. *The Inns of Court under Elizabeth I and the Early Stuarts, 1590–1640.* London, 1972.

Ranke, Leopold von. *A History of England, Principally in the Seventeenth Century.* Vol. 4. Oxford, 1875.

Robbins, Caroline. "The Repeal of the Triennial Act in 1664." *Huntington Library Quarterly,* vol. 12 (1949).

Roberts, Clayton. *The Growth of Responsible Government in Stuart England.* Cambridge, Eng., 1966.

Sachse, William L. "The Mob and the Revolution of 1688." *Journal of British Studies,* vol. 4 (1964).

Schochet, Gordon J. *Patriarchalism in Political Thought.* New York, 1975.

Shapiro, Barbara J. "Law and Science in Seventeenth-Century England." *Stanford Law Review,* vol. 21 (1969).

Skinner, Quentin. "The Ideological Context of Hobbes's Political Thought." *Historical Journal,* vol. 9 (1966).

Tanner, J. R. *English Constitutional Conflicts of the Seventeenth*

242

Century. Cambridge, Eng., 1928.

Thorne, Samuel E. "Dr. Bonham's Case." *Law Quarterly Review,* vol. 54 (1938).

————. *Sir Edward Coke, 1552-1952.* London, 1957.

Tillyard, E. M. W. *The Elizabethan World Picture.* New York, 1943.

Trevelyan, G. M. *The English Revolution, 1688-1689.* New York, 1965.

Usher, Roland G. "James I and Sir Edward Coke." *English Historical Review,* vol. 18 (1903).

Veall, Donald. *The Popular Movement for Law Reform, 1640-1660.* Oxford, 1970.

Wagner, Donald O. "Coke and the Rise of Economic Liberalism." *Economic History Review,* vol. 6 (1935).

Walcott, Robert, Jr. "English Party Politics (1688-1714)." In *Essays in Modern English History: In Honor of Wilbur Cortez Abbott.* Cambridge, Mass., 1941.

Western, J. R. *Monarchy and Revolution: The English State in the 1680s.* London, 1972.

Weston, Corinne Comstock. "The Theory of Mixed Monarchy under Charles I and After." *English Historical Review,* vol. 75 (1960).

Wormuth, Francis D. *The Royal Prerogative, 1603-1649.* Ithaca, 1939.

Index